Town and County

Town and County

Essays on the Structure of Local Government
in the American Colonies

edited by BRUCE C. DANIELS

WESLEYAN UNIVERSITY PRESS
Middletown, Connecticut

Copyright © 1978 by Wesleyan University

The publisher gratefully acknowledges support of the publication of this
book by the Friends of the Wesleyan University Press.

Library of Congress Cataloging in Publication Data
Main entry under title:

Town and county.

  Bibliography: p.
  Includes index.
  1. Local government—United States—History—
Addresses, essays, lectures. I. Daniels, Bruce Colin.
JS311.T68   352.073   77-14834
ISBN 0-8195-5020-5

Manufactured in the United States of America
First edition

For three inspiring teachers
Arthur Allbee
Fred Cazel, Jr.
Henry Duckworth

Contents

Preface

Since the publication, in the 1880s, of the monumental Johns Hopkins University Studies in Historical and Political Science, no systematic attempt has been made to analyze the structures of local government in colonial America. Under the vigorous editorship of Herbert Baxter Adams, the Johns Hopkins series ranged in its examination of local government from articles tracing the New England town back to the German *Tun,* to detailed descriptions of parish government in Maryland. Such giants in colonial history as Charles Andrews and Edward Channing contributed articles on local government. Adams himself contributed three articles on local offices and institutions. By the publication of the last volume on local government, most American historians could feel secure in their knowledge of seventeenth- and eighteenth-century local institutions.

The rich promise of the Johns Hopkins series has not been fulfilled

by the last ninety years of scholarship. The twentieth century has
seen thousands of books and articles on local colonial history but
only a handful of them have been concerned with the general characteristics of local institutions. Most of the local histories tell the
story of one town, one parish, or one county without paying attention to the institutional milieu in which that town, parish, or county
was framed. The few articles in the last generation that have focused
on the structures of local institutions have usually appeared in state
historical journals and in monographs on the history of one colony.
The result of this inattention is that today's students of colonial history have little more knowledge of local governments than did the
generation of the 1890s.

The Johns Hopkins series, while still immensely valuable, no longer
adequately fulfills our needs. Basically, it provided only skeletal
outlines of local governments. One might find out when an office
first appeared in a colony or what formal powers an officer exercised, but the authors in the series seldom went beyond this legalistic dimension. The study of history has changed dramatically since
the late nineteenth century and in particular has benefited from new
questions and new techniques advanced by the social sciences. It is
no longer adequate merely to provide the skeleton of government;
scholars of the past now demand to see the flesh that rounded out
the whole being, the nerves that connected its parts, and the mus-
cles that did its work. Historians now believe that social attitudes,
geography, class, economic influences, and other variables that are
studied by the new "social historians" must be linked to structure
for any meaningful understanding of past institutions. Accordingly,
the essays in this volume examine the dynamics as well as the structure of local government.

With the increased emphasis on nonelitist history among current
historians, many students have turned away from the studies of
royal governors, assemblies, and colony leaders. In the 1960s and
1970s a massive amount of writing has been devoted to the political,
social, and economic leadership in local communities, but still there
is little emphasis on the structures through which these leaders
worked. The new social history has not been effectively linked with
the older institutional history. The nine essays in this volume attempt
to make that linkage and to begin a reevaluation of colonial local
institutions. It would be presumptuous to think that these essays

could achieve the influence of those of the old Johns Hopkins series, but when made available under one cover their high quality of scholarship should add a new dimension to the study of colonial history.

The subjects of the nine essays in this volume were chosen to complement previously published historical knowledge. The first essay on New England examines the founding of institutions in Massachusetts with special reference to the English background and the transference of institutions across the Atlantic. The other essay on New England provides an overall view of the structure of local government in Connecticut because that colony has received less attention than Massachusetts. Similarly, one of the four essays on the South provides an overall view of local government in Maryland, a colony which has been studied far less than Virginia; two others focus specifically on the two crucial local units of Virginia: the county and the parish. The fourth examines local government in South Carolina, a colony that deviates significantly from the experience of the Chesapeake. Two of the three essays on the Middle Colonies are overviews of local government in New York and Pennsylvania respectively because the descriptions they provide cannot be found elsewhere. The third is an analysis of the government of Philadelphia, one of the few incorporated cities in the colonies.

Admittedly, the gaps in this collection of essays are many. The volume is not meant to be inclusive but rather suggestive, to supply knowledge in areas where it does not exist, and to pull together under one cover more essays on local institutions in the colonies than would normally appear in scattered historical journals over a ten-year period.

Acknowledgments

My greatest debt is to the eight talented historians who have joined me in this volume and whose essays grace its pages. They have endured without complaint the long delays that inevitably accompany a book like this and have cheerfully responded to any requests for revisions. I have learned a great deal about professionalism from them.

A number of people have made important contributions to this work although they have not read a word of it. The inception of the book owes much to Professors A. E. Van Dusen and Richard D. Brown of the University of Connecticut. My interest in local government was first stimulated in Professor Van Dusen's graduate seminar on colonial New England, and I sought out contributors for the volume after being encouraged to do so by Professor Brown, then a fellow at the Charles Warren Center at Harvard University. I am grateful to Professor H. V. Rutherford, chairman of the history department at the University of Winnipeg, and to my colleagues in that department for providing an atmosphere conducive to scholarship without sacrificing the congeniality that makes the University of Winnipeg a delightful place at which to teach. I wish also to thank the Research and Travel Committee of the university for providing funds for typing two drafts of the manuscript.

Professors Walter Stein and Wesley Stevens of the University of Winnipeg and my father, Howard Daniels, read the portions of the book that I wrote and made helpful suggestions for revisions in content and style. The primary reader for Wesleyan University Press, whose identity is unknown to me, can take silent pride in knowing he or she has immeasurably improved the product.

Finally, I wish to thank the three men whose names appear on the dedication page for showing me by their examples that fairness and a commitment to excellence are the essential qualities of a good teacher.

Town and County

Introduction

BRUCE C. DANIELS

A historian beginning the study of colonial American local government would rapidly become aware of, and perhaps be puzzled by, the regional differences in local institutions. The terminology used to denote southern local government might sound familiar but irrelevant to someone versed in New England history. Vestry, parish, justice of the peace, and county are all terms the New Englander knows, but he attributes little importance to them. Even in the twentieth century, after living with these differences for three hundred years, New Englanders who move to the South are usually surprised by the vigor and scope of county government. They are used to thinking of counties as mere geographic divisions that have few functions in government—if, indeed, New Englanders think about counties. Similarly, most Southerners feel New Englanders are confusing when they include isolated farmsteads and other

3

outlying areas in a town. A town is, of course, the Southerners would say, a collection of houses and businesses clustered together as a unit—not an aggregate of isolated outposts.

What can account for the great differences between the local institutions of New England and the South? One might expect to find diversity in the Middle Colonies where non-English influences were much stronger, but in both New England and the South the overwhelming influence on institutions was English. Nor can one discover that most New Englanders came with one set of English backgrounds and most Southerners with another. New England towns were often created by men with vastly different experiences. Also, on the level above local government, colony-level government, there existed a great similarity of structures between the differing regions.

Was there something inherent in Puritanism and Anglicanism that inclined a Puritan toward the town meeting and an Anglican toward the county court? Probably there was, and religious differences undoubtedly played a strong role in the separate evolutions. While the words "democracy" and "equality" were anathema to most Puritans, Puritanism encouraged more participation of more men in government than did Anglicanism. The Congregational nature of the New England church polity also fostered an interest in immediate localism that was not as prevalent in the South. Finally, the Puritan concept of the covenant, with its emphasis on community, was bound to manifest itself in different institutions than the institutions of the more individualistic Anglicans.

Probably, geography, climate, and agricultural growing conditions helped develop the town and county systems as much as did Puritanism and Anglicanism. Few parts of the seventeenth-century South were far from the many navigable rivers that traversed the countryside, while relatively much more of New England lay isolated by the difficulties of land travel. Similarly, the winters of the South never isolated Virginians the way the New England snows did the people of Massachusetts. The agricultural growing conditions of New England made small-acreage intensive farming the norm, while relatively large-acreage extensive farming was the norm of the South. All these conditions when coupled with the spirit of Puritanism and the spirit of Anglicanism gave seventeenth-century New England a pattern of nucleated settlements and the seventeenth-century South a pattern of dispersed population. Since village and countryside require different governments, two sets of institutions started to emerge by the mid–seventeenth century to accommodate these divergent needs. By a process of selective borrowing each region emphasized different aspects of the English institutional past. In both regions the early stark contrast of settlement patterns gave way to a softer contrast in the eighteenth century: New England settlement evolved somewhat to the dispersed population pattern of the isolated farmstead and, while the south did not develop a village system, its population density grew and the separateness of each settler was diminished. Nevertheless, the town and county systems of local government, products of the seventeenth century, remained intact throughout the colonial period.

Six essays in this volume, two on New England and four on the South, describe the two systems by examining the general nature of local government in the two regions and by analyzing in depth specific aspects of it. Three essays on the Middle Colonies examine local government in the area where the two systems merge geographically and institutionally. New England and the South differ from each other, yet each region, while containing significant variations, was relatively homogeneous in local institutions. The Middle Colonies combined aspects of both the town and county systems and added to the blend unique ingredients growing out of their particular circumstances.

The Middle Colonies' internal diversity best demonstrates the complexity of local government in the colonies. Towns, counties, manors, boroughs, and cities all existed side by side in New York and Pennsylvania. Because they were not primarily town nor totally county, and because they resemble a bewildering patchwork to the historian, the local institutions of the Middle Colonies have received little study. Even when the patchwork is assembled into a quilt the seams are obvious; mastering a knowledge of local institutions in these colonies is a formidable task. However, as the other essays show, the town system and the county system, which both sound deceptively simple, were actually highly complex structures. Town government was never simply the town meeting and county government was never simply the county court. The town meeting and the county court were the most important institutions in their respective regions except for the colony governments, but both had numerous officers serving them whose duties went beyond the meeting and the court and both coexisted with other local governmental units that also served the vital needs of the community.

Because the essays in this volume range over most of the possible experiences in colonial local institutions, they provide a good basis for some tentative generalizing. Indeed, an editor who did not attempt to identify some themes arising out of a collection as rich as this would be remiss in his duties. After all this particularistic study, what can we comfortably say about local government in the American colonies? What questions appear answered? What problems remain unsolved? Where does the study of local government go from here?

It is clear from the essays that in no colony was local government ever "created"; it evolved over a considerable period of time in response to needs experienced by the first two or three generations of settlers. Counties were not established in Virginia until 1634 or in Connecticut until 1664. The outlines of the county system in Virginia grew slowly and were not codified until 1662. The vestry did not appear in Maryland until 1692 when the Anglican Church was established. In South Carolina not until a significant portion of the colony's settlement was beyond the immediate reach of Charles Town's control did local institutions develop. The proprietors and society were not clearly separated from the town meeting in New England until after 1675. Significant local bodies did not exist in the Middle Colonies until the overweening powers of the proprietors were successfully resisted in New York in the 1660s and 1670s and in Pennsylvania in the 1690s. However, in all the colonies dealt with in these essays, with the possible exception of South Carolina, the basic local institutions that would characterize the entire colonial period were developed by the end of the seventeenth century. Little basic change took place in institutional structure after 1700; the eighteenth century saw a vast elaboration and development of a seventeenth-century model.

It is equally clear that the institutions that had emerged by 1700 were modern in the sense that they had little in common with feudal medieval institutions and were essentially the same institutions that exist in the United States today. Manorial courts and hundred courts, fuedal institutions becoming outdated in England because of the enclosure movement, did not survive their transplantation to the

English new world. The most medieval institution to survive as a meaningful governmental unit, the closed corporation of Philadelphia, became essentially a vestigial organ rendered less and less effective by time and circumstances.

The modern institutions that did emerge by 1700 were thoroughly English in all the colonies. When hammering out the institutional framework best suited to their needs, the colonists took refuge in the familiar. Even in New York where Dutch influences had more than a generation to develop, the impact of the non-English experience was on the social structure and not on the governing institutions. New York was diverse in its local institutions not because of the Dutch but because of its variegated settlement pattern.

A common theme in most of the essays shows that a meaningful role for local government did not emerge as a natural child but had to be fought for everywhere. The colonies were governed first by centralized authorities from whom power for local decision-making had to be wrested. Almost immediately at settlement a tension developed, in each of the colonies studied in this collection, between the powers governing the colony and the settlers aspiring to local self-control. Whether the proprietors in New York, Pennsylvania, Maryland, and South Carolina, the Puritan leadership in New England, or the company and later royal authority in Virginia, a central body governed the first settlers of each colony that had little interest in decentralizing the institutions of government. Yet, the struggle of the colonists proved successful and the subsequent colonial period witnessed a decentralizing process that continued in most colonies until local institutions were the most important part of the political constellation. The bulk of revenue went to local bodies and by the end of the first quarter of the eighteenth century people related more to the close neighborhood institutions than to the more remote central ones. The essays suggest that even the character of the colonial assembly changed: in some colonies local representatives forced it to practice a legislative courtesy whereby the delegates from each area had their wishes respected regarding local decisions; in other colonies it moved away from a strict delegation of powers as practiced earlier and passed general enabling acts giving local officials more discretionary powers.

Each of the historians in this volume seems to feel intuitively, if not state explicitly, that local government in its mature, eighteenth-century form worked reasonably well and satisfied most colonists. While many people appealed specific local decisions to the colony assembly, there was little or no agitation for changes in the system whereby decisions were made. The American Revolution produced cries for reforms in almost every aspect of human activity but very few pleas for changes in government beneath the colony level. The contention of a recent essay elsewhere that the local institutions that had evolved were a sound basis for an experiment in republicanism is borne out by the essays here.[1]

One of the reasons the institutions of local government satisfied so well was that they invited the participation of a large percentage of the responsible adult white males. Perhaps nowhere else is this point made as powerfully as in these essays. The South never had town or parish meetings but its invitation to freemen to attend the levy court which exercised the financial power, and its widespread use of juries to advise county courts potentially involved many southerners in deliberative bodies. Although many local officers were appointed, in all levels of local government in all the colonies under study there were elective elements which generally gained power as the colonial period progressed. One reason for this, as the city of Philadelphia found, was that colonists were loath to allow a body to levy taxes on them unless the body was in some measure representative. The freemen also often played a role in appointing officers since appointments were frequently made from among nominees proposed by the freemen or, owing to legislative courtesy, were made by the localities' elected representatives in the assembly. Although major officeholding was reserved usually for men of distinction, the tremendous growth in secondary local positions offered many "middlin'" men a chance to become involved in the operations of government. All these circumstances produced a system where, even if people did normally "defer" to their social superiors, they still felt a "widespread sense of personal competence to make a difference."[2] The essays in this volume will not cause the profession to question the widely accepted "deferential" model of colonial politics; they will, however, add some perspective to the existing model and show that deference was but one aspect of a complex political world.

In reading the essays in this volume one slowly becomes aware that amid the striking differences among regions there were many similarities; within basically divergent systems, many common officers existed and several patterns manifested themselves in every colony. Sheriffs, constables, highway officers, and justices of the peace operated everywhere in crucial roles. If the essays single out one office as the most significant position in local government, it would be that of the justice of the peace. The power of the magistracy was immense in all the colonies and it was the local justice who brought that power to every neighborhood. The statement made by one of this volume's contributors that it would be difficult to travel ten miles and not cross the path of a justice was true for every colony. Similarly, the body to which the justices related, the county court, played an important role in the governance of every colony with the exception of South Carolina, and the parish played almost as important a role in every colony but Maryland and, in places, New York. A common trend revealed by the essays at all levels of local government was the widespread use of special committees and commissions appointed for specific functions. The New England society and town meetings typically responded to any unusual problem by striking a committee to deal with it. Ad hoc courts which were special committees of the full court often gathered to sit between full county court sessions in the Middle and Southern colonies if something out of the ordinary necessitated it. Philadelphia and Charles Town both relied heavily upon standing commissions and temporary committees to solve specific problems.

Local government bodies generally performed all three functions of government: executive, legislative, and judicial. It is apparent from the essays that because colonists drew no clear line between these functions, historians often cannot now state with any finality what activities comprised each of the functional spheres. Local government existed to promote peace and order, to maintain the moral character of the citizenry, process the records that society wanted kept, and to solve the practical problems of a mercantile or agricultural community. They were governments, in the main, devoid of sharply argued or deeply felt ideologies—governments that existed to keep society functioning smoothly. No one questioned whether a justice's decision to fine a man 10s. for slandering his neighbor and then to supervise the offender's conduct for the next six months was a judicial or executive action or a criminal or civil one. It was an action that had to be taken for the good order of the community. Power was unified, not separated. Most of the operations of local government dealt with matters like ensuring valid titles to land, deciding where roads were to go and who was to build and pay for them, making sure that fences were maintained in good condition, enforcing regulations for the proper conduct of slaves or the proper treatment of indentured servants, or overseeing the care of orphans, widows, and "distracted" persons. Decency and practicality were the sought-after goals of local officials and government institutions were used to promote these goals. A phenomenon too little noticed by historians, that the generation of constitutional theorizing that accompanied the Revolution never engendered a consideration of local institutions, can be understood more fully after reading these essays. Local government was a practical, not a theoretical, affair.

While it is hoped this volume will have brought us a significant way toward a thorough understanding of local government, most areas require additional exploration and some remain to be examined for the first time. Comparative studies are needed that range beyond one colony and one model. Comprehensive histories of differing offices such as the justice of the peace or the sheriff are needed. The present essays, with the exception of the one prepared specifically on the subject, merely scratch the surface of the process of "selective borrowing" whereby the various regions developed their unique institutions; more research utilizing source materials in England has to be done on the transference of institutions across the Atlantic to each of the colonies. Similarly, all the essays deal in a qualitative sense with the important relationship between elite officeholding and the operations of local government, but their conclusions lack the precision that would make a behavioralist feel secure; much good work is being done elsewhere on officeholding patterns but much more remains to be done.[3] We cannot let our knowledge rest on vague generalizations that simply tell us that officeholders were economic and social elites; more typologies that relate officeholding to a host of variables are needed. Another weakness of this volume, resulting from criteria set by the editor in his invitations to contributors, lies in its failure to deal meaningfully with specialized aspects of local government such as poor relief, education, and finances; these subjects and many more like them invite intensive analysis both on a case study basis and in broad treatments ranging over colonies and regions. In addition, while the essays here take a step away from a study of the offices of the traditional elites, the governors, colonial officials, and leaders of assemblies, they turn in the main to offices dominated by a secondary elite, the justices of the peace, selectmen, and vestrymen; the offices that gave the real non-elites an entrée into the governing process have yet to be deeply studied. We need analyses of offices that regulated highways, fences, weights and measures, and so on, if historians are serious about rewriting history "from the bottom up."[4]

As one trumpets the "what we need" call for additional work it becomes hard to imagine any aspect in American colonial history that contains as many fresh subjects for investigation as the immensely important area of local government. Nothing would make this present volume more worthwhile or gratify the editor more than to introduce a host of graduate students and a few seasoned professionals to the problems of the study of local institutions and then to see them exploit the rich research opportunities.

NOTES

1. Patricia Bonomi, "Local Government in Colonial New York: A Base for Republicanism," in *Aspects of Early New York Society and Politics,* ed. Jacob Judd and Irwin H. Polishook (Tarrytown, N.Y., 1974). See the essay by Varga in this volume.

2. "The personal competence to make a difference" is one definition of democracy, proposed by Stanley Elkins and Eric McKitrick in "A Meaning for Turner's Frontier," *Political Science Quarterly,* LXIX (September 1954), 325. See the essay by Diamondstone in this volume.

3. This widely quoted phrase comes from Jesse Lemisch, "The American Revolution from the Bottom Up," in *Towards a New Past: Dissenting Essays in American History,* ed. Barton Bernstein (New York, 1967).

4. See, for example, Edward Cooke, Jr., "Local Leadership and the Typology of New England Towns, 1700-1785," *Political Science Quarterly,* XCVI (December 1971), 586–608; Bruce Steiner, "Anglican Officeholding in pre-Revolutionary Connecticut: The Parameters of New England Community," *William and Mary Quarterly,* XXXI (July 1974), 369–405; and Bruce C. Daniels, "Democracy and Oligarchy in Connecticut Towns: General Assembly Officeholding, 1701-1790," *Social Science Quarterly* LVI (December 1975), 460–75.

English Legal Change and the
Origins of Local Government
in Northern Massachusetts

DAVID THOMAS KONIG

In 1645 Hugh Peter addressed Parliament, the mayor and aldermen of London, and the Assembly of Divines to celebrate a victory of the Parliamentary Army. An army chaplain, Peter had been "eye-witnesse to many of [God's] Glorious works," and much of his sermon concerned military triumphs. However, Peter had witnessed another example of "God's bounty" that his listeners had not. He had been to Massachusetts Bay "where," he said, "in seven years I never saw beggar, nor heard an oath, nor lookt upon a drunkard." Peter was exaggerating; he had spent less than six years in the colony, and in that time he could scarcely have avoided the begging, swearing, and drunkenness that existed there. But Peter was trying to make a point to illustrate the difference between "Gods Doing" and "Mans Duty": despite Parliament's providential military successes, many Puritan goals still remained only theoretical proposals which had to be implemented by man. Referring to Massachusetts—and particularly to its legal system—Peter was appealing to an example of Puritan intentions translated into practice.[1]

What was the actual shape of the Puritan colony's sytem of law and local government which Peter had left behind in 1641? Recent historiography emphasizes the centrality of the town and congregation. By that interpretation, it was the conscious and immediate goal of the founders to abandon the English system of county and oligarchical government and to replace it with communal village utopias capable of serving as the primary units of government and social control.[2] Such a portrait may well be appropriate to a later generation. But during the first decade of settlement the founders departed very little from the patterns of English local government. Their "towns" were not established as autonomous or self-contained entities, but remained very much within the traditionally narrow confines of manorial and parochial practice. Above them, the colony erected institutions much like those of an English county, or of a borough incorporated as its own county. While the founders put a Puritan gloss on their product, they nonetheless followed the contours of the system with which they were familiar, and whose virtues they recognized as essential to their uninterrupted effort to create a godly society both in England and America.

To understand the impulse behind the creation of legal and governmental institutions in Massachusetts, one must recognize the dominant concept in the Puritan view of man and society, that of mankind's innate depravity after the Fall. As described by Calvin, man is a corrupt creature in need of constant restraint and direction. "We know," he wrote, "that man is of so perverse and crooked a nature, that everyone would scratch out hs neighbor's eyes if there were no bridle to hold them in."[3] Calvin's view of mankind reflected his understanding of sixteenth-century France, but it was applied to seventeenth-century England by Thomas Hobbes, in whose portrait of a society at war ("of every man against every man") Puritans saw much truth.[4]

By the time the Puritans would found Massachusetts, England had been experiencing social, economic, and political crisis for generations. The civil wars of the fifteenth century had been succeeded by a period of economic dislocation and rapid population increase in the next, leaving the seventeenth century an ongoing legacy of disorder. To contemporary observers, the symptoms of these vast economic and demographic changes were manifest. Englishmen appeared to sue each other avidly, while their communities seemed beset by thieves, drunkards, "common hedge-breakers, common peace-breakers, ray-lers, and sowers of discord between neighbours, keepers or haunters of baudy houses, common scolds," and the ubiquitous vagabond. The wandering poor were most worrisome, as the enclosure of common fields had dispossessed thousands and produced a population of "sturdy Beggars" who streamed into London or wandered about the countryside. Many of these "night-walkers and day-sleepers" turned to crime as a way of life, and their frequently illegitimate offspring were a heavy drain on local institutions of relief. Seventeenth-century English thought was conditioned by these realities and was, not surprisingly, pervaded by a fear of crime and an anxiety over social instability.[5]

Assuming ever more authority and responsibility, the monarchy and its Parliaments developed a comprehensive system of social regulation to meet the crisis. New statutes on felonies and misdemeanors poured out of Parliament, while Privy Council orders strengthened and reinvigorated the institutions necessary to enforce them. The famous Elizabethan Poor Laws, which sought to force idlers and vagabonds to work, were but one phase of this effort to bring order out of perceived chaos, and to eradicate offensive behavior.[6]

Though Puritans opposed crown attempts to impose conformity to an insufficiently reformed Church of England, they supported the general Tudor-Stuart desire to discipline an unruly population. Once the early leaders of the movement reconciled themselves to legal institutions as a way of reshaping England, they in fact became keen participants.[7] As such, they were able to observe at first hand the available English instruments of social control and to evaluate their relative effectiveness. English legal institutions, they saw, ranged from the central courts of Westminster to the local courts of individual manors in a system of overlapping and sometimes conflicting jurisdictions. Nevertheless, the salient distinction among them—and a factor responsible for their varying degrees of effectiveness—was the kind of power on which they relied for enforcement: royal, oligarchical, or popular pressure.

The central courts were the most direct agents of royal authority, and because they could draw upon the power and prestige of the sovereign, their impact was felt across the kingdom. Tudor and Stuart monarchs employed the prerogative Star Chamber and, through the archbishop of Canterbury, the ecclesiastical High Commission. But it was through the common law courts that central power was brought more regularly to bear on the general population, when the assizes brought their circuit jurisdiction to the counties. Despite the antagonism between the common law and prerogative courts, both relied ultimately on the power of the crown, whose authority made the assizes formidable weapons against disorder. Puritan ministers recognized this fact, and their sermons at the opening of assize terms expressed their hope that London's authority could impose the order necessary for a reformed England. At the Hertford Assizes in 1619, for example, William Pemberton spoke of the judges there as the "masters and pilots in the ship of the commonwealth, who sit at the stern and guide it forward through their wisdom and fidelity . . . unto the desired haven of peace and prosperity."[8]

Though potent, the assizes were not always practicable as a ready or easily available agent of direct social regulation in local communities. The assizes visited the localities only semiannually, and brought with them a relatively small staff.[9] In addition, the assize courts were expensive ones in which to seek redress of civil grievances. In their *nisi prius* capacity[10] they dealt with a veritable storm of civil litigation in this period, but the benefits of royal authority came only at a high price. On the eve of the Civil War, Sir Edward Coke estimated that Englishmen were spending a million pounds every year on litigation before such courts, while Sir Matthew Hale later observed that costs were so outrageous that they were "often forty times more than the principall." Altogether, the costs of litigation were such that John Winthrop, later the first governor of the Massachusetts Bay Colony, listed them in 1624 as one of England's "Common Greavances Groaninge for Reformation."[11]

Englishmen concerned about disorder, then, appreciated the authority of the assizes, but they had to look to other institutions rather than rely on those powerful but expensive semiannual courts. For hundreds of years justice had been available in the localities in the form of the sheriff's tourn, the county and hundred courts, and the manorial courts leet and baron. However, the same historical

changes that had weakened all feudal structures and helped precipi-
tate the general crisis of the age also had undermined these institutions. The Tudors, of course, accelerated this process of decline in
their program to eliminate those vestiges of the feudal system that
challenged royal power. A chief casualty of Tudor policy was the old
sheriff's tourn, at one time the primary instrument of local administration and social control; by Stuart times it was rarely the
agent of "even the most elementary police tasks."[12]

Yet Tudor opposition was hardly necessary, for the old baronial
and popular courts could flourish only in a social context of communalism which was steadily disappearing in England. There were
undoubtedly backwaters in the varied English social and legal geography where communal institutions and ways of life persisted, but
they had faded most completely in areas where Puritanism—perhaps
in reaction—was strongest. The strength of these courts had been
the ideal of unanimity which governed the medieval manor. In conformity to the needs of common field husbandry, decisions had to be
collective. Tenants had to decide on what crops to plant in the field
where their individual strips of land lay, or what part of it should be
left fallow; these were decisions which, once made, had to be followed by all. Similarly, the tenants acted in a body to discharge their
obligations to the lord, such as yoking their oxen together to plow
his demesne. Working in close and repeated proximity with one
another, they had known their neighbors all their lives and were
aware of whatever happened in their community.[13] Manorial institutions reflected this familiarity and collective effort in their procedures. Attendance at the manorial courts was mandatory for all
tenants, both as a means to confer legitimacy on their decisions and
to bring forward all persons who could contribute information to
guide them.

Theoretically, the courts leet and baron were distinct bodies, but
they were often combined in practice. Leet jurisdiction was concerned with public nuisances and "evill members, and persons of ill
behaviour that are dangerous to their neighbours." The lord's steward
sat there as judge, presiding over a "presentment jury" elected from
those in attendance.[14] This body combined the functions of discovery, indictment, trial, and sentencing. While some manors em-
paneled two juries—a grand jury for indictment, and a petit or
traverse jury for trial—most empowered a single group to perform all

these tasks. Once a presentment was made by a unanimous jury, explained a seventeenth-century treatise, "it is said to be as Gospell, and no Traverse lyeth to it, but in some speciall case, as when it doth concern freehold." After these jurors had accused and convicted, they then set the penalty. This amercement, or fine, was set by "afferers," who might be the entire jury or a few chosen among them.[15]

Like the court leet, the court baron had been established to make justice available to villeins "at their own doors." Its purpose was not to "enquire of any offence against the state," but rather "to take care and inquire of causes concerning the Mannor," and it handled matters pertaining to the lord's own rights as well as to disputes among his tenants.[16] The court baron was truly an instrument of, by, and for a manor's residents, for the steward presided only on matters concerning the lord's rights or conveyance of freehold among copyholders. In all other cases, this court was conducted by twelve "suitors" chosen from the manor; they alone decided disputes over refusals to keep promises or pay debts, up to the value of 40s. When manorial management required it, they might make bylaws for the regulation of manorial business, and set penalties for their violation.[17]

Though suitors of the court baron had little legal expertise and lacked the authority of the lord's steward to enforce their decisions, they possessed other strengths. For one, the weight of tradition was a guide to the rules that should be followed. In addition, their process of making decisions, like that of the leet, drew heavily upon the community's acquaintance with the parties. If, for instance, a man were accused of taking another's livestock as his own, he might bring to court a dozen neighbors to attest to his honesty; their "oath helping," or "wager of law," was sufficient to acquit him of the demand. This sytem worked in a society where a community trusted the knowledge a man's closest acquaintances had of him, and where it was confident that patently false swearing would be recognized sooner or later.[18]

The medieval local courts, therefore, rested mainly on the community to be effective—for bringing actions, making decisons, and finally for enforcing their orders. But enforcement was the crucial element in the structure, for it was the ultimate standard by which the effectiveness of the medieval system of local justice could be measured. The county and hundred courts, for example, were also local medieval courts, and had been established to bring the King's justice to the shires. Conducted by twelve suitors, their jurisdiction was broad, ranging from debts and promises to the "chasing of hoggs with doggs" and other trespassers.[19] While these courts relied less on the community than did the others by not permitting wager of law, they were little less dependent ultimately on the pressures of the community for enforcement. This was so because these bodies were not "courts of record"; that is, their decisions had no standing with outside institutions such as the royal machinery of government. Also unable to obtain adequate support from the impotent sheriff, they had to draw upon the fact that their decisions had been made in the presence of numerous involved members of the community who, it was hoped, would assure compliance through local pressures.[20]

The ideal behind this entire system was described by Sir Thomas Smith in 1565. "These courtes doe serve rather for men that can be content to be ordered by their neighbors, and which love their quiet and profit in their husbandrie, more than to be busy in the law."[21] By that time, however, the wishfulness of this view had become apparent, primarily because the medieval community—especially in Puritan areas—had been eroded by political, economic, and demographic change. Quite simply, many people were no longer part of meaningful communities in the old sense. Uprooted by enclosure or the need to seek work in areas less severely hurt by unemployment, they were unfamiliar with local customs and not well known by any "vicinage," or neighborhood. In sum, writes Christopher Hill, society was changing "from a hierarchy of communities to the agglomeration of equal competing individuals depicted in *Leviathan.*"[22] Without the habits of collective activities and the modes of thought endemic to communalism, the medieval local courts were shrinking to insignificance, doing little more than electing knights to Parliament (at the county courts) and managing the economic affairs of the manor.[23] But, when disputes involved difficult issues, the courts lacked the social foundation to function adequately. Typical of their limited capacity was the way in which the court of a manor near John Winthrop's in Suffolk[24] could amerce only when "everyone in the village knew whether Samuel Ware let his trees 'overdreep' the highway or left his chimney in disrepair, and he could hardly deny the charge."

Where denial or contention existed, the community was as reluctant as it was unable to act. The Elizabethan justice of the peace William Lambard had complained of this problem when he lectured a grand jury that people "vex and overcrow their neighbors . . . bastards be multiplied in parishes, [and] thieves and rogues do swarm the highways," but "scarcely any man [is] found that will once move his finger" to promote order. William Sheppard, writing in 1657, commented that "there are many good Laws" against disorder, "but there is little execution of them: Not one Oath of a thousand that is sworn," he protested, "is punished."[25]

Punishment, of course, requires officials and institutions capable of exercising adequate sanctions against offenders.[26] Only the crown and the powerful country gentry, however, possessed such sanctions in the early seventeenth century. As a result, only those institutions able to draw upon these sources were able to function as effective instruments of social control or conflict resolution when the Puritan migration began. The court leet, for example, was able to continue even its "humble" existence mainly because of such external assistance. If its judgments were resisted, the justices of the peace were available for support because the leet was a court of record. As such, its decisions and orders were recognizable by the royal bureaucracy, while those of the court baron or county court were not. Perhaps equally important was the interest of the manor lord in its continued existence for his personal gain: as his franchise, its fees were a steady source of income.[27]

Gaining a much greater role, for this reason, was the parish, which was coming under the control of the "select vestry," a self-perpetuating oligarchy of the "chief men" of the parish whose prestige and financial weight helped promote the ends of parochial administration. Although the parish was an ecclesiastical division with no original basis in statute, royal decree, or commission, the Tudors had given it responsibilities beyond its traditional duties of maintaining church property and punishing its parishioners' moral or religious transgressions. From its power to tax came a responsibility to repair highways, destroy pests, aid disabled soldiers and sailors, and build workhouses for the unemployed.[28]

Yet the parish, according to Sidney and Beatrice Webb, "was regarded by no one as an organ of autonomous self-government,"[29] and its capacity to cope with the broad spectrum of seventeenth-

century disorder and community disruption was significantly limited
by two factors. In the first place, its jurisdiction stopped sharply at
the end of the list of duties specified by statute. The informal pressures which the locally eminent vestry may have been able to exert
were considerable, but were nevertheless limited to those affairs over
which it had legal jurisdiction, such as implementation of the poor
laws.[30] Second, the vestry was forced to rely on the so-called "customary parish officials" to carry out its will—the constables, churchwardens, tithingmen, overseers of the poor, and surveyors of highways.[31] It was their lot, for example, to collect taxes, detect sabbath
violations, and set vagrants to work or warn them to another parish.
Unfortunately, the men delegated to perform these unwelcome
duties were in many cases hardly those who could do them well.
Constables in particular were drawn from the lower ranks of society.
Their low social standing weakened their efforts to command obedience, and if they did attempt to preserve the peace they might be
sued or humiliated for their pains. Ordered in the King's name to
come to the aid of a Middlesex constable in 1614, one Paul Jefferson embellished his refusal by telling the officer, "I charge you in the
Kinge's name to kiss my tayle."[32] Left to its own devices, therefore,
the parish was unable to overcome its legal shortcomings and to assume a greater role as an instrument of local control.

Yet the parish was not the moribund institution in the early Stuart
period that the manor was. On the contrary, the parish functioned
relatively well for the circumscribed tasks assigned to it. That it did
so, however, was ultimately owing to the supervision and assistance
of the justice of the peace, without whom it would have lacked much
of its ability to act. It fell to the justices of Middlesex, for instance,
to punish Paul Jefferson for his conduct toward a parish official trying to do his job. Indeed, much of the work of a county's justices
was supervision of local affairs.

A county's justices all met in a body quarterly and, more frequently,
they met in smaller groups as "petty sessions." The latter meetings
were held at locations in different "divisions" of the county, but
even the quarterly sessions might adjourn to meet at different
towns "so that nobody," writes a historian of local government in
Norfolk, "ever needed to travel outside his 'division' to attend
quarter sessions." In addition, any one of the dozens of justices living in a county could act individually out of sessions at his resi-

dence.[33] Enforcing many statutes through summary conviction, he was utilizing what Lambard called "the advantage and facilitie that they have to dispatch the affaire by meanes of their nearness and dwelling." As Tudor monarchs assumed more responsibility for establishing and maintaining civil order where local officials had failed, Tudor Parliaments delegated an ever greater share of this burden to the justice of the peace, sending him "not Loads, but Stacks of Statutes," as Lambard wearily observed.[34]

Unlike most other local officials, justices of the peace possessed the powers necessary to bear this burden and to perform their duties effectively. As members of the gentry, they could draw upon their wealth and social standing to command deference and compliance.[35] Among their most important assets, however, was a specific royal grant of power denied to the others—the "commission of the peace," issued by the chancellor under the Great Seal. The reformed commission of 1590 ordered justices to hold regular sessions where they were to enforce all statutes of the peace and try indicted offences.[36] Given the authority to order corporal punishment, commit offenders to gaol, or call upon the physical might of the crown if necessary, the justices possessed the legal powers required to bring peace to an unruly population. As a result, they did not have to rely on the sanctions of the community. They were not limited to imposing the dubious restraint of an oath, moreover, but could enforce any oath to keep the peace by further obtaining a surety bond. As Lambard explained, "Our Governours, knowing that evill men be more restrayned by losse of goods than by conscience of an oath, have used to take sure bonds, and that to the Prince, for the securitie of such as be in feare."

The threat of forfeiting a sum of money was a considerable deterrent, and its effectiveness was increased by the procedures governing its application. To begin with, a justice need not have awaited a complaint in order to act. Lambard pointed out that if a justice "see menne contending in hotte wordes, and threatening the one to hurte (or kill) the other, he may of discretion and ought of Duety (as I thinke) to commaunde them to finde Surety of the Peace." Such persons were required to answer and post bond, and faced commitment to gaol if they refused. Further, the justice was protected from retaliation in a way that other local officials were not. One of the most annoying weaknesses of parish and manor officials had been their vulnerability to vexatious litigation—usually actions of trespass —brought by those against whom they had exercised authority. By contrast, writes Lambard, "no Action would lye against that Justice for so doing."[38]

Justices of the peace commonly supervised local officials in petty sessions. At these meetings, two or more justices (one a member of the quorum)[39] brought their power to bear on inefficient, corrupt, or reluctant local government. This system had been emerging for some time, and in 1605 the Privy Council gave it more formal shape by ordering that "convenient and apt divisions be made through every county and riding, and that fit Justices of the Peace be assigned to have the special charge and care of every such division, and these to be answerable for such defects as through their default shall happen therein." To a hard-working and hard-pressed local official, the presence of the justices was a welcome source of support. On the other hand, their presence was less welcome to someone like High Constable John Crosbie, who was sent to quarter sessions and then removed from office in 1609 for his "evil."[40]

The supervisory responsibilities of the justices were broad but explicit. Overseers of the poor, for instance, as well as surveyors of highways were accountable for the performance of assigned tasks and were required to report to the justices. The parish had to demonstrate that its whipping post, pillory, and other instruments of punishment were serviceable. Even in the administration of the poor laws—a major force behind the "rise of the parish"—the justices were indispensible, for they appointed overseers, examined financial records, and levied rates on wealthier parishes to assist less able ones in bearing the charges of the poor laws. With the power to punish specific officials for nonperformance, the justice of the peace and the petty sessions brought the power of the crown and gentry into local affairs and made resistance inadvisable, whether by recalcitrant parishioners or lazy officials. Even the vestry itself was subject to presentment at quarter sessions for neglecting its duty.[41]

Although the justices had statutory tasks of their own with regard to some local matters,[42] their primary contribution was not direct administration but rather their work above and through subordinate local officeholders. Frequently, disagreements arose in a manor or parish over where responsibility lay for performance of a specific task, and it was the justices who assigned the unwanted job. Similarly, they might have to arbitrate the "many disputes arising out of rating, enclosure, and right of way."[43] Prodding reluctant officials, punishing corrupt ones, or assisting others, they saw to it that local government worked.

Statute granted the justices of the peace only "inconsiderable" civil authority (generally confined to matters between masters and servants),[44] but justices occasionally construed their peace-keeping obligation broadly enough to cover many civil affairs. While any local official or institution might try to do the same and employ informal pressures to expand formal jurisdiction, the justice of the peace was better equipped by his power to take bonds. If, for example, someone believed that a dispute would become violent and endanger the peace, he could ask a justice to intervene and require a peace bond of the person threatening him. Even where the parties admitted that there had been no "threatening words or blows," as several people of Chester did in 1635, they might approach a justice and receive his "lawful favour and assistance for the speedy ending of the differences, the poor men being freed of any further charge." The justice could arbitrate on his own, or he could refer it to other justices or eminent men of the locality, and could then take bonds for adherence to the decision.[45]

It is not surprising, therefore, that many proposals for reform in this period placed much of the burden for bringing order and efficiency to the legal system upon the justices of the peace. To be sure, the variety of suggestions matched the political variety of the times, and there was also much support for reviving the older communal institutions.[46] But William Sheppard integrated the stronger features of many systems to suggest a much greater supervisory role for the justice of the peace over local institutions. Like Lambard before him, Sheppard cited the "tediousness, charge and difficulty" of prosecution, the "neglect of Officers in execution of their Offices," and the fact that "men will not complain one against another, but do conceal the faults of each other." Sheppard's remedy drew upon his observation of the justice's role in local government, and he proposed "that there be more Justices of the Peace, one at least in every Hundred; and that they sit once a Month in every Hundred." Their authority should include all crimes but treason and felony, while conviction should be made an easy, prompt matter upon the testimony of one or two witnesses.[47]

Sheppard also called for extending the justices' jurisdiction to civil issues, for in that area they had been notably restricted. He suggested that the county and hundred courts and the courts baron and leet would function more effectively if supervised by the justices and conducted by "able Judges setled and kept in them." He also proposed that there be "set up a Court of Judicature in every County, to be kept by some of the Justices of the Peace, with a Lawyer, for some special matters" such as probate, tithes, and "poor mens Causes, matters of Equity."[48] John Winthrop, himself a justice, proposed that "any two Justices of Peace (one being of Quorum)" be given authority to make summary judgments in "all Actions suites and demandes touchinge debt trespass batterye defamation or other cause not concerninge matter of tenure or title of or to any maners landes ten[emen]tes or hereditaments nor exceeding the value of x li [£10]. wherein any artificer husbandman labourer servant or spinster" was involved.[49]

Many Puritans supported these reforms. Although the justices were nominally the agents of a monarch who attacked nonconformity, Puritans did not fear the magistrates themselves. They recognized that justices could be useful allies in resisting the church and the crown. Many justices, for instance, refused to enforce unpopular statutes, while others protected Puritans who were presented at quarter sessions.[50] This experience of witnessing "lesser magistrates" oppose the will of the crown, in fact, led Puritans to assign a central role to them. "They alone," Calvin had written, "might defend true religion against heretical kings."[51] Puritan doctrine, of course, required freedom from sinfulness, and the justice was seen as protecting the Puritan community in that important sense as well. While Puritans emphasized the communal watchfulness of the covenanted, they knew that their communities contained the unregenerate who would require discipline from "grave and religious magistrates." Even the radically presbyterian classis of Dedham, which tried to eschew all civil authorities in its affairs, sometimes had to enlist their aid. As they discovered in 1586, it had become necessary "to compleine to the magistrates" about "some careles persons that had no regard of the word or Sacraments."[52]

Puritans in England and America recognized the interdependence of godliness and civil order. Hugh Peter believed that the two were inseparable and went so far as to say that justice was "more necessarie to the immediate subsistence of a Commonwealth" than either "religion or mercie." The reason, he explained in the preface to his tract on law reform, was that "manie Common-wealths subsist without true Religion, and much Mercie; but without Justice, no Commonwealth can long subsist; and it is this, of the three, the most immediate and proper work of the Magistrate's office, to see true Justice executed."[53] Peter's view of the orderly and godly society was a typically Puritan attempt to fuse older communal values and institutions with contemporary institutions of social control. He suggested that disputes be handled by the community, for example, before recourse to the justices of the peace. To implement this plan, he proposed that "there bee in everie Citie, town, and hundred, appointed five, or seven able fit men, to determine all Controversies for Debts, and strifes."[54]

Responding to the concerns and goals of a shared experience, Massachusetts Puritans tried to revive old communal methods and combine them with an expanded magistracy. The settlers of the first towns of the colony—and in particular those spinning off from Salem, where Peter had preached for several years—translated many of these proposals into reality. As some of them stated in the covenant of the First Church of Salem in 1629, "Wee promise to walk with our brethren and sisters in the Congregations with all watchfulness, and tendernis avoyding all jealousies, suspitions, backbyteings, conjurings, provoakings, [and] secret riseing of spirit against them, but in all offences to follow the rule of the Lord Jesus, and to beare and forebeare, give and forgive as he hath taught us."[55]

At the same time, the founders agreed with their contemporary Michael Dalton that the situation "most commonly" occurred that peace "is rather a restraining of hands, then an uniting of minds, And for the maintenance of this Peace chiefly, were the Justices of Peace first made."[56] Dalton's thumbnail analysis of English legal history would have applied to the earliest years at the Bay, for the colony's founders knew that they were organizing a community composed of factious sectarians as well as many other persons who were outcasts from England for decidedly nontheological reasons. Understandably, the founders took full advantage of their charter privileges to make laws "for setling the formes and ceremonies of government and magistracy," which included the right to make "impositions of lawfull fynes, mulcts, imprisonments, or other lawfull correction, according to the course of other corporations in this our realme of England."[57]

Their right to act as a corporation was significant, for it meant that the Massachusetts Bay Company was not, like the old Dorchester Company, merely a type of business partnership with few powers of self-government. Rather, it possessed an authority granted only to corporate bodies and denied to lesser units of government: in the words of the Webbs, this was the right to give "one or more members . . . the well-known powers and authorities elsewhere conferred by the Commission of the Peace,"[58] and thus to hold its own county quarter sessions. The members of the company were well acquainted with the commission of the peace as it was exercised in English counties or corporate boroughs, for many of them had had either direct or indirect experience with it.[59] John Winthrop had been a justice of the peace of the quorum in Suffolk, and Richard Bellingham had held the like position in Lincolnshire. Sir Richard Saltonstall, another justice of the peace, was also a nephew of an Elizabethan lord mayor of London. Additionally, there were close connections among these men and others who became the first magistrates of the colony, such as the obvious one between the John Winthrops, Senior and Junior, or the Richard Saltonstalls, Senior and Junior. Isaac Johnson and John Humfrey were both sons-in-law of the earl of Lincoln, whose steward was Thomas Dudley, the father-in-law of Simon Bradstreet. The Winthrops, Emmanuel Downing (the governor's brother-in-law), Bellingham, Humfrey, Dudley, and Nathaniel Ward all had had some legal training in England, which stood them in good stead as preparation for wielding the extensive legal powers they received from the charter.[60]

While English county oligarchies did not migrate en bloc to America Massachusetts did not lack an incipient oligarchy of its own. To the contrary, the governor, deputy governor, and the assistants (that is, the entire group of company members migrating to America) quickly constituted themselves as a tightly knit and powerful magistracy. With their English experience in law and government, and with their particular social, religious, and political goals to advance, they voted on August 23, 1630 that they were "in all things to have like power that justices of peace hath in England for reformation of abuses and punishing of offenders." These magistrates spent much of their time in the first years of the colony's existence in exercising magisterial powers as broad as those wielded by the justices of any county or corporation in England. They took their status and powers seriously and guarded them jealously. When Israel Stoughton had the temerity in 1635 to challenge them by "affirmeing the Assistants were noe magistrates," he was barred from office for a year. Their meetings were important affairs, and as a group they would fine those among them who were even late for their morning assembly.[61]

Retaining such power proved to be as much a necessity as it had been a product of experience and foresight. Many of the problems that had led reformers to demand that the legal system confer upon the justices of the peace greater powers of swift and certain punishment were duplicated in Massachusetts. The assistants (meeting together in their judicial capacity as the Court of Assistants) had to punish drunkenness, manslaughter, theft, cursing, fornication, and various forms of idleness during the early years of the colony.[62]

Emigration did not solve these troubles, but new conditions in Massachusetts produced a different pattern of problems. To begin with, vagrancy and poverty were less common where labor was dearly short. But this same labor shortage also created difficulties. In a situation directly contrary to that of England, servants were no longer a surplus economic commodity but had become one desperately sought after. Servants were aware of this, and their ill behavior toward masters demonstrated that traditional patterns of deference would have to be reinforced by legal authority. Discipline of servants by the justices of the peace was explicitly authorized by statute in 1630, and was a large part of the assistants' early business.

That servants were brought to Boston for trial indicates the control which central authorities exercised over local affairs as well as the weakness of the satellite communities beyond the capital. The English experience had demonstrated the peril of placing too great a reliance on local institutions, as well as the consequent need to impose magisterial control. Emigration to the New World, where the Puritans had to deal with Antinomians and adventure-seekers alike, heightened this awareness. Even before the Massachusetts Bay Company had received its charter in 1629, those officials who led a vanguard group to Naumkeag (Salem) for the short-lived New England Company in September 1628 exerted close control over the separate settlements hugging the coast to the south. These vestiges of earlier enterprise shared few of the Puritans' goals, and John

Endecott, at the head of the Salem settlement, was suspicious of
their heterodoxy. Samuel Maverick at Winnisimet (Chelsea) dis-
liked Puritanism, while William Blaxton at Shawmut (Boston) and
Thomas Walford at Mishawum (Charlestown) leaned toward episcopacy. Most seriously upsetting, of course, were Merrymount and
Passonagessit (Braintree), where the revellers Thomas Morton and
Captain Wollaston compounded their sins by selling guns to the
Indians. Endecott had no authority to act as a "governor" because
the New England Company was not a chartered corporation, but he
nonetheless managed to command their obedience—and with force
when that became necessry.[63]

Endecott's personal control of affairs at the Bay was brief—it was
reduced when the New England Company was reestablished and
incorporated as the Massachusetts Bay Company in March 1629—
but the role he had played anticipated the centralized direction of
local affairs which his successors would continue. For the first six
years of the colony's existence, the only legal authority (outside
of church discipline) was the General Court, consisting of the Court
of Assistants and those freemen admitted to sit as delegates after
1632. Although the General Court experienced a great deal of
internal turmoil as the governor, assistants, and deputies struggled
over a division of power, centralized control over local government
was not reduced.[64] Rather, it remained firmly with the assistants,
who—sometimes meeting together as a court, and at others acting
singly or in pairs—virtually ran the small settlements that were
taking shape outside Boston. These enterprises, initially referred to
interchangeably as "severall plantations" or "towns," had no legal
status and possessed no machinery of government. As such, they
stood under the control of the Court of Assistants or those assis-
tants/justices of the peace who resided among them. These men
assumed the major responsibility of keeping the peace, resolving disputes, and carrying out the policies of the colonial government in
Boston. They were, to use Edward Johnson's description, "able
Pilots to steere the Helme in a godly peaceable Civill Government."[65]

Their work became progressively heavier as the Great Migration
brought thousands of newcomers—and attendant social problems—
to Massachusetts Bay. Under the impact of this increased business,
the legislature had to concede the need for decentralization and the
delegation of some duties or powers to subordinate units of ad-

ministration. Yet the founders of the colony were not about to create autonomous bodies that would rival their authority or become bailiwicks (literally, as well as metaphorically) of nonconformity. When the General Court dealt with this matter on March 3, 1636, therefore, it constituted town governments closely to resemble the weak and limited structure of English parochial or manorial administration. The famous Town Act of that date is worth quoting in its entirety in order to demonstrate the strictly and traditionally circumscribed nature of town powers:

> Whereas particular townes have many things, which conerne only themselves, and the ordering of their owne affaires, and disposeing of businesses in their owne towne, it is therefore ordered, that the Freemen of every towne, or the major parte of them, shall onely have power to dispose of their owne lands, and woods, with all the previlidges and appurtenances of said townes, to graunt lotts, and make such orders as may concerne the well ordering of their owne townes, not repugnant to the lawes and orders here established by the Generall Court; as also to lay mulks and penaltyes for breach of theis orders, and to levy and distreine the same, not exceeding the some of xx s [20 shillings] ; also to chuse their owne particular officers, as constables, surveyors for the highwayes, and the like; and because much busines is like to ensue to the constables of severall townes, by reason they are to make distresses, and gather Fynes, therefore that every towne shall have two constables, where there is neede, that soe their office may not be a burthen unto them, and they may attend more carefully upon the discharge of their office, for which they shalbe lyeable to give their accompts to this Court when they shalbe called thereunto.[66]

The act did no more than confer on the colony's towns the same limited powers of agricultural and economic management exercised by English manors and parishes; it contained the unmistakeable emphasis on disposing of lands and woods, the petty bylaws with the amercements for their breach, and the choice of parochial officials.

In no sense was the General Court constituting anything resembling the English system of borough corporations as a pattern for these new towns.[67] To have attempted that would not only have been politically unwise; it also would have been flagrantly illegal,

because the Massachusetts Bay Company, as a corporation, had no
authority to create other corporations. "For one corporation cannot
make another Corporation," wrote Sheppard in his treatise on the
subject, "much lesse may it make many Corporations out of itself."
Of course, the governor and company did not always adhere to the
strict letter of only those privileges specified in the charter. But on
close examination it appears that the contours of the colony's governmental system did remain consistent with county or general
corporate practice in England.[68]

The colony's corporate status has been one of the most commonly misunderstood aspects of its early development. Yet it is
essential to understand because English corporate practices dictated the general course to be followed as the colony set up its
system of government in the 1630s. When the Massachusetts Bay
Company was chartered in 1629 it was incorporated as a joint-
stock company; but because its true impulse was the establishment
of a Puritan society beyond the reach of royal or episcopal control, historians have interpreted the events of the first decade as the
acts of a sovereign state. It is an article of faith in the existing scholarship, therefore, that immediately on arriving at the Bay the founders embarked on a policy of shedding their corporate status and
assuming that of a "commonwealth."[69]

In point of fact, the colonists did not even arrive at the Bay as a
joint-stock enterprise. The company had undergone a complete financial reorganization in 1629 when a group of "undertakers"
assumed control of the original capital stock. This effectively divided
the trading and governmental aspects of the venture, and at that
point it "ceased to exist as a joint-stock body." The undertakers
became trustees of the stock with no role in managing the colony,
while the colonists took with them a charter divested of its business character and whose sole purpose remained that of governing
a plantation in the new world."[70]

But once there, the colonists did not use their remoteness or the
collapse of the old financial arrangements to erect a "commonwealth," if by that is meant an independent state. Rather, they
interpreted their surviving charter as that of an English borough
corporation, and they set up a system of government consistent with
it. Though still known as "governor" and "assistants" (terms associated with trading companies), they functioned like a mayor and

burgesses or aldermen—or, more specifically in some situations, like a borough's justices in their quarter sessional capacity. Freemanship followed borough practice in manner as well as name: just as some boroughs predicated membership upon prior admission to a particular guild or fraternity, the colony required admission to a Puritan congregation before anyone could be sworn before its General Court. Even taxation of all residents, which has been cited as the primary example of "commonwealth" right and charter violation, was in fact only a duplication of the traditional assessment made by many boroughs on all householders through a variety of methods available to a corporation, such as the levy of a tax equivalent to the "county rate."[71] When the General Court assessed £60 for defense in 1632, therefore, Watertown leaders might protest that the government "as a mayor and aldermen . . . have not power to make laws or raise taxations without the people," but their legal argument was weak against a background of corporate or county practice in England.[72]

Answering the protest, Winthrop denied that the colony was bound by corporate practice, but reaction against his rule led to his defeat as governor in 1634. His successors Dudley, Haynes, and Vane made no such claims, for external events were combining with internal factors to force the colony to conform to corporation practice. In the same year that Winthrop was defeated, the colony learned that the powerful Laud Commission for Regulating Plantations was investigating it. A year later Sir Ferdinando Gorges, who had rival land claims to the area, filed suit against the patentees and made numerous accusations about charter violations, while the Laud Commission added its complaints about Puritan heterodoxy and intolerance. With the outcome pending in litigation, the colony had to demonstrate that it was not the refractory, independent commonwealth that its opponents said it was. On the contrary, it had to solidify its position by showing that it was doing no more than what many other English corporations were entitled to do. Just as the colony's leaders publicly admonished John Endecott for cutting the cross of St. George from the English flag, they were careful not to usurp any privilege denied to a corporation. True, they did not stay within the *specific* limitations of the 1629 charter, but they did nothing that they could not later defend, if necessary, as being generally accepted corporate practice in England. The Standing Council created in 1636 was a case in point, as its members were to

serve for life. Such a body was not warranted by the charter, but
neither was it an uncommon feature of English corporations, many
of whom had groups of "principal burgesses" with life tenure.[73]

This strategy was, to a degree, successful, because when the court
of King's Bench finally did revoke the charter in 1637 it did not do
so because of charter violations. Rather, it acted only on the grounds
that the charter had been "surreptitiously obtained," and it permitted
the colony to continue with its existing government until Gorges
could be sent over as "General Governor" with a new charter.[74]
Fortunately for Massachusetts, its enemies were later distracted by
the Civil War, and Gorges never arrived at the Bay. But until that
became clear, the colony was left in a position of precarious survival,
and it had to pursue a strategy of giving no further provocation
by acting like a rebellious commonwealth and exercising royal
prerogative.

The creation of corporations was a privilege clearly reserved to the
crown or Parliament and not generally possessed by English corporations. The General Court seems to have been well aware of this
limitation, for while it did vote funds for Harvard College in 1636,
it did not specify any type of government for it until 1642 and did
not confer "corporation" status until 1650—by which time Charles I
was dead and his sons in flight.[75]

Nor did the General Court make Massachusetts towns into corporations, although some historians believe that town land policy suggests
corporate practice.[76] However, their actual handling of the land
suggests unincorporated tenancy in common and hints strongly at
manorial procedures. When towns reserved to themselves the privilege of buying back a parcel of land before it was sold, for instance,
their action corresponded to the manorial procedure of conveying
all copyhold through the lord: a seller technically conveyed the
parcel first back to the lord, who then conveyed it to the actual
recipient. Another corporate privilege would have been the towns'
ability to sue as a collective entity, but they did not do this in practice in the 1630s. Instead, they appear to have followed the parochial method of designating a particular individual to appear privately
for them.[77]

The town was thus not intended to be a corporate entity nor, for
that matter, a very autonomous one. To assure that fact, the General
Court passed the Town Act (General Court Order no. 285) only

after it had created a supervisory level of government above the towns earlier that same day.[78] Before the legislature delegated manorial or parochial powers, it created the rules and institutions — drawn from English precedent — sufficient to oversee that authority. As a first step, the General Court repeated a rule made by the Court of Assistants acting alone in 1630 that the "sitting downe of men in any newe plantation" had to be approved by a majority of the magistrates. Order no. 280 expanded on this, requiring that any new gathering of churches also receive their permission, in addition to that of the "elders of the greater parte of the churches in this jurisdiction."[79]

Order no. 281, however, was the most important limitation on the newly constituted towns, because it created a system of quarterly courts exercising civil, criminal, and administrative jurisdiction in the major population centers of Boston, Cambridge, Salem, and Ipswich. They could hear and determine civil causes of up to £10 in value and try all crimes but those punishable by banishment or by loss of life or limb.[80] The colony possessed no authority to create additional courts, but the quarterly courts were not, strictly speaking, an entirely new judicial system. In reality, they were a type of circuit court composed of those magistrates living in or near the four locations of the court, and any magistrate who wished to join them. The magistrates were assisted by "assotiates" appointed by the General Court on nomination by the freemen of the towns, but who were explicitly subordinate to the magistrates and had no authority to act on their own. Individual associates had none of the magistrate's powers, nor could they collectively hold a quarterly court without a magistrate present.[81]

Almost as soon as the acts of March 3 took effect, the courts had to assist the towns. The weak institutions of the towns were barely able to manage land arrangements, and the courts had to punish commoners who failed to maintain adequate fences in defiance of town orders, others who resisted constables or poundkeepers, and even the officials who were negligent in their duty.[82] In addition, the courts assumed such traditionally parochial functions as appointing constables, enforcing church attendance, and punishing moral delinquency, as well as the clerical responsibility of performing marriages and recording births and deaths.[83]

If the substance of quarterly court business is suggestive of both

petty sessions and quarter sessions, their procedures also suggest
a combination of the two. Like petty sessions, small groups of magistrates brought justice and administrative efficiency to the general
area of their residences. Because they had no grand juries of their
own, they often acted on referral from the Assistants Court, much
in the traditional manner that petty sessions received cases from
quarter sessions. But the Massachusetts courts did have petit juries
of their own, and, also like quarter sessions, they held four regular
meetings each year. By statute and in practice, these were even held
at similar times: the English courts met at Easter (between March 22
and April 25), the Translation of St. Thomas (or "Midsummer," in
June), Michaelmas (September 29), and after Epiphany (January 6),
while those in Massachusetts met in March, June, September, and
December.[84] In addition, the selection of locations had precedent
in the English magisterial practice of holding quarter sessions at
different sites in a county to assure accessibility. The Privy Council
Order of 1605 had specified that courts be no further from anyone
seeking justice than seven or eight miles—approximately the distance
from any settled area in the colony in the 1630s to either Boston,
Cambridge, Salem, or Ipswich.[85]

As the quarterly courts operated in Massachusetts, they embodied
elements of quarter sessions practice, reform proposals for greater
magisterial involvement in civil matters, and Puritan desires for
greater reliance on arbitration in conflict resolution. For instance,
the quarterly courts and the Assistants Court appear to have divided
criminal jurisdiction in roughly the way that quarter sessions and
the assizes in England did. Save for statutory differences, there was
much overlapping of jurisdiction in both legal systems, and many of
the same type of cases could be tried at either level in them. Nevertheless, similar implicit rules of practice governed both: just as
the more difficult or serious English cases were reserved to the assizes,
the Assistants Court heard the more serious offenses in Massachusetts.[86] While the Assistants Court punished John Davies in 1639
"for grosse offences in attempting lewdness with divers woomen,"
the Salem quarterly courts more commonly acted as they did that
same year in admonishing James Downing "to take great heed" in
his choice of companions.[87]

The civil jurisdiction of the quarterly courts was a novelty for
justices of the peace (who quickly came to be referred to in Massa-

chusetts as "magistrates"), but it also had English impulses behind it. In the first place, the quarterly courts of northern Massachusetts referred many civil matters to arbitration, following the practice of English justices: between 1636 and 1643, the magistrates of Salem an Ipswich dispatched twenty cases in this way.[88] Second, the involvement of magistrates in local civil disputes was actually the embodiment of the reformist desire in England to confer such authority on the justices. While this arrangement fulfilled the Puritan goal of greater community involvement in conflict resolution, the intervention of the magistrate was also a means of assuring that the decision would stand.

Like the quarter sessions in relation to English manors or parishes, the quarterly courts of northern Massachusetts handled many problems beyond the legal or practical abilities of the towns there, allowing, of course, for the different social problems in the New World. Northern Massachusetts towns appear to have had particular difficulties with servants and children, and magistrates often had to be called upon to impose order in domestic relations. They might be required to whip recalcitrant servants or, conversely but less frequently, to punish masters who had been too severe in their own exercise of discipline.[89]

It is clear from the records of the towns north of Boston—those which became Essex County in 1643—that the quarterly courts there were filling a need resulting from inherent town weaknesses, and that the role of magistrate was essential to town order. One obvious reason for their indispensability in Salem, for instance, was that town's initial reliance on the leet practice of requiring unanimity to make a presentment and amercement for violation of town orders. The difficulty of this procedure became evident in 1637 when John Pickering enclosed a part of the town common "without Consent from the Towne." Elias Stileman, one of the town's seven selectmen, refused to concur in a decision by the other six to levy a 20s. fine, and the six were left vainly to record, "we therfore whose names ar underwrit doe protest ageanst all disorderlie Lay[ing] out of Land in thes Limitts of Salem."[90]

Even with unanimity the towns—like English manors and hundreds —lacked the sanctions necessary to make their decisions meaningful. They might send malefactors to the quarterly court or to Boston, but their own sanction of a 20s. fine was weak—indeed, it was only half the sum allowed in manorial courts. Salem, the largest town in the colony after Boston, fined only two men as much as 20s. in the 1630s, both for fencing town common: Gervas Garfor by the selectmen in 1637, and Edmund Giles in 1640 "by the generall towne meeting." When the selectmen fined John Gatchell 10s. for the same offense, they agreed to refund half that sum "in case he shall cutt of his lonng har of his Head in to a sevill frame." It seems that Salem was still less stern in disciplining the negligence of its officeholders. In 1637 it assessed insignificant sixpence fines against Thomas Scruggs and Daniel Ray "for disorderlie standing and neglecting to spek to T[own] busines." When an "agitation of matters which concerne the neatherd" also occurred that year, the town only voted its "sensure" should he fail to do his job. Otherwise, Salem had to enlist the aid of a magistrate, as it did in 1640 when constables were not collecting rates and it voted to obtain "helpe from the Magistrate to [di] straine for such summes as are behinde."[91]

While English parochial administration and manorial justice were susceptible to partiality, the quarterly courts contained several features to minimize this abuse, at least, and to impart a relative degree of impartiality. Juries were not confined to the men of a single town, but included others as well. Customarily, the court at Salem consisted of seven men of that town and five from Lynn.[92]

The dependence of northern Massachusetts towns on the magistrates and quarterly courts for peace-keeping, conflict resolution, and administrative effectiveness can be drawn from the many examples of court intervention in town disputes and problems.[93] While Salem selectmen were able to refer to arbitrators issues related to town land, other problems went directly to the courts. Between 1636 and 1640 the Salem court punished twenty-nine men of that town for various offenses including pound breach, use of false weights, illegal sale of liquor, and abuse of constables. This figure constitutes fully 7 percent, or one out of fourteen, of all adult males known to have taken up even temporary residence in Salem during this period.[94] During those same years the court heard 192 civil causes; of these, almost 75 percent (145) were intratown disputes between residents of Salem, Ipswich, or Lynn.[95] These percentages bespeak severe weaknesses within those towns for resolving petty disagreements among townsmen, while the available town records are correspondingly devoid of such activity.[96]

Northern Massachusetts may not be typical of all New England, nor even of Massachusetts. Its low percentage of church members weakened the role of the church, and its alternately rocky and marshy topography made it a less than affluent farming region. As a result, it became a fishing and pasturing society which stood apart from Boston and other towns to the south.[97] But these features did not dictate the precise shape of local government that its leaders John Endecott, Simon Bradstreet, and Richard Saltonstall would erect. Drawing upon their English experience with corporate or county government, they did not attempt to gain political power from Boston in order to vest it in their town meetings or boards of selectmen.[98] Indeed, the colony government would have resisted such an attempt, for the memory of nonconformists like Roger Williams or Anne Hutchinson was a lesson in the dangers of excessive town or congregational autonomy. Instead, political leaders in Boston as well as to the north were satisfied with the devolution of power upon the quarterly courts, which were more effective institutions of local governance than the towns. Regionalist rather than town-centered, the magistrates at Salem and Ipswich gained a further measure of power in 1641 when their courts were given their own grand juries and a jurisdiction virtually equal to that of the Assistants Court. Two years later their incipient regional identity was strengthened when the towns between the Mystick and Merrimack Rivers were grouped together as Essex County.[99] Their English experience before emigration had demonstrated the effectiveness of corporate or county magisterial government; Massachusetts conditions, while they altered some details, confirmed it.

NOTES

1. Hugh Peters [sic], *Gods Doings, and Mans Duty* (London, 1646), dedication, 44–45.

2. See, as representative, Kenneth A. Lockridge, *A New England Town. The First Hundred Years: Dedham, Massachusetts, 1636–1736* (New York, 1970).

3. Cited in Michael Walzer, *The Revolution of the Saints: A Study in the Origins of Radical Politics* (Cambridge, Mass., 1965), 33.

4. Cited ibid., 202. This view of mankind is incompatible with the liberal utopianism depicted in Lockridge, *New England Town*. Lockridge, p. 1, compares Dedham with the nineteenth-century experiments at Amana, Oneida, and Brook Farm, settlements whose positive idea of human nature derived from a post-Enlightenment world view, and which the founders of Massachusetts would not have accepted.

5. William Sheppard, *The Court-keepers Guide* ([1641] London, 1654), 14–15. Christopher Hill, in explaining the pre–Civil War period, warns, "We shall often misinterpret

men's thoughts and actions if we do not continually remind ourselves of this background of potential unrest" (*The Century of Revolution, 1603-1714* [New York, 1961], 28).

6. For new statutes, see Sir William Holdsworth, *A History of English Law,* 17 vols. (London, 1922-73), IV, 503-21; John H. Langbein, "The Historical Origins of the Sanction of Imprisonment for Serious Crime," *Journal of Legal Studies,* V (1976), 35-60.

7. For John Winthrop's activities in this regard before emigration, see Edmund S. Morgan, *The Puritan Dilemma: The Story of John Winthrop* (Boston, 1958), 26. On the early Puritan ambivalence toward legal institutions, see M. M. Knappen, *Tudor Puritanism: A Chapter in the History of Idealism,* paperback ed., (Chicago, 1965), 402-3.

8. Cited in Walzer, *Revolution,* 179. See also 174, 233.

9. J. S. Cockburn, *A History of English Assizes, 1558-1714* (Cambridge, 1972), 70. Assizes were held only annually in the three most remote counties of the north (ibid., 19).

10. *Nisi prius* civil jurisdiction was technically distinct from the gaol delivery authority of the assize courts. See Sir Edward Coke, *The Fourth Part of the Institutes of the Laws of England* (London, 1809), chapter 56.

11. Donald Veall, *The Popular Movement for Law Reform, 1640-1660* (Oxford, 1970), 37-38; Sir Matthew Hale, "Considerations touching the Amendment or Alteration of Lawes," in *A Collection of Tracts Relative to the Laws of England,* ed. Francis Hargrave, 2 vols. (Dublin, 1787), I, 283; Winthrop Papers, vol. 1, *1498-1628* (Boston, 1929), 309-10. Figures on civil causes at *nisi prius* can be found in Cockburn, *Assizes,* 137.

12. Thomas G. Barnes, *Somerset, 1625-1640: A County's Government during the "Personal Rule"* (Cambridge, Mass., 1961), 124.

13. H. S. Bennett, *Life on the English Manor: A Study of Peasant Conditions, 1150-1400* (Cambridge, 1960), 44-49.

14. Sheppard, *Court-keepers Guide,* 14; John Kitchin, *Jurisdictions; or, the Lawful Authority of Courts Leet, Courts Baron, Court of Marshalseyes, Court of Pypowder, and Antient Demesne* (London, 1663), 16.

15. For a description of the presentment jury, see Sheppard, *Court-keepers Guide,* 20-22; Kitchin, *Jurisdictions,* 83ff; and John P. Dawson, *A History of Lay Judges* (Cambridge, Mass., 1960), 191-92.

16. Trespass by force and arms was not within its jurisdiction. For the court baron in general, see Coke, *Fourth Institute,* chapter 57; Kitchin, *Jurisdictions,* 344-69; and Sheppard, *Court-keepers Guide,* 3, 66.

17. Sidney and Beatrice Webb, *English Local Government* (London, 1906-29), *vol. 2, The Manor and the Borough,* 13n, 18.

18. For a description of this procedure, see Bennett, *English Manor,* 207-16; and Holdsworth, *English Law,* I, 305-8, for the pleas in which wager of law was permitted. Oath-helpers were also subject to penalty if a man's later behavior made it clear that their oath had been false swearing.

19. William Greenwood, *Curia Comitatus Rediviva, or the Pratique Part of the County-Court Revived* (London, 1657), 108-55. Usually limited to actions under 40s., the court could hear higher claims upon obtaining a writ of *justicies* from the chancellor.

20. Coke, *Fourth Institute,* chapters 60, 61.

21. Cited in Dawson, *Lay Judges,* 232.

22. *Society and Puritanism in Prerevolutionary England* (New York, 1964), 487.

23. Geoffrey Elton, *The Tudor Constitution: Documents and Commentary* (Cambridge, 1965), 451; David G. Hey, *An English Rural Community: Myddle under the Tudors and Stuarts* (Leicester, 1974), 228. On Puritan avoidance of the leet, see Veall, *Popular Movement,* 37-39.

24. Dawson, *Lay Judges,* 191-92, describes Redgrave, near Bury St. Edmunds.

25. *England's Balme* (London, 1657), 25–26. This book was subtitled *Proposals by Way of Grievance and Remedy; Humbly Presented to His Highness and Parliament; Towards the Regulation of the Law, and better Administration of Justice. Tending to the great Ease and Benefit of the good people of the Nation.* Veall, *Popular Movement,* 84, refers to this as "the most comprehensive set of law reform proposals put forward during the whole of the period covered by the Civil War and Interregnum."

26. For a theoretical discussion of this general point, see Harold Lasswell and Richard Arens, "The Role of Sanction in Conflict Resolution," *Journal of Conflict Resolution,* XI (1967), 27–39.

27. Holdsworth, *English Law,* IV, 127–30.

28. Ibid., 155–57.

29. Webb and Webb, *English Local Government, vol. 1, The Parish and the County,* 40.

30. W. E. Tate, *The Parish Chest: A Study of the Records of Parochial Administration in England* (Cambridge, 1960), 249ff; Eleanor Trotter, *Seventeenth-Century Life in the Country Parish, with Special Reference to Local Government* (Cambridge, 1909), 23.

31. Trotter, *Seventeenth-Century Life,* 23. Strictly speaking, the constable was an officer of the hundred, but his duties concerned parish affairs, and by a statute of 22 Henry VIII, c. 12, sec. 3, parishes were made liable to fine if he did not perform his duties (Holdsworth, *English Law,* IV, 124, 158).

32. William LeHardy, ed., *County of Middlesex: Calendar to the Sessions Records,* vol. 1, *1612–1614* (London, 1935), 371. Barnes, *Somerset,* 77, describes constables in that county as "lazy, disobedient, and negligent."

33. A. Hassell Smith, *County and Court: Government and Politics in Norfolk, 1558–1603* (Oxford, 1974), 88. The authority of the justices acting individually, in petty sessions, or in quarter sessions, is distinguished in Holdsworth, *English Law,* IV, 138–49.

34. William Lambard, *Eirenarcha, or of the Office of Justices of Peace* (London, 1581), 34, 246. More justices were commissioned to handle the load. The Commission of the Peace for Somerset in 1613 named forty-three justices (twenty-six of the quorum), while that of 1625 named fifty-nine (thirty-seven of the quorum) (E. H. Bates Harbin, ed., *Quarter Sessions Records for the County of Somerset,* vol. 1, *James I, 1607–1625* [London, 1907], xxiii; vol. 2, *Charles I, 1625–1639* [London, 1908], xviii–xix).

35. G. M. Trevelyan, *English Social History* (London, 1941), 171, cited in J. H. Gleason, *The Justices of the Peace in England, 1558–1640* (Oxford, 1969), 1.

36. The reformed commission of the peace can be found in Elton, *Tudor Constitution,* 460–62. In practice, the justice had jurisdiction over all crimes but treason (D. H. Allen, ed., *Essex Quarter Sessions Order Book, 1652–1661* [Chelmsford, 1974], xii).

37. *Eirenarcha,* 83. There were two types of bonds: peace bonds, taken to prevent threatened or potential disorder, and the bond "of good abearing," to prevent recurrence of an offense (ibid., 124–25).

38. Ibid., 86.

39. A specially designated group among the justices, originally distinguished by their superior learning in the law, and later by their greater experience, who were to be present at each petty session. Most Elizabethan social and economic legislation required the presence of a quorum member. (Allen, *Essex Quarter Sessions,* xii.)

40. Conyers Read, ed., *William Lambarde and Local Government: His "Ephemeris" and Twenty-Nine Charges to Juries and Commissions* (Ithaca, 1962), 98; J. H. E. Bennett and J. C. Dewhurst, eds., *Quarter Sessions Records Records of the Justices of the Peace for the County Palatine of Chester, 1559–1760* (Chester, 1940), 70.

41. Holdsworth, *English Law,* IV, 141; Webb and Webb, *Parish and County,* 31. A re-

cent study of Norfolk in this period concludes that parish officials "would have achieved little without oversight by the magistrates" in poor law administration (Hassell Smith, *County and Court*, 105–6).

42. Holdsworth, *English Law*, IV, 138–42; Lambard, *Eirenarcha*, 198ff.

43. Trotter, *Country Parish*, 214–15.

44. Holdsworth, *English Law*, IV, 139–41, fails to go beyond these explicit grants and ignores the wider capacity available in practice.

45. *Records of Chester*, 89; see also D. E. Howell James, ed., *Norfolk Quarter Sessions Order Book, 1650–57* (Norwich, 1955), 17; and Trotter, *Country Parish*, 210n.

46. For example, see Veall, *Popular Movement*, 75.

47. *England's Balme*, 25–28, 35–36.

48. Ibid., 62–63.

49. Winthrop Papers, I, 310.

50. Hassell Smith, *County and Court*, 112. Smith cites M. G. Davies, *The Enforcement of English Apprenticeship* (Cambridge, Mass., 1956), 162, that justices enforced a new apprenticeship law "only when it met an urgent need of the local community or was in harmony with strong public sentiment." See also Allen, *Essex Quarter Sessions*, xiii.

51. Walzer, *Revolution*, 59–60. It appears that these "godly justices" were not removed from office because of such efforts or their religion. According to Gleason, *Justices of the Peace*, 73–74, there were recurring rumors that this would occur, but "the absence of all pertinent evidence argues that the Puritans as such were not systematically excluded from the county benches."

52. Patrick Collinson, *The Elizabethan Movement* (Berkeley, 1967), 54–55, 174, 204, 354–55; Hill, *Society and Puritanism*, 224–25; R. G. Usher, ed., *The Presbyterian Movement in the reign of Queen Elizabeth as illustrated by the Minute Book of the Dedham Classis* (London, 1905), 55.

53. *Good Work for a Good Magistrate. Or, a Short Cut to great quiet* (London, 1651), 27–28.

54. Ibid., 39.

55. Richard D. Pierce, ed., *Records of the First Church in Salem, Massachusetts, 1629–1736* (Salem, 1974), 3–4.

56. Michael Dalton, *Countrey Justice* (London, 1619), 7.

57. Nathaniel B. Shurtleff, ed., *Records of the Governor and Company of the Massachusetts Bay in New England*, 4 vols. (Boston, 1853–54), I, 16, 17. (Hereafter, *Mass. Rec.*)

58. *Manor and Borough*, 279.

59. The following draws in large part from Robert E. Wall, *Massachusetts Bay: The Crucial Decade, 1640–1650* (New Haven, 1972), 31–32.

60. Thomas G. Barnes, *The English Legal System, Carryover to the Colonies*, Papers read at a Clark Library Seminar, November 3, 1973 (Los Angeles, 1975), 78–79; Charles M. Andrews, *The Colonial Period of American History*, 4 vols. (New Haven, 1934–38); *Note Book Kept by Thomas Lechford, Esq., Lawyer, in Boston, Massachusetts Bay, from June 27, 1638 to July 29, 1641* (Cambridge, Mass., 1885), xv, 45.

61. *Mass. Rec.*, I, 74, 136, 181, 182. For a comparison with the powers of an English borough corporation, see Webb and Webb, *Manor and Borough*, 280.

62. John Noble and John F. Cronin, eds., *Records of the Court of Assistants of Massachusetts Bay, 1630–1692*, 3 vols. (Boston, 1901–28), II, 4, 7, 9, 13, 14, 18, 26, 28, 48, 50, 64. (Hereafter, *Assts. Rec.*)

63. Andrews, *Colonial Period*, I, 340, 361–62; A. C. Goodell, "The Origin of Towns in Massachusetts," *Proceedings of the Massachusetts Historical Society*, 2nd ser., V (1890), 328. Endecott also drafted a set of laws. "Captain Indicotts Lawes" have been lost, how-

ever, and there is no evidence as to their content or effect. (James Duncan Phillips, *Salem in the Seventeenth Century* [New York, 1933], 81.)

64. This control was held fast even during the more serious political debates of the next decade. Wall, *Crucial Decade*, 21-22, interprets the debates over the Standing Council and the negative voice as efforts to confer greater powers on the lower house *and* the town boards of selectmen. Actually, nothing in those debates would have enhanced the authority of the latter. Whatever powers the deputies wrested from the assistants, they retained them for the lower house of the legislature and granted none of them to the towns. Judicial powers, moreover, were held securely by the assistants themselves. The lower house collectively shared some judicial power with the assistants, but its individual members had no magisterial authority.

65. *Wonder-Working Providence* [1653], ed. J. F. Jameson (New York, 1910), 30-31; Darrett Rutman, *Winthrop's Boston: Portrait of a Puritan Town, 1630-1649* (Chapel Hill, 1965), 43-44.

66. *Mass. Rec.*, II, 172.

67. For the contrary view that the towns were modeled after corporations, see T. H. Breen, "Persistent Localism: English Social Change and the Shaping of New England Institutions," *William and Mary Quarterly*, 3rd ser., (1975), XXXII 3-28.

68. William Sheppard, *Of Corporations, Fraternities, and Guilds* (London, 1659), 9. General corporate powers are described in *La Graunde Abridgment, Collect and Escrit per le Iudge tresreuerend Syr Robert Brooke*, 2 vols. (London, 1573), I, 188-92.

69. See, for example, Wall, *Crucial Decade, 6.;* or *Andrews*, Colonial Period, I, chapter 20, "From Charter to Commonwealth in Massachusetts."

70. William R. Scott, *The Constitution and Finance of English, Scottish, and Irish Joint-Stock Companies to 1720*, vol. 2, *Companies for Foreign Trade, Colonization, Fishing, and Mining* (Cambridge, 1910), 314-15.

71. Webb and Webb, *Manor and Borough*, 703n; Martin Weinbaum, ed., *British Borough Charters, 1307-1660* (London, 1943), passim.

72. John Winthrop, *The History of New England from 1630 to 1649*, ed. James Savage, 2 vols. (Boston, 1853), I, 84.

73. See, for example, the charter of Dorchester, in Weinbaum, *Borough Charters*, 29-30. Julius Goebel, in his classic article "King's Law and Local Custom in Seventeenth Century New England," *Columbia Law Review*, XXXI (1931), 416-48, shifted the focus in Early American legal history from Westminster to the great variety of practice found in the localities. However, he overlooked the justice of the peace—especially in his quarter sessional capacity within an incorporated borough—as an institution of some uniformity throughout local government which could serve as a model for New England.

74. W. N. Sainsbury and J. W. Fortescue, eds., *Calendar of State Papers, Colonial Series, America and West Indies*, vol. 1, *1574-1660* (London, 1860), 204-5; vol. 5, *1677-1680* (London, 1896), 129-30; *Acts of the Privy Council, Colonial Series*, vol. 1, *1613-1680* (London, 1908), 217; Andrews, *Colonial Period*, I, 423.

75. London, by unique prescription, ("lusage de Lond"), had created lesser corporations such as guilds. On London's exceptional character in this regard, see *Graunde Abridgement*, under "Prescription," I, 149. Harvard College was referred to as "The Society" in its early years. (Andrew M. Davis, "Corporations in the Days of the Colony," *Publications of the Colonial Society of Massachusetts*, vol. 1, *1892-94*, 184n, 190; *Mass. Rec.*, II, 30; IV (part i), 12-14.)

76. Viola F. Barnes, *The Dominion of New England* (New Haven, 1923), 184, expresses this view.

77. In 1639 Thomas Oliver sued George Harris for trespass, "according to ord. of Towne,

Jos. Woodbury, tres." Microfilm of Essex (Massachusetts) Quarterly Court Recordbook (Salem), 1636–41, 25 (hereafter, Salem Recordbook, 1636–41). Conversely, a year later "Augustin Calem, Goatkeeper," sued "Mr. Conant and Divers others" over a matter which the "towne ordered" (ibid., 39). For an English comparison, see *Quarter Sessions of Somerset*, I, xlviii, 156.

78. At this meeting the legislature also created the Standing Council and formalized the negative voice (*Mass. Rec.*, I, 167). Although the town act is generally considered by historians to be a single enactment, it was merely part of a larger comprehensive plan for effective local government in the colony. Perhaps one reason for isolating the Town Act is an oversight committed by the clerk of the General Court when it was passed: he failed to enter the act with that day's business and later had to insert it where space allowed— with the business of April 5, 1636 (ibid., I, 172).

79. Ibid., I, 168.

80. Ibid., I, 169.

81. Ibid.

82. Salem Recordbook, 1636–41, 3, 5, 25.

83. Fusing magisterial and clerical roles had some English county precedent in the person of the "clerical justice," the minister commissioned as a justice of the peace. Because Massachusetts Puritans—contrary to their former reputation as "theocrats"—distrusted secular power in clerical hands, they vested these combined responsibilities in *lay* justices alone. On the "clerical justice," see Webb and Webb, *Parish and County*, 250-60.

84. Quarter sessions met according to 2 Henry IV, c. 4 (Salem Recordbook, 1636–41, 2–48, *passim*). These dates of the Salem term found in the manuscript differ from those listed by George F. Dow., ed., *Records and Files of the Quarterly Courts of Essex County*, 9 vols. (Salem, 1921–75), I, 3–60. They were set by statute on March 3, 1636, and manuscript records show practice conforming to the law.

85. Holdsworth, *English Law*, IV, 147.

86. Allen, *Essex Quarter Sessions*, xxii, comments on the "marked similarity" between the business of the assizes and quarter sessions, and Barnes calls them "indistinguishable." Nevertheless, they point out that capital crimes were reserved to the assizes.

87. *Assts. Rec.*, II, 81; Salem Recordbook, 1636–41, 33.

88. Salem Recordbook, 1636–41, 2–48. Records of the Ipswich terms of the quarterly court are lost before 1641. The earliest records of that court can be found included with the town records of Ipswich, on a microfilm at the Essex Institute in Salem, labeled "Ipswich Town Records, 1634-[1660]."

89. See, for example, Salem Recordbook, 1636–41, 17.

90. *Town Records of Salem, October 1, 1634, to November 7, 1659* (Salem, 1868), 46.

91. Ibid., 34, 38, 41–42, 55, 101, 106.

92. Salem Recordbook, 1636–41, 2–48.

93. Records are sparse for the early years of these towns, but enough exist to indicate that town weaknesses are not a fallacious inference drawn from negative evidence; the ineffectiveness of town sanctions are explicit in the town records, and strongly implicit in the quarterly court records. In addition to the *Salem Town Records*, see *Wenham Town Records, 1642-1706*, comp. William P. Upham (Wenham, 1930); Salisbury Town Records, 1638-1902 (typescript at the Essex Institute); "Marblehead Town Records" [1648-1683], comp. William H. Bowden, in *Essex Institute Historical Collections*, 69 (1933), 207-329; and "Ipswich Town Records."

94. This author's estimate of 419 adult male arrivals through 1640 is drawn from records of the town, congregation, quarterly courts, and Assistants Court. The quarterly court also punished fifteen women and fourteen male servants, but no reliable estimate can be made for the total population of those groups.

95. When available for litigation at the Ipswich court in 1641, the figures are not as dramatic, but still suggestive: 47 percent of the cases that year were between Ipswich residents, a figure which may be artificially low because 35 percent of the sample were of unknown residence.

96. Town records devoid of serious dispute have been presented as evidence of a successfully utopian communalism which obviated conflict in the early seventeenth century. However, historians of Tudor-Stuart England have proposed more plausible explanations for similar evidence found in contemporary English records. Dawson, *Lay Judges,* 254, maintains that this was not proof of *effective* local institutions, but rather the product of a "contracting circle of topics dealt with" by communal bodies; a court might record *"omnia bene"* when in fact much difficulty was being handled elsewhere. In a superb study of early seventeenth-century political practices, Derek Hirst points out that localities may have concealed their disputes in order to create "the illusion of unanimity" where none existed (*The Representative of the People? Voters and Voting in England Under the Early Stuarts* [Cambridge, 1975], 15).

97. Wall, *Crucial Decade,* 35–38, discusses the distinctiveness of this area, but he interprets the political efforts of its leaders as part of a colony-wide effort by local gentry to place power within the towns.

98. *Mass. Rec.,* II, 138. It is true that the founders of the colony brought with them an impulse toward "persistent localism" as suggested by Breen (see note 67). Yet "localism" did not mean antipathy to, or independence of, county institutions. Rather, the word in its contemporary English usage more accurately meant *county* localism against the centralizing attempts of London. See, in this regard, Hassell Smith, *County and Court,* esp. vii.

99. *Mass. Rec.,* II, 285–86; I, 325–26.

The Political Structure
of Local Government
in Colonial Connecticut

BRUCE C. DANIELS

It is often asserted that the political structure of the colony of Connecticut stemmed from the unusual origins of the colonial government. Charles Andrews wrote that the Connecticut towns organized the colonial government, instead of the government organizing the towns as happened in most of the other colonies.[1] Chronologically, he was correct: towns were born in Connecticut before the colonial government. But the original three towns of Connecticut deliberately gave up their sovereignty to a General Court, and it was under this court's guidance that the towns were organized. The court formed those towns in substance and not vice versa as the chronology would indicate. Only this conclusion can explain the similarity in the governments of the first three towns.

Local government in the early seventeenth century was relatively simple. It originally developed under the supervision of the General

44

Court, but the subsequent history of local government in Connecticut's colonial period saw a constant evolution toward more complexity and greater power.

It was with the Fundamental Orders of Connecticut that the first enduring outlines of a government were constituted. The Fundamental Orders set up a General Court which consisted of a governor, a deputy governor, four assistants called magistrates at that time, and an unspecified number of deputies from each town. The General Court took upon itself the "supreme power of the commonwealth to make laws or repeal them" and the powers to admit freemen, to dispose of lands, and to call any person into question for any misdemeanor.[2] The Fundamental Orders really created a de facto government of the colony with extremely broad and vague powers.

Under this constitution the towns were given the power to dispose of all lands within their territory and to control all assets within their boundaries with the exception of rivers. The towns were given the authority and power to choose their own officers and "make such orders as may be for [their] well ordering." They had legal powers to impose penalties for breach of peace or of colony or town laws as well as the power to levy any taxes the town's administration might require. All the towns' earliest officers were created specifically by the Fundamental Orders; they were told, for example, to elect three, five, or seven of their "chief inhabitants" as townsmen who would have the executive authority within the town.[3]

Connecticut's Charter of 1662 from the British government basically reaffirmed the powers of the colony government and legalized beyond question what had already been a fact for twenty-four years under the Fundamental Orders. Under the charter, the General Court served the dual functions of a particular court which passed on individual cases and a General Assembly which promulgated laws. The General Court consisted of one governor, one deputy governor, twelve assistants, and no more than two deputies from each of the towns. The charter gave the colony almost a full measure of self-government, allowing the General Court to make any laws that were not contrary to the laws of England and were wholesome and reasonable. Unlike most colonies, Connecticut had no provision specified for disallowance of any laws. The colony was also empowered to set up an independent judicial system. The

Charter of 1662 actually made the colony in practice a self-governing state.[4]

There were two levels of government in early seventeenth-century Connecticut: the General Court and the towns. Constitutionally, the towns had no power other than that delegated to them by the colony government in Hartford, and most town offices were created by the central government—although many of the first towns did create an eclectic minor office or two.[5] In practice, the towns did administer their own daily affairs. The General Court could, in theory, interfere in any internal town matter, and the towns always operated with the knowledge that the court would be quick to interfere if the local peace were threatened or if local events went contrary to the judgment of the colony magistrates; and they knew that the court would insist that its superior authority be acknowledged.[6] Connecticut towns were much more subordinated to the central government than were their counterparts in Rhode Island and probably more so than Massachusetts towns.[7] The General Court and the towns practiced "dual localism," in the words of one scholar; and even though the same men were usually involved in both bodies, a tension developed between the two as a "persistent localism" brought with the English colonists tended to cause villagers to assert their local interests to the detriment of the tribal spirit of the larger Puritan community.[8]

As the seventeenth century progressed, a third element was added to the colony's political structure. County government was created and grew in power throughout the rest of the colonial period. Theoretically, of course, the General Court still held all the power, but in practice both county government and town government increased their powers. The first four counties were created in 1666: Hartford, New Haven, New London, and Fairfield. At first they were merely judicial units of government, with county courts having only judicial powers. The only administrative position was that of a county clerk to whom the town clerks were directed to send their vital records. The county court was presided over by a chief judge appointed by the General Court and by three other town magistrates called commissioners, who were also appointed by the General Court. After 1698 when commissioners were superseded by justices of the peace, the office of justice of the peace and quorum was created to fill the posts of judges of the county courts. In 1699 an additional court, the probate court, was created as a separate body at the county level.[9]

In the first decade of the eighteenth century county government was considerably strengthened as the General Assembly created other administrative positions and powers for it. A county surveyor of highways, appointed in 1700 to take care of all roads between towns, supervised the highways of each county. Later, this office was given the power to measure and lay out all grants of land made by the General Assembly within each county. In 1700 the assembly ordered each county to keep a Latin grammar school to prepare students for the university. In 1703 the county courts were given authority to license and supervise all inns and taverns within their respective jurisdictions. Commissioners and then justices of the peace had possessed this power before it was turned over to the county courts. Military matters were often coordinated by counties, as for instance when county commissaries were set up to supply soldiers, and committees of safety were appointed for each county to supervise their defense in time of war. The General Assembly in 1704 ordered each county court to appoint an attorney for the Queen whose function was that of a prosecuter to "suppress vice and immorality," and both a financial arm and a police arm were added by the creation of the posts of county treasurer and county sheriff. The treasurer, appointed by the court he served and subject to its supervision, was responsible for the financial affairs of the county and supervised the collection of a tax on every town. The rates were set by the county court in consultation with the collected grandjurymen of each of the towns. The sheriff had constabulary duties over the entire county, was the police arm of its court, and even had the power to raise the militia if needed to carry out his duties. The full scope of the sheriff's job can be demonstrated by the fact that in Hartford County he was allowed to appoint ten deputies.[10]

After the interjection and strengthening of county government, the colony's governing organization remained basically the same throughout the eighteenth century. The three levels, colony, county, and town, all survived into the early national period. However, while the structural relationship remained fairly constant, changes did occur within all three levels of government.

The method of electing the members of the General Court was officially set and communicated to the freemen of the colony in 1689.

The freemen of each town met in April and each freeman handed to the constable a list of twenty men that he wished to nominate as assistants. The constable then tallied all the votes and submitted the twenty leading candidates to the county sheriff, who in turn forwarded them to the colony secretary. The secretary pooled the votes of all the towns and sent back to each town a list of the top twenty men. These men were now candidates for assistants. Out of these twenty candidates, each freeman could choose one for governor, one for deputy governor, and twelve of those remaining for assistants.[11] Hence, the governor and deputy governor, not nominated specifically for their offices but nominated instead as assistants, were not designated by the freemen to their respective offices until after the nomination process. This system gave unusual stability to the governor's office. There were only seven different governors between 1700 and 1783, and five of them died in office.

The General Court's structure was changed in 1698 when an act divided it into two houses: the upper house being the council composed of the governor, deputy governor, and assistants, and the lower house being the assembly composed "of such deputies as shall be legally returned from the several towns within this colony." Previously, the assistants and the deputies had met together in General Court twice a year and at the second of these two meetings had voted to allow the assistants alone to meet with the governor and have the full power of the court while it was not in session. Usually, this power was only used during an emergency such as war. However, after 1698 the two houses regularly met separately and any law had to be passed by both to be effective.[12]

The powers of the General Assembly were practically unlimited and restrained only by the "reasonable and wholesome" clause of the Charter of 1662. In practice, as the eighteenth century progressed the General Assembly allowed the towns more and more power. Yet the colonial government still reserved for itself the right to create all new ecclesiastical societies within towns and to arbitrate all differences among towns over problems such as boundary disputes. Any intertown problems were of course taken care of by the General Assembly. It exercised all powers of commerce and even, for instance, ordered the town of Norwalk to build a new bridge over a river. Many things considered minor at later times in Connecticut, such as divorces and militia exemptions, could be granted only by the General Assembly.[13] The trend, however, in the eighteenth century was constantly toward greater town power.

One of the greatest powers over local government that the General Assembly had was its appointive power. It appointed all judges of the county courts, all justices of the peace, all judges of probate courts, and all justices of the peace and quorum. This appointive power gave the General Assembly almost complete control over the judiciary. Another major appointive power was that of special ad hoc committees. Often, when a town became embroiled in a controversy such as where to build a new meeting house or school, the General Assembly would appoint a special committee to recommend a settlement which the colony would enforce. Usually, the committee would be made up of three or four men, often deputies or assistants, from another part of the colony. Many important disputes were settled this way by neutral arbitration.

The judicial structure of the colony, as would be expected, functioned on all three levels of government. The Fundamental Orders originally gave the selectmen, or townsmen as they were then called, judicial powers. They were the first judiciary on the local level and were empowered to hear all cases of crime and all suits of debt, provided neither the fine nor the amount of the suit exceeded 40s. and provided that both parties in the case were from the same town. They could issue a summons to any person to come before the entire town meeting or before the selectmen's meeting. In 1665 the General Court created the office of commissioner to take over the judicial functions of the selectmen.[14] Commissioners, appointed one per town for one-year terms, had all the judicial powers townsmen had previously exercised and were usually reappointed year after year.

The office of justice of the peace, created in 1697, superseded the post of commissioners.[15] Unlike commissioners, justices of the peace were appointed for the county in theory but in practice each town had one justice while many of the larger ones had two. The functions of a justice of the peace in Connecticut must not be confused with those of a seventeenth-century justice in England. In England the justice of the peace, besides being a judge, was also an administrative official who supervised lesser officials and acted as a liaison between local government and the Privy Council.[16] The justice of the peace in Connecticut was instead a strictly judicial figure. Originally, he did have the administrative duty of licensing inns but this was transferred to the county courts very early in the eighteenth century. Many of the English justices' functions were performed by the selectmen and constables in Connecticut. The constable was inextricably tied to the Connecticut local judicial system since he was the administrative arm of first the townsmen, then the commissioner, and finally the justice of the peace as the progression of local magistrates evolved.

County courts, set up with the creation of the four counties in 1666, at first consisted of one assistant from the General Court and two of the local commissioners. This changed with the abolition of the commissioner's office, and henceforth the county courts consisted of one county court chief judge and three justices of the peace and quorum, all of whom were appointed by the General Assembly. The county courts, higher courts to which local judicial decisions could be appealed, exercised original jurisdiction over all criminal cases and suits that involved more than 40s. or suits between men of different towns within the county. No appeal was allowed from a justice of the peace to a county court in cases involving less than 10s.[17] This restriction, enacted by the General Assembly in 1725, was probably intended to cut down the heavy case load on the higher courts. The load, so heavy that it suggested colonial men sued one another at the drop of a hat, was growing constantly; while the population of the colony increased about three and one-half times between 1700 and 1730, the debt cases in county courts increased nineteenfold.[18] The courts were constantly full of litigation over debt disputes, many of them involving seemingly insignificant sums of money.

The sheriff, the judicial counterpart on the county level of the constable on the local level, was the legal arm of the county court and actually took over some of the functions of the constable, such as serving writs to the selectmen from the county courts. Up until 1724 the sheriff was appointed by the county court that he served, but in that year the General Assembly assumed his appointment in one of the few instances in the eighteenth century where the assembly increased its powers over local officials.[19]

Probate courts were an integral part of the judicial system. Originally, one probate court served each county, but by 1775 seventeen separate probate districts existed and their records indicate very crowded dockets. Probate judgeships were very lucrative since the judge received a percentage of every case he handled. In many cases when men could be judges of either the probate or the county court, they chose the more lucrative over the more powerful office.

The first regular court higher than the county or local one, the Court of Assistants, constituted in 1665, was also known as the Superior Court of Common Pleas, and consisted of a quorum of at least seven assistants. It held sessions twice yearly, heard cases on appeal from the county courts, and had original jurisdiction over all cases involving capital punishment or banishment. The Court of Assistants had a relatively short life and was replaced by the Superior Court of Judicature in 1711. The Court of Assistants, apparently unwieldy with over seven judges, did not hold enough sessions to meet the case load and had a difficult time assembling seven different men for a sitting. The new Superior Court inherited the powers of the previous one but consisted of one chief judge and four other judges, any three of whom would be a quorum. The chief judge was the deputy governor and in practice almost all the judges were assistants, although in theory they did not have to be. The new court increased its sessions and met twice a year in each of the county seats.[20]

In Connecticut's judicial system, unlike that of most mainland colonies, the court of the council or the superior court made up of assistants was not the highest appeals court in the colony. Any case that could be appealed to the Superior Court could also be further appealed to the General Assembly. The General Assembly, besides being a legislative body, was also the highest court in the colony and this was true in practice as well as in theory. The records of the assembly are studded with appeals from the lower courts.

Before examining town government, it might be interesting to ask to what ends, besides justice and peace, these sophisticated judicial and legislative systems were directed. If one word had to convey the philosophy of government in Connecticut in the seventeenth century and at least the first third of the eighteenth, it would be *control*. Economic control of the colony's activities was almost complete. The General Assembly stipulated in the middle of the seventeenth century that a bushel of corn could not be sold for more than 5s. 6d. and that board sawyers had to charge precisely 5s. per hundred feet of lumber. These were not general economic guidelines but specific measures, perhaps the most specific being the act of the General Assembly that allowed a shoemaker to charge 5d. for all shoes size seven and under and 7d. for all shoes size eight or larger. As another example, all inns regardless of degree of comfort were required to charge the same price for boarding of men and horses.[21]

Social control was also an important goal of the government. Just as today, a tavern's hours were strictly regulated but, unlike today, a man had to leave if he consumed a half-pint of wine or if he spent a half hour there—whichever came first. Men known as "tavern haunters" would be brought before the local magistrate to answer charges. Idleness was also a crime: the law stated that no time should be spent "unfruitfully." A man caught in the act of lying was liable to receive thirty lashes and a 40s. fine. No one was allowed to live alone or keep a bachelor residence—all single people had to live with a family. Some measures were extreme by today's sensibilities; one such prohibited all criticism of selectmen engaged in their official duties.[22]

As the eighteenth century progressed, there can be no doubt that the degree of control by the government dwindled greatly. In the seventeenth century enjoinders to town officials to enforce "tippling" laws were passed at least once every other year by the General Assembly. In the eighteenth century the repetition of the law became less and less frequent and ceased altogether after 1735. The laws that banned gaming were changed so that it was banned only on Sunday. Control of prices also lessened and supply and demand regulated the market much more than previously. The penalties for crime were reduced; the punishment for adultery, for instance, was changed from death to thirty lashes.[23] It should not be suggested that there was no government control of personal morality by 1760, but it should be clear that much less existed than in 1660. The story of Puritan controlling legislation and its subsequent breakdown is well known to historians, but along with this evolution toward less governmental control over individuals' lives came a concomitant relaxation of control by the General Assembly over the towns.

It was, of course, ultimately in the towns that the principles of strong government were put into effect. The origins of the English colonies' town governments have been debated by historians. Herbert Baxter Adams summed up late nineteenth-century attitudes on the origins of New England town government when he stated that "town institutions were propagated in New England by old English and German ideas, brought over by Puritans and Pilgrims and as ready to take root in the free soil of America as would Egyptian grain which had been drying in a mummy case for thousands of years."[24] Opposed to Adams' prosaic belief in the European origins of town government is Alexis de Tocqueville's thesis that town government in New England came out of the reaction of nature and colonist.[25] This is a Turnerian approach to the origins of town government that predates Turner by a half-century. Sumner Chilton Powell recently complemented and strengthened this thesis in his study of Sudbury, Massachusetts, where he found that many English town, parish, and manor officials were left out of the New England town structure.[26] This of course is true, but what is undeniable also is that most New England town officers do have English counterparts.[27] Charles Andrews came closest to a true appreciation of the origins of Connecticut towns when he stated that they were a "twice purified" or "second sifting" of English antecedents.[28] This explanation recognizes that Connecticut towns were the product of English origins that had interacted with practical problems once in Massachusetts and then again in Connecticut. To deny either the forces of English origins or the interaction with New World conditions is to miss the essentially dual origins of the Connecticut town. Of course, Puritanism, the fundamental factor of seventeenth-century New England, shaped town government directly by insisting that local government maintain a well-ordered community and that authority be near, easily exercised, and respected, and indirectly by instituting the nucleated form of settlement.[29]

Local government in the colonial Connecticut town was infinitely more complicated than folklore would have the casual student of history believe. There were, besides the town meeting government, three other deliberative bodies in the town: the proprietors, the freemen, and the societies. Early in the seventeenth century this complexity may have been lacking since the membership of the four bodies was almost identical. However, as towns grew and social distinctions became more apparent, the membership of each of the four bodies became unique and thus the separateness of the four groups became more real.

The proprietors, usually between thirty and sixty heads of household, were the first group since they received the actual grant of land for the town from the colony government.[30] Seventeenth-century proprietors, always actual residents of their towns, received the land at no cost after petitioning the General Court for a "plantation," while eighteenth-century proprietors paid the assembly for the land and could be either residents or absentee speculators.[31] All the undivided land of the town, of which there was usually a great deal, remained in the legal hands of the proprietors, not under the control of the town meeting. The proprietors, required to meet once a year, frequently met more often and exercised strong economic power in the community through their periodic divisions and allotments of new land. Proprietors enjoyed political equality insofar as voting on issues since each one could cast a ballot on decisions, but practiced inequality in allotment of land; respected town leaders and men with large families received larger shares.[32] In Norwalk's original distribution the largest parcel allotted was fifty-two acres, while the smallest was seventeen.[33] In Fairfield the ratio of largest to smallest was three to one and in no town did it exceed four to one.[34]

In the early days of resident proprietors the town meeting usually served as the proprietors' meeting since the constituency of the two bodies was virtually identical.[35] Sometimes a town meeting would shift gears and become a proprietors' meeting without anyone's changing seats.[36] Starting as early as 1665, however, some proprietors started meeting as a group apart because immigration to town caused the membership of the town meeting to diverge from that of the proprietors' meeting.[37] This tendency toward separating the two, accentuated by the old towns' growth of nonproprietors and by the phenomenon in the new towns of absentee proprietors with different interests from the town residents, finally resulted in colony laws in 1727 and 1732 requiring separate proprietor meetings. The 1732 enactment also gave the proprietors the power to set taxes or "rates" to defray their expenses.[38] Most groups of proprietors, once they acted separately from the town meeting, elected a clerk, treasurer, surveyor, and a proprietors committee whose membership varied between three and seven. Elections, unlike those of the towns, were not annual and officers served as long as they had the electorate's confidence; proprietor officers usually served many consecutive years. The proprietors committee made the crucial decisions regarding land divisions, although their tenuous position presumably made them responsive to the meeting.[39]

The seventeenth-century proprietors carefully husbanded their resource, land, and parceled it out slowly over the years. Farmington, Middletown, and Norwich had active proprietors and undivided lands almost one hundred years after their founding. Proprietors of later towns, however, disposed of their land more quickly, and once all the land was divided the proprietors had no reason for existence. Kent, founded in 1739, divided 32,000 of its 50,000 acres within two years, and Lebanon, founded in the 1690s, had divided all its land by 1730.[40] During the speculative-land mania that swept Connecticut in the 1730s, most proprietors divided away their power with their land; proprietors remained important factors only in new towns.[41] They often continued as social clubs and one lasted in Middletown until 1882 when it dissolved itself.

The second deliberative body of the town was the freemen. The Fundamental Orders established two types of voters in the colony: freemen and town voters.[42] Only freemen could vote in any election on the colony level for deputies to the General Assembly, for assistants, and for the governor and deputy governor. At this time there were no religious or property qualifications for freemanship, and admission into the freemen's circle was granted by the General Assembly. In practice if not in theory, there were probably both religious and property qualifications. The Charter of 1662 empowered the General Court to set qualifications for freemen and admit them, saying only that they must be of "honest conversation" and must have £20 of property.[43] In 1729 the duty of admitting freemen was voluntarily delegated by the General Assembly to the individual freemen of each town.[44] This was probably forced by the difficulty of admitting freemen in large numbers and from distant parts of the growing colony. For at least thirty years before the freemen in the towns were given the right to choose their own members, the selectmen of each town controlled their admission because the General Assembly made people freemen on the written recommendation of their home selectmen.[45] Under the new law the freemen met twice a year to admit new members and had the right to determine whether the prospective freemen were of "honest conversation."[46] In these meetings the collected freemen also elected their deputies to the May and October sessions of the General Assembly. The freemen nominated twenty men for the assistants list and finally voted for twelve assistants, the governor, and deputy governor. Consequently, it was the freemen in each town who controlled their own membership and the colony-level government.

The percentage of an average Connecticut town's adult white males admitted to freemanship changed over time. Prior to 1662 when it was not important to be a freeman, few men were recorded in the colony records as admitted, but many men never known to be admitted exercised the rights of freemanship. The distinction between the freemen's meeting and the town meeting was thus blurred. After 1662 when strict qualifications for freemanship were set and the General Court carefully recorded all those admitted, there were no more casual freemen. Because traveling to Hartford, the capital, was a time-consuming process, the percentage of adults admitted from a town varied proportionately with the town's distance from Hartford. Thus, in towns near the capital about 63 percent of adult white men were freemen in 1669; in Middletown, halfway down the Connecticut River, only 50 percent were admitted; in Saybrook, at the mouth of the river, only 33 percent were; and in remote Norwich freemanship dropped to 25 percent.[47]

A broad sampling of probate inventories reveals that at least 80 percent of eighteenth-century Connecticut men satisfied the property qualifications for freemanship, and after 1729 when the power of admittance was transferred to each town's freemen's meeting, few barriers stood in a man's way to register.[48] Yet in six towns of varying age and size where the percentage of adult white males becoming freemen has been calculated, it ranged from approximately 50 percent in each of Farmington, Kent, Lebanon, and Norwich, to 64 percent and 79 percent in East Haddam and East Guilford.[49] Undoubtedly, the percentage of men who were freemen was lower than the percentage of men who could have been freemen because those who lived long distances from the meetinghouse did not normally attend meetings. A positive correlation between proximity to the meetinghouse and freemanship can be established.[50] Connecticut towns were often geographically large and men frequently felt that the disadvantages of a long trip over bad or nonexistent roads outweighed the advantages of freemanship.

Only freemen could be deputies to the General Assembly or other colony officials, and it was clear that the deputies represented the *freemen* of a town and not the town government. As an example, the town meeting of Middletown addressed a petition to the Middletown freemen asking them if their deputies would act as agents for the town meeting.[51] Towns sometimes took advantage of the convergence of people in town in April and September on "Freemen's Day" to hold a town meeting, but the two meetings were always clearly separated.

The third deliberative body in the town's governing structure was the society. The society corresponded to the parish in England. Like the parish, the society had ecclesiastical origins but rapidly became a political governing body.[52] Originally, each town had one parish whose functions were administered by the town meeting. However, when a town grew in size, it usually divided into more than one parish, and once the town and parish were no longer coterminous a level of government beneath the town was needed. The society filled that need. By 1720 more than half of Connecticut's towns had more than one parish and almost all the earliest settled ones had multiple societies.[53] By 1760 over three-fourths of Connecticut's towns had at least two societies operating as governmental units, and two towns had as many as six societies. Hartford, with a population in 1774 of 4,881, had five different societies. An average society would have about two hundred families and a population of about one thousand people.[54]

One of the society's major functions was choosing a site for a meeting house, building it, and maintaining it. The society also had the duty of hiring and paying a minister. For these functions they were allowed to levy a society rate, usually expressly worded for the financial obligation, such as minister's rate or meeting house rate. The societies also had the obligation of maintaining schools within their districts, which were paid for both by levying a special school rate and from student fees.[55] For all of these functions the society elected a slate of officers.

The chief officers elected were the society committmen whose duties corresponded roughly to some of those of the churchwardens in the old English parish. The society committee was the executive and administrative arm of the society. Besides the committee, the society elected a clerk, treasurer, and rate collector. The rate would be fixed by the committee on assets of the society members as listed by the town officials but was collected by the society rate collector. To vote for officers in a society, a person had to be a duly registered freeman or a full communicant of the church.[56] The society was in fact a neighborhood governing body that had its functions reduced to certain specified areas. Very often, town officials were designated as coming from one society or another and a conscious effort was made to spread the town offices out among the societies. In this manner, societies as units often had a direct influence on town meeting elections.

The town meeting government was the major and most important unit of local authority. In Connecticut any adult white male could vote at a town meeting for town officers if he was a legal inhabitant of the town and possessed 50s. of taxable property, a financial requirement so low that only outright paupers would be disenfranchised by it. Town meeting voters were the second class of voters, different from and more numerous than freemen. However, being a legal inhabitant of a town involved more than just living within the town limits; a person had to be legally recognized by the selectmen in writing. It was not possible merely to move into a town on one's own volition and thus qualify as an inhabitant. The General Assembly required any new resident in a town who desired to be admitted to furnish written character references from the selectmen of his old town to those of the new town.[57] Only when the selectmen were satisfied with the character of the new resident would he be admitted as an inhabitant. Thus, even the more open town meeting voting had some restrictions on it.[58]

The activity of the town meeting in Connecticut evolved through a discernible pattern in the colonial period. New towns always had an active meeting that could meet as frequently as twelve times a year.[59] After about ten years of existence, town meetings would taper off until often they would be held only once or twice in a year.[60] While in the early active years a meeting would concern itself with many minute and specific issues and be a vital decision-making body, in its inactive mature years it usually concerned itself only with elections of town officers. Should a controversial issue surface in a mature town, however, the town meeting could be suddenly propelled from a state of quietude of perhaps twenty years' duration which saw only one meeting a year to a state of extreme activity witnessing six or seven meetings in a year until the issue was settled, at which time the meeting would lapse back into inactivity. In this manner the meeting was always a potential if latent force in town government. Generally, the meeting was more active in the seventeenth century than in the eighteenth, and in the period from 1720 to the American Revolution town meetings were exceptionally inactive except for those in new towns. Almost all the towns did have extremely active meetings during the revolutionary years, obviously a crisis situation.

Meetings were run differently in different towns, but in every meeting in most of the eighteenth century the first order of business was always to choose a moderator who would preside over it. In the seventeenth century moderators were not chosen and apparently one of the selectmen presided over the meeting. The office of moderator was probably borrowed from the Presbyterian Church government. First appearing in most Connecticut towns between 1690 and 1730, the moderator was often but not always a selectman. Between meetings the position of moderator was normally defunct, but some towns would hold a second meeting months after the first one, call the second one an "adjourned" meeting, and have the previously elected moderator preside. One town elected a man to preside as moderator at every meeting until the town saw fit to elect a replacement.[61]

Town meeting elections were usually held in the latter part of December. As might be expected, the elections progressed from a few basic offices in the early seventeenth century to over two hundred in one town in the revolutionary period. As the sheer size of Connecticut's population increased during the colonial period, so also did the size and complexity of the town meeting government. Hartford, with a population of almost five thousand people in 1774, had a total of 76 town meeting officers, while Norwich, the colony's second largest town with over seven thousand people, had 116 officers. Farmington, with a decentralized population of fifty-six hundred spread over a huge land mass, elected 206 men in 1776. Of thirty towns sampled for the year 1776, all of which were over thirty years old, New Hartford with 38 officers elected the fewest. Medium-size towns with populations between twenty-five hundred and four thousand usually elected 60 to 80 officers at the end of the colonial period.

The towns' selectmen, or "townsmen" as they were called in the seventeenth century, were the most important figures in town government throughout the colonial period. Around the first of the eighteenth century they began to be called selectmen. In periods

TABLE 1.
Size of Town Meeting Government.

Hartford[a]

Elections of 1640		Surveyors	5
Townsmen	4	Fenceviewers	8
Constables	2	Haywards	7
Surveyors of highways	2	List and rate makers	7
		Tithingmen	8
Total officers	8	Collectors of rates	4
		Leather sealers	3
Elections of 1681		Measure sealer	1
Townsmen	4	Packer of meat	1
Constables	2		
Surveyors of highways	2	Total officers	62
Fenceviewers, north side	2		
Fenceviewers, south side	2	*Elections of 1770*	
Fenceviewers, east side		Moderator	1
of river	2	Selectmen	7
Chimneyviewers, north side	2	Treasurer	1
Chimneyviewers, south side	2	Clerk	1
Leather sealers	2	Constables	4
Packer	1	Grandjurymen	7
List and rate makers	4	Tithingmen	9
		Listers	6
Total officers	25	Raters	4
		Surveyors	10
Elections of 1730		Leather sealers	7
Moderator	1	Measure sealers	2
Clerk	1	Weights sealers	1
Selectmen	7	Fenceviewers	10
Constables	4	Packers	3
Treasurer	1	Collectors	3
Grandjurymen	5	Total officers	76

Norwich[b]

Elections of 1770		Gagers	3
Moderator	1	Surveyors	36
Selectmen	7	Leather sealers	8
Treasurer	1	Measure sealers	1
Clerk	1	Weight sealers	1
Constables	6	Fenceviewers	4
Grandjurymen	11	Packers	3
Tithingmen	15	Collectors	8
Listers	10	Total officers	116

Ridgefield[c]

Elections of 1750		Elections of 1775	
Moderator	1	Moderator	1
Selectmen	3	Selectmen	5
Treasurer	1	Constables	4
Clerk	1	Grandjurymen	3
Constables	2	Treasurer	1
Surveyors	9	Listers	8
Listers	5	Surveyors	11
Collectors	2	Fenceviewers	4
Sealer of weights and measures	1	Branders	2
Grandjurymen	3	Sealers	2
Tithingmen	3	Key keepers	2
Fenceviewers	4	Tithingmen	2
Branders	2	Inspectors	12
Poundkeeper	1	Collectors	2
		Sealer	1
Total officers	38	Total officers	60

New Hartford[d]		Waterbury[e]	
Elections of 1776		Elections of 1776	
Moderator	1	Moderator	1
Clerk	1	Treasurer	1
Treasurer	1	Clerk	1
Selectmen	7	Selectmen	7
Constables	2	Constables	7
Grandjurymen	2	Grandjurymen	13
Listers	4	Tithingmen	15
Surveyors	10	Listers	14
Tithingmen	2	Agent	1
Sealers	3	Surveyors	39
Packer	1	Branders	8
Ratemakers	4	Sealers of leather	3
		Sealer of weights and measures	1
Total officers	38	Key keepers	4
		Total officers	105

a. Founded 1636. Population 4,881 in 1774.
b. Founded 1659. Population 7,032 in 1774.
c. Founded 1708. Population 1,673 in 1774.
d. Founded 1738. Population 985 in 1774.
e. Founded 1686. Population 3,498 in 1774.

between town meetings they enjoyed and exercised the executive and legislative powers of the whole town meeting. Their power was subject to review by the town meeting but in fact this seldom happened and the selectmen's orders or decisions were rarely appealed.

The selectmen held many of the powers the churchwardens and justices of the peace had in England, such as serving as overseers of the poor and administering a general program of welfare. They had the duty of taking care of poor and maimed people, idiots, and distracted persons and if need be would administer such persons' financial affairs to maintain the income necessary to support them. If a person had no estate, he would be bound out to someone who would be paid for taking care of him. The selectmen had the power to grant sums of money to widows or to suspend the collection of the town rate upon a maimed householder.[62]

Besides being the welfare administrators of each town, the selectmen served as the major keepers of morality. In the town they, along with other officers, were the main forces behind the tight social control. They were the chief inspectors of the town's morals and were enjoined by the General Assembly to watch out for tavern haunters, beware of strangers in town, be suspicious of young people congregating, and in general to keep a sharp eye on all activity. If any person had a chance of becoming a public charge through idleness, the selectmen were empowered to put him to work. It was the selectmen who had the duty of making sure that every child was taught reading and writing, a basic knowledge of religion, and an "honest lawful calling" by his parents. If children were not properly raised in the selectmen's view, they could swear out a warrant against the parents. As a measure of extreme control, the selectmen had the right to inspect any house in the town whose inhabitants they suspected of violating laws.[63]

Between the seventeenth and the eighteenth centuries the selectmen lost some of their functions but actually grew more powerful as the towns increased in size. As tight social control progressively lessened, they lost some of their power as the towns' chief moral keepers but more than made this up with increases in executive authority. In the seventeenth century the board of selectmen often served as the financial arm of the town and assessed estates for taxing, decided on the taxing rate, and sometimes even held the treasurer's books. Originally, they also, as has been mentioned, held judicial powers. With the eighteenth century came the addition of town offices such as listers, raters, and treasurers. These officers took over many of the selectmen's direct functions, but the selectmen gained a much greater indirect power over an ever-increasing town organization. Instead of acting as town handymen, the selectmen became the overseers of a larger structure. The assembly passed an act in 1690, crucial to the selectmen's power, that gave them the supervisory authority over all other town officers. They were told "to take cognizance of such as do neglect the duties of surveyor, hayward, fenceviewer . . . etc."[64]

The increase in the number of towns in the colony also increased the selectmen's powers. In the early seventeenth century the General Court kept a tight rein over the selectmen of each town and often required them to submit individual petitions to the colony government if they wanted to act on something. In the eighteenth century there were fewer individual petitions from selectmen and more general enabling acts of power from the General Assembly to them. For instance, to reduce a colony rate on a sick person in the seventeenth century the selectmen had to apply specifically to the General Court. In the eighteenth century the size of the colony precluded activity like this and the selectmen were allowed to reduce the rate directly. Selectmen were also given broad military powers in 1703, power to raise taxes in 1708, total control of local welfare problems in 1719, and strong war-time emergency powers at the end of the colonial period in 1775.[65]

As the power of the selectmen increased during the colonial period, the power of the other major seventeenth-century town officer declined. The constable's status declined so much that by the end of the first decade of the eighteenth century, instead of being one of the major ones, he was the most important of the minor officers. In the seventeenth century the constable had a plethora of functions and was the chief law enforcement officer of the colony. He cooperated with the selectmen, the commissioner, or the justice of the peace to ensure social conformity. When the General Assembly passed general control laws, it was always the constable who was the chief official ordered to enforce them. When the General Assembly passed any law, it was sent to the constable to be read aloud at the next town meeting. He was the link between the colony government and the town and the right arm of the General Assembly in each particular town. When the colony wanted an action taken in a particular town in the seventeenth century, such as selling a man's estate to pay the colony rate, it was the constable who was given the job.[66]

The constable had several specific functions in the seventeenth century that were either taken away from his office or made superfluous by changing times. At first, under the Fundamental Orders the constable was the chief military figure in the towns and made sure that every adult male had a firearm and knew how to use it. The strict watch kept in all towns was under the constable's supervision. As the chief militia officer, he organized and executed all the different militia exercises. All this military power and prestige were taken away from the constable in the Code of 1650.

Only the constable had the power to raise a "hue and cry" for any crime. Like the selectmen and some other officials, the constable could arrest people for such varied offences as tippling, Sabbathbreaking, vagrancy, and lying. He also enforced inn regulations, watched out for "tobacco-takers," and seized any heretical book and presented it and its owner to the magistrate.[67] As all these systems of control broke down, the constable's power and prestige declined proportionately and nothing was added to upgrade it.

The ever-expanding town and county governments absorbed other functions of the constables. The sheriff took over many of the tasks that had been the constable's responsibility prior to county government. Before 1700, in most towns, the constable collected the colony rate. The difficulty in carrying out this job was attested by the numbers of acts passed for fining constables who did not collect the rates on time. Around 1700 most towns started creating rate collectors who collected not only the town rate but the colony rate as well. They then gave the proceeds to the constable, who was reduced to being a delivery boy, and he carried it to the General Assembly. As the eighteenth century progressed, the constable became less and less the General Assembly's right arm in the town. As towns gained more autonomy, the constable's position as the agent of the colony government declined in status. Beyond this, the General Assembly much more often communicated its wishes to the selectmen of the town directly or to the sheriff of the county. The constable declined in executive status as these offices increased.

The other major officers of the town meeting government were the town clerk and town treasurer. In the early days of the seventeenth century the selectmen performed both these functions, but rather early a need was discovered for a town clerk. The 1644 General Assembly created the office of clerk and in 1680 his oath was ordered in a way that provided a good description of his duties: "Swear by the dreadfull name of the ever-living God that you will keep an entry of all grants, deeds of sale or mortgages of lands, and all marriages, births, deaths and other writings brought to you and deliver copies when required of you."[68] The town clerk was the indispensable man of the local government. Then, much as today, he bore the burden of a great deal of work and received little glory. However, he must be recognized as a major officer. Often, when the duties of treasurer first became separated from the selectmen, the town clerk assumed the dual office of clerk and treasurer. That the clerk could assume another such position of importance strongly suggests that he was a man of unusual repute. By the end of the first quarter of the eighteenth century most towns elected separate treasurers and clerks. The duties of taking care of the towns' financial affairs increased proportionately with their size.

Certainly, the creation of the offices of listers and their subsequent increase in numbers bears out this conclusion. The colony tax rate was set by the General Assembly and the county tax rate by the county court, but there yet remained a town rate to be set. Originally, the selectmen of the town did this, but by the 1670s most towns were electing men to the dual office of lister and rater. The lister's part of the dual job was to list or assess the personal and real wealth of each town inhabitant. It was on this list that the colony, county, society, and town tax rates were based. Lister findings could be appealed first to the selectmen, who had the power to set them aside, and then to the justice of the peace. Apparently, listing all these goods was a difficult task because in the early eighteenth century the General Assembly adopted a new law for regulating the process. Under this law every taxpayer estimated his own list and submitted it to the town lister, who either accepted or rejected the estimate. If he accepted it, this was then the amount that the different rates would be levied on. However, if the lister rejected the estimate and upon investigation found that it was an underassessment, he was required to multiply the difference by four and add this to the taxpayer's list.[69] The colony records published a survey of "fourfold lists" each year for every town. The duties of list and rate makers increased as did other jobs, for by the middle of the eighteenth century virtually every large town had separated the two jobs. Yet, they would both be considered lesser offices since they were under the supervision of the town selectmen and treasurer.

Other lesser offices at about the same mid-level position as the raters and listers were those of grandjurymen and tithingmen. Both offices, created as a conservative response to the declining piety and morality of the second and third generation of settlers, possessed essentially constabulary functions. Grandjurymen, created by the colony government in 1667, at first were appointed for each town by the county courts and told to "make presentments of ye breaches of any law." In 1712 the assembly ordered the towns to elect the grandjurymen and in 1721 the assembly created the office of tithingman also to help combat moral laxity.[70] Massachusetts had elected tithingmen as early as 1679.[71] The two assisted the constable and selectmen in enforcing the colony's social code and were the eyes and ears of the commissioner and justice of the peace. They would report to the justice of the peace such diverse incidents as cruelty to animals or tippling or Sabbath-breaking. Both officials were social constables whose importance declined directly with the decline of the constable and with the system of social control. Tithingmen declined more than grandjurymen because they had no other basic duties. Grandjurymen did have an additional function at the county level; all juries at the county court were chosen from among the towns' grandjurymen and they collectively advised the county court on the matter of the county rate. The grandjurymen were lesser officials by the revolutionary period, but since they still had duties at the county level they were slightly more important than the tithingmen.

Many other lesser officials were elected in Connecticut's mature towns. The surveyors of highways, the largest group of town officers elected, had their English antecedent in the waymen of the English parish. They took care of the roads within a town and had the power to commandeer any town man to work on the highways a certain number of days every year. In addition to being accountable to the selectmen, they were supervised by the county surveyor on all intertown road problems.[72]

Fenceviewers, first established in 1643, were another large class of minor officials in all towns. Keeping animals properly fenced within particular confines was a major problem, and the fenceviewers had the obligation of making sure all the fences of a town were of proper standards and in good repair. They, like surveyors, could commandeer any town man to work on the common fences a number of days a year. Fenceviewers also had the authority to fine delinquent fence keepers and could even fix improper fences and charge the owner twice the cost.[73] Theirs was a rather mundane and unprestigious job but, like the surveyors of the highways, of extreme practical importance.

Other lesser positions within the framework of town meeting government were those of the sealers of leather, weights, and measures, the packers of beef, and the hayward. The sealer of leather put his mark on all leather processed in the town to certify that it was of a respectable quality. The packers of beef did the same with processed meat. Both the leather sealer and the beef packer protected the buyer from inferior or tainted goods. The measures and weights sealers, sometimes combined and sometimes elected separately, were to make sure that the measures and weights used in sales in the town agreed with colony standards. Usually, the last officials elected at town meetings were the haywards who, similar to the packers of beef and pork, had the duty to decide on the "goodness or badness" of corn in any controversies over the selling of grain.[74] The haywards, the sealers, and the packers really enjoyed very little leadership prestige in town, and all these lesser officials acted more as functionaries than as political leaders.

With the election of these lesser figures, the chain of the power structure in Connecticut ends. The political structure of local government in the colony was infinitely more detailed and complex than most historians have chosen to acknowledge. The town governments, under the guidance of the General Court and according to the needs of the times, had evolved from the simple days of the earliest settlements of Hartford, Windsor, and Wethersfield to the highly sophisticated structures of 1776.

A second evolution took place in local government, more subtle and perhaps more important than mere growth. This was the constant trend throughout the colonial period toward greater town power. The first towns, once they had surrendered their powers to the General Court, were firmly under the colony government's supervision, but the next century and a half witnessed a steady decline of external control over the towns. By the outbreak of the Revolution the towns had reached a semi-autonomous stage of development. As the local structures increased in size and complexity they correspondingly increased in power and independence. The increase in local power did not necessarily mean that the General Assembly did not act in local matters. Many people disagreed with the decisions of local officials and the Assembly became deluged with an ever growing number of appeals from disaffected townspeople.[75] But the Assembly and colony government seldom took the initiative in local affairs and became a place for the disgruntled to carry their complaints.

The shift in the locus of power from the colony to the towns can be explained by three phenomena: the general decline of the Puritan philosophy of strict control and authority, the increasing difficulty of maintaining tight administrative control over such a burgeoning system, and the "persistent localism" that survived the trans-Atlantic crossing. The decentralization process was never articulated and occurred without any specific major battles between the towns and the colony that can be identified as turning points, though individual towns did have jurisdictional squabbles with the Assembly. Power was transferred away from the center in the same organic way that the towns grew steadily in size.

NOTES

1. *The River Towns of Connecticut* (Baltimore, 1889), 28.

2. J. Hammond Trumbull and Charles Hoadley, eds., *The Public Records of the Colony of Connecticut*, 15 vols. (Hartford, 1850–1890), I (April 1638), 24 (hereafter, *Col. Recs*).

3. *Col. Recs.*, I (October 1639), 36, 37.

4. *Charter of the Colony of Connecticut of 1662* (Hartford, 1900), 6, 7, 8, 14.

5. A few examples of early eclectic officers were chimney cleaners in Hartford, a treasurer in Norwalk, and a sheepmaster and man to beat the drum for town meetings in Fairfield. Windsor elected a hayward in 1641 and the General Court ordered all towns to do so thirty-one years later.

6. Thomas Jodziewicz, "Dual Localism in Seventeenth-Century Connecticut," Ph.D. diss. (College of William and Mary, 1974), makes the strongest possible case for the independence of the towns, but even he agrees that the court insisted the towns acknowledge its sovereignty. As late as 1698, when Windham was short of money to pay bills, the court ordered the town to raise its tax rate. See *Col. Recs.*, IV (October 1698), 270.

7. Bruce Daniels, "Contrasting Colony-Town Relations in the Founding of Connecticut and Rhode Island Prior to the Charters of 1662 and 1663," *Bulletin of the Connecticut Historical Asociety* (April 1973), 60–64, shows the almost completely autonomous state of

Rhode Island towns. Sumner Chilton Powell, *Puritan Village* (Middletown, Conn., 1963), 140, passim, and Kenneth Lockridge, *A New England Town: The First Hundred Years* (New York, 1970), 4, passim, both present a picture of semiautonomous Massachusetts towns, but Michael Zuckerman, *Peaceable Kingdoms: New England Towns in the Eighteenth Century* (New York, 1970), argues that Massachusetts towns were closely controlled prior to the loss of the charter.

8. Jodziewicz, "Dual Localism," passim. T. H. Breen, "Persistent Localism: English Social Change and the Shaping of New England Institutions," *William and Mary Quarterly*, XXXII (January 1975), 3–28, develops this theme for Massachusetts and shows the localism that New Englanders brought with them.

9. *Col. Recs.*, II (May 1666), 34, 35; II (May 1666), 35; IV (January 1697), 235; IV (October 1699), 309, 310, 311.

10. *Col. Recs.*, IV (October 1700), 331; IV (October 1703), 439; IV (March 1704), 459; IV (May 1704), 462, 468; V (May 1712), 328, 329; VI (October 1722), 354; XII (October 1766), 499.

11. *Col. Recs.*, IV (October 1689), 11, 12.

12. *Col. Recs.*, IV (October 1698), 267, 282. It is proper to refer to the colony government as the General Court prior to the October 1698 session and as the General Assembly afterward.

13. *Col. Recs.*, III (May 1680), 50; II (October 1668), 95.

14. *Col. Recs.*, I (October 1639), 37; II (May 1665), 14.

15. *Col. Recs.*, IV (January 1697), 235.

16. Wallace Notestein, *England on the Eve of Colonization* (New York, 1954), 218, 219.

17. *Col. Recs.*, II (May 1666), 35; IV (January 1697), 235; VI (October 1725), 559–60.

18. Richard Bushman, *From Puritan to Yankee: Character and the Social Order in Connecticut, 1690–1765* (Cambridge, Mass., 1967), 136.

19. *Col. Recs.*, VI (October 1709), 133; VI (May 1724), 46.

20. *Col. Recs.*, II (July 1665), 29; V (May 1711), 239–41.

21. *Col. Recs.*, I (April 1638), 18; I (June 1641), 65; II (October 1677), 325; II (May 1674), 244.

22. *Col. Recs.*, I (Code of 1650), 527, 533, 538, 540.

23. *Col. Recs.*, VI (October 1717), 27.

24. *The Germanic Origins of New England Towns*, Johns Hopkins University Studies in Historical and Political Science, I (Baltimore, 1882), 8.

25. John Sly, *Town Government in Massachusetts, 1620–1930*, (Cambridge, Mass., 1930), 53, 54, discusses the Tocqueville thesis at length but uncritically.

26. Powell, *Puritan Village*, 142.

27. Kenneth Lockridge believes that Powell in *Puritan Village* tended to overemphasize the uniqueness of the Massachusetts town. See Lockridge, *New England Town*, XIII. Connecticut's example causes me to concur in that judgment. The most recent historian of the English origins of New England institutions has performed more research on both sides of the Atlantic than any previous scholar interested in the subject, and concludes that the Puritans "gave up as little of their former ways of doing things as possible" and that the seventeenth century was more of a New "England" than a "New" England. See the unusually well written and thoroughly researched thesis by David Grayson Allen, "In English Ways: The Movement of Societies and the Transferal of English Local Law and Custom to Massachusetts Bay, 1600–1690," Ph.D. diss. (University of Wisconsin, 1974), iii, vi.

28. Andrews, *River Towns*, 27.

29. Bushman, *From Puritan to Yankee*, chapter 1, discusses the immense effect the

desire for order had on the philosophy of government in seventeenth-century Connecticut. See also Edmond Morgan, *The Puritan Family* (New York, 1966 ed.), 17–21.

30. The near-definitive work on New England's town proprietors is Roy Akagi, *The Town Proprietors of the New England Colonies* (Philadelphia, 1924). Anthony Garvan, *Architecture and Town Planning in Colonial Connecticut* (New Haven, 1951), 41, gives fifty as an average number.

31. Akagi, *Town Proprietors,* 46. Bushman, *From Puritan to Yankee,* 84, 85, 87, states that the Narragansett War in 1675 demarcated the resident proprietor era from the speculative era.

32. Lockridge, *A New England Town,* 10, 11, discusses how one Massachusetts town made its decisions concerning land divisions.

33. Erna Green, "The Public Land System of Norwalk, Connecticut, 1654–1704: A structural Analysis of Economic and Political Relationships," M.A. thesis (University of Bridgeport, 1972), 41, 42.

34. Joan R. Ballen, "Fairfield, Connecticut, 1661–1691: A Demographic Study of the Economic, Political, and Social Life of a New England Community," M.A. thesis (University of Bridgeport, 1970), 157–62; Akagi, *Town Proprietors,* 108; and Garvan, *Architecture and Town Planning,* 41.

35. This can be seen in *Hartford Town Votes,* I, 1638–1716, *Connecticut Historical Society Collections,* VI (January 1638), 2; and in *Some Early Records of and Documents Relating to the Town of Windsor, Connecticut, 1639–1703* (Hartford, 1930), 107. Middletown, Farmington, Norwalk, and Fairfield were the same.

36. The Middletown town meeting simply changed the introduction of bylaws from, "At a Town Meeting" to "At a Proprietors' Meeting" all at the same session. Middletown Proprietor Records, City Hall, Middletown, 1717–1733, passim.

37. *Hartford Town Votes,* 1665.

38. *Col. Recs.,* VII (October 1727), 137; VII (May 1732), 379.

39. Akagi, *Town Proprietors,* 63–66.

40. Charles Grant, *Democracy in the Connecticut Frontier Town of Kent* (New York, 1972 ed.), 15; and Bruce P. Stark, "Lebanon, Connecticut: A Study of Society and Politics in the Eighteenth Century," Ph.D. diss. (University of Connecticut, 1970), 349.

41. Farmington, Middletown, and Norwich, three old towns with significant unallotted land, divided almost all of it by 1740.

42. Albert McKinley, *The Suffrage Franchise in the Thirteen English Colonies in America* (Philadelphia, 1905), 382–84.

43. Ibid., 408.

44. *Col. Recs.,* VII (October 1729), 259, 260.

45. This can be seen by the way the freemen's admissions are worded in the Assembly records.

46. *Col. Recs.,* VII (October 1729), 260.

47. This paragraph is based on David Fowler, "Connecticut's Freemen: The First Forty Years," *William and Mary Quarterly,* XV (July 1958), 312–33.

48. The probate inventories are listed in Bruce Daniels, "Money-Value Definitions of Economic Classes in Colonial Connecticut, 1700–1776," *Social History–Sociale Histoire,* VII (November 1974), 346–52. Over 90 percent of the men recorded in inventories satisfied the requirement, but this must be adjusted downward slightly because not all men were included in probate records.

49. Figures for Farmington and Norwich are from calculations I have made based on freemen admission recorded in the town records; for Kent, Grant, *Kent,* part III; for Lebanon, Stark, "Lebanon," 208; and for East Haddam and East Guilford, Chilton Williamson, *American Suffrage: From Property to Democracy, 1760–1860* (Princeton, 1960), 27.

50. Stark, "Lebanon," 217-19; Grant, *Kent,* 113.

51. Middletown Town Meeting Minutes (March 1779).

52. Notestein, *England on the Eve,* 241.

53. Bushmen, *From Puritan to Yankee,* 292. Samuel Rankin, Jr., "Conservatism and the Problem of Change in the Congregational Churches of Connecticut, 1660-1760," Ph.D. diss. (Kent State University, 1972), 116, 117, discusses at length the growth of societies in numbers and in independence from the colony government's control.

54. Ibid., 293.

55. *Col. Recs.,* VII (October 1728), 211.

56. *Col. Recs.,* VII (October 1729), 211.

57. The records of the town meetings are studded with these references.

58. Lockridge, *A New England Town,* 8, 9, shows how important a part of town policy it was in Dedham to carefully screen new candidates for admission.

59. This paragraph is based on a study I have made of town meetings in eighteen different Connecticut towns, which included towns from all counties and of all ages.

60. This appears to have been the pattern also in Massachusetts, but unlike Connecticut the meeting appears to have made a comeback there in the late seventeenth and eighteenth centuries. Powell, *Puritan Village,* 99; Zuckerman, *Peaceable Kingdoms,* chapter 5; Kenneth Lockridge and Alan Kreider, "The Evolution of Massachusetts Town Government, 1640 to 1740," *William and Mary Quarterly,* XXXII (October 1966), 557.

61. Derby Town Meeting Minutes, City Hall, Derby (December 1707).

62. *Col. Recs.,* IV (May 1699), 286; XII (May 1765), 355.

63. *Col. Recs.,* V (May 1716), 563; II (May 1676), 281; II (May 1667), 66; VI (May 1719), 112; I (Code of 1650), 521.

64. *Col. Recs.,* IV (May 1690), 32.

65. *Col. Recs.,* XII (May 1765), 355; IV (October, 1703), 455, 456; V (October 1708), 73; VI (May 1719), 112; XV (December 1775), 193-94.

66. Andrews, *River Towns,* 110.

67. *Col. Recs.,* I (Code of 1650), 552, 528; II (May 1668), 88.

68. *Col. Recs.,* III (May 1680), 53.

69. *Col. Recs.,* IV (May 1703), 409; IV (May 1705), 502, 503.

70. *Col. Recs.,* II (May 1667), 61; V (May 1712), 324; VI (October 1721), 277.

71. Herbert Baxter Adams, *Saxon Tithingmen in America,* Johns Hopkins University Studies in Historical and Political Science, IV (New York, 1973, reprint of 1881 ed.), 8.

72. *Col. Recs.,* I (July 1643), 91.

73. *Col. Recs.,* V (October 1713), 403, 404.

74. *Col. Recs.,* II (May 1674), 224.

75. Allison Olson, "The Colonial Assemblies and their Constituents, 1700-1764," paper delivered to the American Historical Association (Chicago, 1974), shows that in most colonies local government experienced a growth of power in the eighteenth century and petitions and appeals to the central government increased.

The Foundations
of Social Order:
Local Government
in Colonial Maryland

LOIS GREEN CARR

How is social order established in a new settlement? How do people of diverse social origins and experience find ways of cooperating that produce workable and long-lasting institutions? How are disagreements voiced and grievances settled without disrupting daily routines or paralyzing the decision-making process? What changes take place as the population grows, becomes native born, and communities acquire a history? These are basic questions in the evolution of colonial local governments; they underlie this study of local government as it developed in Maryland.

Maryland local government developed over the second half of the seventeenth century, after Calvert hegemony was firmly established and population had begun to spread beyond the first settlement. The Calverts in part followed Virginia precedent in giving powers of local government to the county court.[1] This court derived from English quarter sessions and in both colonies absorbed also the powers of the manorial courts and the English sheriff's courts. Unlike the Virginia courts, however, the Maryland county courts did not share powers of any importance with the parish vestries; these did not appear in Maryland until the Anglican Church was established in 1692. In seventeenth-century Maryland all local administration and decision-making was concentrated in the county courts.

A look strictly at institutions as legally defined might suggest that in Maryland a strong centralized government gave way to a looser decentralized distribution of power as counties were erected. Reality was different. The governor and Council of the early settlement sat as a court, enforced the laws, adjudicated disputes, and made administrative decisions, although some powers were delegated to other magistrates, especially on distant Kent Island. But the councillors served a tiny population, about five hundred people in 1642. In effect, the government was a local government and not yet at all secure, as Richard Ingle proved when with one ship and a handful of men he nearly destroyed the colony in 1645. A major expansion of population in the Chesapeake that began just after Ingle's raid helped to save the Maryland colony, although Calvert authority was briefly challenged once more in the 1650s. With the spread of settlement came the need for additional centers of government. By 1658 there were about three thousand people in Maryland organized into five counties. These developments brought more differentiation of central and local functions and as time went on a clearer hierarchy of authority. In part, the evolution of local government accompanied rather than followed the evolution of central government.

The first standard commissions that empowered county magistrates to sit as a court appeared in 1658. That year began three decades of peaceful growth for Maryland under firmly established Calvert rule. By 1674 population had more than tripled and five more counties had appeared. Over the same time the county courts had gained most of the administrative powers that made them into local governments. When, in 1689, a revolution overturned the proprietary government, well-functioning county courts and conscientious magistrates could maintain order and provide public services in the absence of any central government.[2]

Seventeenth-century Maryland was a land of immigrants, largely from England, who brought English attitudes and traditions with them. "Order," "well ordering," "quiet rule"—these words often appear in Maryland court records of the seventeenth century.[3] They were key words in the thoughts of English and Maryland rulers and ruled. Everyone was considered obligated to help the community maintain this order. Individuals were supposed to stop an affray, though without themselves using violence, and to assist officers in making arrests. Men of sufficient estate filled the public offices to which their stations in life both obligated and entitled them. A poor man of low degree and a rich one who stood high had the best chances of escaping these obligations, but participation of the whole community was the assumption that underlay the operations of local government and justice.

The methods by which the county magistrates carried on local administration showed their judicial origin. What today would be an executive order to professional employees was then a judicial proceeding, and often against conscripted and unpaid citizens. Since public service was obligatory, refusal to serve or neglect of duty was subject to presentment and trial as an offense against the community.[4]

For these reasons, the judicial responsibilities of the county courts are not easy to separate from their administrative functions. As courts of justice they had jurisdiction over all accusations and over trial and sentencing of most offenders against the peace, although not the major felons, and they adjudicated many categories of civil disputes between individuals. As administrative agencies the county courts enforced various regulations—those that set the terms of servants, for example, or established liquor controls—and provided services still familiar to Maryland county residents: appointing and overseeing guardians of minor orphans, supplying relief for the poor, and constructing and maintaining roads and other public works. These services often entailed expenditures that had to be covered by local poll taxes which the magistrates levied. Thus these administrative functions led to the exercise of executive and even legislative powers by a body organized to operate as a court of justice.

The visible structure of county government was simple. The justices of the peace, commissioned together by the governor, sat as a county court, but in effect were also a committee which made executive decisions and issued orders. The justices had the assistance of several paid administrators: the sheriff and the coroner, appointed by the governor, and two clerks, one appointed by the provincial secretary and one by the attorney general. These magistrates and administrators, together with unpaid local officers and juries that they in turn appointed from among the county householders, carried on all local governmental functions until the 1690s. The creation then of parish vestries did nothing of importance to alter the functions and organization already developed.

The sheriff was an arm of the central government as well as of the county court. He delivered all orders from the governor and Council. He conducted elections of delegates to the Assembly. For the central courts, as well as the county court, he served all process, took bail for appearance, made arrests, impaneled juries, and in other ways acted as an agent. Since he had custody of prisoners, he ran the county jail. And he collected and disbursed, within the county, provincial and county taxes upon Assembly or county court order. Above all, the sheriff was the representative of the proprietor, the Keeper of the County, with power to raise a posse when necessary to quell disorder. In consequence he was a figure of great local authority and usually had been or would be a justice.[5]

In any court proceeding to which the sheriff was himself a party, a coroner acted in his place. In addition, coroners impaneled juries to inquire into mysterious deaths and reported the findings to the county or Provincial Court. By the late seventeenth century there were usually two or more coroners for each county. Often they were also justices.[6]

The clerks provided professional assistance without which the courts could not have operated. The clerk of court issued all process, kept the records, and organized the agenda of the court. Since his duties required considerable education and since the fees were lucrative, he, too, often was or became a man of local standing. The clerk of the indictments, whose office appeared in the 1680s, was the court prosecutor and general legal officer. He was necessarily an attorney and during the first two decades after his appearance, some of the ablest attorneys held the office. They must have influenced the development of county court procedures, which began to cleave more closely to English precedent than earlier.[7] All attorneys were officers of the courts, admitted to practice by the justices. By 1700 several practiced in every county.[8]

Various minor unpaid officers performed many necessary functions of local government. The court yearly appointed constables and highway overseers for each hundred, or subdivision, of the county. Constables broke up affrays, reported various offenders to the court, and prepared the lists of taxable inhabitants. Highway overseers impressed inhabitants to work on the roads and directed their labor on court order.[9] In addition, the justices appointed two pressmasters for each hundred (after 1699 two for each county), who could impress goods for the use of the militia on order of the governor.[10] Also essential to governmental process were many kinds of juries. Sheriffs impaneled petit juries to decide the guilt or innocence of those accused of offenses or to determine the liability of those sued for breach of a contractual obligation.[11] Special juries of inquiry served various purposes. They investigated mysterious deaths in conjunction with the coroner,[12] determined uncertain land boundaries,[13] determined whether land was escheatable,[14] valued land taken for public purposes,[15] and established the amount of damages due for various kinds of injury.[16] Whenever there was information needed, a jury of men of the neighborhood was the device inherited from the English legal and administrative system for inquiring into and reporting the facts.

The most important jury of inquest was the grand jury, which was usually called three times a year.[17] These jurors determined whether those accused of offenses were indictable and in addition presented to the court the jury's knowledge of various community needs: what roads or bridges needed repair, what orphans needed protection, and the like.[18] In some counties by the 1690s the grand jury had become a watchdog of the court. A Baltimore County grand jury forced election of parish vestries by parishioners according to law, although the justices had already made choices, and on another occasion protested public expenditures for salaries of clerks. A Somerset County grand jury sent up a "paper of grievances" to the Council asking that per diem for the justices be lowered and that some freeholders be added to the court when it decided on expenditures.[19] This power to draw public attention to court action or inaction provided some check on the power of justices who were not otherwise much subject to local supervision.

At the provincial level of government were the Provincial, Chancery, and Probate Courts, the Assembly, and the governor and Council. The Provincial Court tried all offenses punishable by loss of life or limb and all actions concerning ownership of land. It had concurrent original jurisdiction with the county courts over most offenses and over civil causes in which the amount demanded was 1,500 pounds of tobacco or more. It could also hear appeals. To this court would be taken civil actions brought against county justices for false imprisonment or any criminal accusations brought against them. Until the early 1680s, appeal from the Provincial Court was to the upper house of the Assembly, which consisted of the Council and was usually also identical with the Provincial Court itself. From 1692 the governor and Council heard cases on review, in effect adding the governor to this court and an act of 1694 formally established them as a Court of Appeals. At the same time, Provincial Court justices ceased usually to be councillors and hence judges of appeal from their own decisions.[20]

The governor and Council heard complaints against unpopular administrative action of the county courts, especially before 1700.[21] Thereafter, objections to county court administration were often taken to the lower house of the Assembly. From 1670, this consisted of four delegates from each county, elected by men with a fifty-acre freehold or £40 of any visible estate.[22] In the Assembly, the rules of legislative courtesy, which early developed, ensured that the wishes of the local delegation would be respected on all purely local matters. Consequently, the Burgesses of the eighteenth century acquired a decision-making role in local government sometimes competitive with that of the county court.[23]

At the pinnacle of the Maryland polity was the lord proprietor, whose charter gave him regal powers within his province. He granted land in fee simple, held of him, not the crown. He appointed his own governor, Council, and superior judges. He created the courts, from which there was no appeal to England. The charter required that he allow an elected Assembly to pass laws, but he—and not the crown—had the power to disallow them. On the other hand, laws were to be so far as possible agreeable to those of England—the English settlers remained English subjects with the rights and privileges of Englishmen. Doubtless the political realities of establishing and maintaining a colony gave the proprietor considerably less independence of the crown than his charter would imply.[24]

The governmental and legal institutions that developed under that charter proved acceptable over the whole colonial period. The common law was transferred immediately and English statute law was adopted as needed, although there was occasional conflict over its reception.[25] From 1692 to 1715 Maryland had a royal government, the result of an anti-Catholic revolution in 1689, but except for the decrease in plural judicial appointments, the structure of government as it had evolved by then underwent no basic changes. However, two modifications of the charter resulted which gave the crown a measure of official control. The crown could disallow an act of the Maryland assembly; and actions or suits for sums of £300 sterling or more could be appealed to the King in Council. These charter modifications had no effect on local government. There, the only alteration was the creation of the parish vestries, which in general did not acquire functions already vested in the county courts.[26]

The local government that had emerged by 1700 had survived the test of revolution and was to provide an institutional structure that changed very little until another revolution brought independence from the crown of England. How and why this government functioned successfully are questions important to the study of social and political history.

Magistracy was at the heart of colonial Maryland local government. The basis of authority of the county justices lay in their magistratical powers, which their English-style commission assigned to each individually as well as to them collectively.[27] The most important was the power grounded in English common law to take a peace bond or recognizance: that is, to require that an individual find sureties who would agree to pay the proprietor — or, during the royal period, the crown — a specified sum if he did not appear at the next court and in the meantime keep the peace toward all men. The justices could require the bond from anyone who broke or threatened to break the peace in their view, or they could act on the complaint of another. If a man could not find sureties, the justices committed him to prison. A justice acting alone could take a bond, but once the person bound appeared in court, the responsibility for continuing or releasing him from the bond belonged to the court.[28]

By an early English statute this power had been expanded to enable the justices to take bond for good behavior. From long usage, this power allowed them to demand bond of wanderers and of those of generally scandalous reputation, though not accused of an indictable offense. This bond was more easily forfeited than the bond to keep the peace and the Maryland justice acting singly used it primarily as a form of bail to ensure the appearance in court of men accused of specific offenses.[29] Nevertheless, bond for good behavior was a potent weapon in his arsenal should he be faced with a flagrant disregard for his authority.

A further reinforcement of magistratical authority was the power of the justices sitting in county court to punish for contempt. At common law they could order summary punishment by whipping or fine for insolent words or behavior in the courtroom, and they could send evidence of defiance reported to them—scurrilous language, refusal to obey court orders or assist in arrests—to the county grand jury for indictment.[30] In addition, Maryland law defined various neglects of duty as contempts, which county justices could punish summarily by fine—refusal to serve in various local offices, for example, or failure of men to appear when summoned as jurors or witnesses.[31] Such powers were essential for ensuring a minimum of efficiency in law enforcement and in the performance of public services.

Compared with the justices of England, those of Maryland exercised few administrative functions out of sessions of the full county court,[32] but the peace-keeping powers of the single justice, based on common law and presettlement statutes, were fundamental to maintaining law and order. There were no policemen to investigate statutory offenses. Instead, any inhabitant who suspected another could report him to the justice of the neighborhood. The justice would then issue a warrant to the constable to bring the accused before him, interrogate both the accused and the witnesses, and either bind over the accused to appear in court or order him to prison, depending upon whether the offense was bailable and sureties could be found. The justice certified all such proceedings to the county court or to the Provincial Court, where those imprisoned or bound to appear could be heard. The certainty of appearing before a higher court was the main protection of an innocent man, although he could also bring an action for damages against a justice for false imprisonment.[33]

The Maryland justice sitting singly had only slight powers to punish free white citizens for indictable offenses, although such jurisdiction increased over the eighteenth century; but from the 1690s he could hear and determine and issue execution in small civil causes that in England were heard in a manorial court baron or sheriff's court.[34] With a second justice, he also performed various functions ancillary to litigation in the higher courts, such as probating accounts or issuing stays to prevent the sheriff from collecting on a judgment before the tobacco crop that could pay it was ready.[35] The justices out of court, as well as when sitting on the bench, played a necessary role in the credit system that enabled the tobacco economy to function.

The county justices shared some of this jurisdiction with the justices of the Provincial Court. The latter also had magistratical powers and they could act singly in the administrative duties that required two county justices to act.[36] Nevertheless, they probably became less and less powerful as local officers. During the first proprietary period (until 1689) these men were also councillors with power to sit in any county court. In any neighborhood they could make themselves felt to whatever degree they wished. But after 1692 councillors and Provincial Court justices lost their automatic right to act as county justices at the same time that the county justices sitting singly began to increase their powers (see below). The language of the laws often does not make clear whether new jurisdiction extended to single Provincial Court justices, but the power to hear a small cause, for example, was probably not a burden put upon them.[37] They became less important to the daily life of their neighbors as the functions of the county justices increased.

To be effective a justice needed more than his magistratical and administrative powers; he also needed the respect of his neighbors. When possible, men with status or wealth or education—and preferably all three—were chosen. Since the social origins of most seventeenth-century immigrants to Maryland were at best the yeoman or small tradesman classes,[38] qualifications depended more often on wealth than on inherited rank or even education. Those who brought with them or achieved wealth were selected, but in the early years planters of no great substance sometimes dominated the bench.[39] Throughout the seventeenth century a gentleman's son establishing a New-World fortune might share power with a man who had begun a successful career as an indentured servant.[40] As late as the 1690s some justices were illiterate,[41] and men of lesser fortune might receive appointment in a neighborhood where no one better qualified was available (see table 1). High mortality helped to delay the formation in Maryland of established families from which leadership could be recruited and kept opportunity open for men with the talent to accumulate wealth or the luck to marry it.[42] At the same time most men of major wealth were likely to have the opportunity to be justices thrust upon them, whether or not they sought it.

The justice's house was a focal point that helped define a neighborhood in a land where farms were scattered and human interaction was not naturally organized around clustered settlements. In his hall —the usual term for the main room of a seventeenth- or eighteenth-century house—he would hold his court, and here his neighbors would come to seek his advice and support on any business likely to bring them before the full county court. A man of the justice's own standing might do this for convenience; one farther down in the social scale would do this to help ensure success. The justice's functions, whether formal or informal, trivial or central, made him a key man in the lives of the neighbors he both served and disciplined.

Justices sitting singly had few decision-making powers, but as members of the county bench they were the county rulers. Their power derived from their combination of judicial and executive powers granted in part by commission and in part by English and Maryland statute.

The commission gave the justices most of their judicial powers. The governor issued it to the justices jointly, and with any new appointment, a new commission had to issue. At least six or eight justices were usually named, even when county populations were small, to ensure sufficient attendance at each session and because large areas had to be serviced by justices acting singly. Three or four were designated justices of the quorum, one of whom had to be present if the court were to undertake any business beyond the powers of the justices out of full court. Until 1689 the commission explicitly allowed any member of the Council to sit on any county court, making possible some central control.[43] In practice, however, councillors did not often exercise this privilege after the early 1670s.[44]

At first the courts met in private houses, but in 1674 the Assembly ordered the construction of courthouses and jails in every county.[45] Legislative acts set court days, staggering them from county to county to enable the small number of attorneys to practice in several courts. During the seventeenth century, courts theoretically met six

TABLE 1.
Characteristics of Justices of Three Maryland Counties, 1660–92.

County	Number[a]	Immigrant	Native	Servant	Title on Arrival or at Majority[b]	No Title, Same	Title Unknown, Same	Literate or Probably Literate[c]
Charles								
1660–69[e]	18	18	0	8	3	13	2	13
1670–79	12	9	3	1	5	6	1	10
1680–89	11	10	1	3	3	7	1	8
1689–92	6	6	0	0	0	4	2	5
Total	47	43	4	12	11	30	6	36
Talbot								
1660–69[e]	11	9	2	0	4	1	6	11
1670–79	11	9	2	1	4	6	1	10
1680–89	9	8	1	0	2	0	7	9
1689–92	8	8	0	2	0	5	3	4
Total	39	34	5	3	10	12	17	34
Kent								
1660–69[e]	25	24	1	2	8	11	6	17
1670–79	11	9	2	1	2	3	6	9
1680–89	11	9	2	1	3	4	4	11
1689–92	2	1	1	0	0	1	1	2
Total	49	43	6	4	13	19	17	39

Source: Menard File, Hall of Records, Annapolis, Md. Russell R. Menard has compiled information on the careers of all governors, councillors, burgesses, justices, and sheriffs appointed in Maryland, 1634–92. He had made his file available to many researchers and plans, when finished with his work, to deposit the file at the Hall of Records, Annapolis. Information on terms that extended beyond the 1680s is from the references supplied with table 2 and from the records of the three counties from 1697, when the commissions generally cease to appear in the Council records.

Illiterate	Roman Catholic	Protestant	Religion Unknown	Disappears from Record	Dismissed for Cause	Dropped on Request	Dismissed or Refused Service at Revolution[d]	Dropped, Reason Unknown	Served Until Death, Removal, Disability, Promotion, or 25 Years or More of Service
5	3	4	11	0	1	0	0	2	15
2	2	4	5	1	0	1	1	2	7
3	0	5	5	0	2	0	1	0	8
1	0	6	0	1	0	0	0	1	4
11	5	19	21	2	3	1	2	5	34
0	0	3	8	2	0	0	0	0	9
1	0	5	6	2	0	0	1	1	7
0	3	6	0	0	0	0	5	0	4
0	0	8	0	0	0	0	0	4	4
1	3	22	14	4	0	0	6	5	24
8	0	5	20	4	1	0	0	8	12
2	0	5	6	1	1	0	1	3	5
0	0	7	4	1	1	0	3	2	4
0	0	2	0	0	0	0	0	1	1
10	0	19	30	6	3	0	4	14	22

a. Quakers who refused service have not been counted.
b. Titles counted are: Mr., Gentleman, Esquire, Doctor, Captain, Major, Colonel.
c. Literacy refers to the ability to sign one's name.
d. Of the 12 dropped or unwilling to serve during the Revolution, 4 were probably Catholic, 5 were reappointed later, 2 died.

times a year, although often one or more sessions were adjourned
without transacting business because bad weather or illness had
cut attendance. In 1708 the sessions were reduced to four.[46]

In full court the justices acquired criminal and civil jurisdiction
over most of the offenses or civil disputes likely to arise, except
those over real property. Swearing, sabbath-breaking, fornicating,
fighting, and assaults of various kinds were offenses that occurred
at all social levels and came to the attention of the courts at nearly
every session. The county courts had no jurisdiction over felonies,
for which English law specified penalties that required loss of life
or limb, but in 1681 an act of Assembly changed the penalties for
simple theft of property worth less than 1,000 pounds of tobacco
and thereby greatly expanded the criminal jurisdiction that the
county commission granted.[47] Horse theft and killing of livestock
not branded with one's own mark were by far the most frequent of
the major offenses. Thereafter, these could be handled locally
on the first two offenses—later first offense only—as if they were
misdemeanors.[48]

Just previous to this extension of criminal jurisdiction, the county
commission greatly expanded the civil jurisdiction of the county
courts, although it never included disputes over rights to land. This
jurisdiction over actions to enforce contractual obligations was unknown to the English justices of the peace. In England, most actions
to collect debts were tried in the Court of Common Pleas or King's
Bench, which went on circuit. Maryland had partly followed Virginia
precedent in granting limited civil jurisdiction to the quorum justices
of the courts, and in 1679 this was extended to the whole bench and
to causes that concerned debts to any amount.[49] During the early
eighteenth century this jurisdiction was somewhat reduced, but not
to a point that excluded any large number of causes. The concurrent
jurisdiction of the Provincial Court in causes over 1,500 pounds
of tobacco or £6 5s. sterling protected those creditors who wished
the benefit of more experienced judges or the convenience of collecting debts from scattered areas without traveling to distant courthouses.[50] But most creditors clearly preferred the county courts,
where costs were lower.[51]

Between 1654 and 1671, various acts of Assembly gave the county
justices most of the administrative responsibilities that made their
courts into local governments exercising basic social controls.[52]

Some duties gave the justices power to regulate economic activity. They adjudicated conflicts between masters and servants,[53] granted license to keep ordinary, where travelers could lodge and liquor could be sold, set prices for liquors not determined by the Assembly,[54] and maintained county standards of weights and measures.[55] Other duties obliged the justices to provide and finance public services. They appointed and oversaw guardians of minor orphans;[56] they dispensed poor relief;[57] they supplied a transportation network through construction of roads and bridges and subsidy of ferries;[58] and they provided and maintained jails and courthouses.[59]

In combination, their various responsibilities made the county justices the local decision makers. Some decisions primarily affected individuals: who still owed service or could claim his freedom, who could be a guardian, who must allow an easement, who could keep ordinary, who should care for a helpless widow, who must contribute time in conscripted unpaid service. Some affected the community as a whole: how much poor relief to allow, what prices the ordinary keeper should charge, what roads to lay out, what ferries to subsidize, what bridges or courthouses or prisons to build. All influenced the convenience, security, or property of some or all inhabitants.

Nevertheless, the justices were weak administrators. They did little planning for public services. Instead they responded to petitions —for extra service from runaway servants; for freedom dues for servants who had completed their terms; for poor relief, road location, and ordinary licenses; and for various reimbursements for outlay of time or money in the county's service. In addition, the most effective weapon for disciplining public officers, threat of removal, was generally not available. The justices could not appoint, or usually dismiss, the clerks or sheriffs or their deputies, who provided essential administrative support in return for lucrative fees, although removal of the clerk of court for gross misconduct became possible for a while in the eighteenth century.[60] Nor was the unpaid citizen appointed by the justices to be constable or highway overseer likely to fear dismissal. The problem instead was to see that he served. Besides, fear of dismissal could not necessarily make a highway overseer a better road engineer or a constable more effective in reporting breaches of the law or more precise in preparing the tax lists. The justices might have ensured greater efficiency by keeping men of proven capacity in these offices over long periods of time, but instead tended to rotate the obligations.[61] The notion that everyone should contribute his share, regardless of his talents or inabilities, took precedence over the notion of efficiency.

Still, on the whole what the local government provided was adequate to the needs of small rural populations. Tobacco reached ships, the poor did not starve, orphans found homes, servants were disciplined and also protected, public records were housed, public creditors were paid, and those believed to be wrongdoers were brought to justice. These were the recognized wants that local government supplied.

As decision makers and administrators, the justices acted primarily in an executive capacity. Like English justices at quarter sessions, those of Maryland had no authorized power to pass by-laws, which would create new offenses or put new obligations on inhabitants. In the 1690s the upper house of the Assembly suggested a law that would confer these powers on the county courts, but it did not pass. Instead, the same Assembly passed an act to prohibit the "striking of fish" in Dorchester and Somerset counties.[62] This was the first county law passed by the Maryland Assembly, and it set a precedent that has lasted until today.

Yet the justices had power of a legislative nature, in that they determined what county expenditures, and hence county taxes, were necessary for many purposes not explicitly authorized by act of Assembly. The power was founded on an act of 1671, which allowed the justices to levy tobacco to pay the "Publick Charges of their . . . Counties."[63] This statement of power was ambiguous in that it did not expressly permit the courts to decide what the public charges should be. Nevertheless, by the 1690s it was assumed to cover all decisions and expenditures that concerned poor relief, bridges, subsidies for ferries, and construction and maintenance of jails and courthouses.[64]

There were some checks on this power to raise and spend public funds. The levy court was held in public, and when the seventeenth-century justices strayed too far from what the people they served found acceptable, individuals or the grand jury could and did protest. During the 1690s such protests reached the governor and Council.[65] Any illegal payment, furthermore, could be challenged in the Provincial Court, and from 1704 the county levy account was sent to the Council each year for possible review.[66] Finally, as time went on the Assembly enacted limitations on expenditures too often found to be excessive (see below). Within these restrictions, however, the power granted to the justices provided essential flexibility for meeting specific local needs.

Their concentration of judicial and executive powers gave the justices far more control over individuals than any single agency of government has today. This control was also a consequence of great decentralization of authority. The higher courts, the governor and Council, even the Assembly could hear complaints or call for reports and issue orders; justices who abused their power could be dismissed or prosecuted. In the 1690s Governor Francis Nicholson was especially active in calling county justices to account and preaching the responsibilities of public service.[67] But these checks were slow and they usually required initiative and sometimes expensive outlay of individual citizens. Most men were at the mercy of their local rulers, as well as under their protection.

The opportunity to exercise such local power must have provided a major incentive to accept appointment as a justice, for there was no significant financial reward; nor for most men was the office a road to positions of major profit. Since from 1692 a sheriff could serve only two—later three—consecutive years, this office was regularly available, but the Maryland justices did not acquire the right held by those of Virginia to rotate it among themselves.[68] The great majority of justices were never sheriffs and some sheriffs were never justices.[69] At the same time, the major provincial offices of profit went to members of the Council.[70] While any man who aimed for a seat on the Council would likely start by acquiring appointment to the county bench, only a handful of justices achieved such promotion. Hopes of major office can hardly have motivated most justices of the peace.

The political advantages of serving as a justice were slightly greater. During the last quarter of the seventeenth century more than half of any assembly was likely to consist of justices (see table 2.) But this fact probably reflected the small size of the pool from which leadership could be drawn more than the use of appointment to the bench as a step toward an Assembly seat. These seats had less value in the seventeenth century than they acquired under the royal governors, when the lower house more firmly established its claim to the lawmaking powers and the privileges of the House of Commons.[71]

TABLE 2.
Justices in the Assembly, 1676–97.

Assembly	Justices	Not Justices
1676–82:		
May 15–June 15, 1676	24	17
Oct. 20–Nov. 14, 1678	26	17
Aug. 16–Sept. 17, 1681	24	18
Nov. 1–Nov. 12, 1681	24	18
April 15–May 13, 1682	24	18
1682–84:		
Oct. 26–Nov. 17, 1682	17	6
Oct. 2–Nov. 6, 1683	12	8
April 1–April 26, 1684	10	7
1686–88:		
Oct. 17–Nov. 19, 1686	15	6
Nov. 14–Dec. 8, 1688	15	6
1692–93:		
May 10–June 9, 1692	28	13
Sept. 20–Sept. 26, 1693	28	12
1694–97:		
Sept. 20–Oct. 18, 1694	30	12
Feb. 28–March 1, 1694/5	27	15
May 8–May 22, 1695	27	15
Oct. 2–Oct. 19, 1695	26	15
April 30–May 14, 1696	26	17
July 1–July 10, 1696	22	16
Sept. 16–Oct. 2, 1696	26	18
May 26–July 11, 1697	27	19

Source: Lois Green Carr and David William Jordan, *Maryland's Revolution of Government, 1689–92* (Ithaca, N.Y., 1974), 289–91, lists the delegates by session through 1688. David William Jordan, "The Royal Period of Colonial Maryland, 1689–1715," Ph.D. diss. (Princeton University, 1966), 356–57, lists the delegates by session, 1692–97. Information on justiceships through 1689 is from the Menard File (see table 1). Thereafter the data are found in *Md. Archives*, VIII, 324, 472, 474; XX, 65–67, 106–11, 138, 190, 386, 465, 466; XXIII, 126–30, 198; Baltimore County Court Proceedings F no. 1, 233–34; G no. 1, 320–21, 658; Charles County Court and Land Records R no. 1, 424; V, no. 1, 20, 205–6, 403; Dorchester County Land Record 0 no. 4 1/2, 59–60; Kent County Court Proceedings I, 402–3, 405, 481–82, 592–93; Prince George's County Court Record A, 1, 167–69; Somerset County Judicial Record, 1690–93, 221; 1692–93, 78, 227–28; Talbot County Land Record NN no. 6, 37b–38a (rear).

Exercise of power and the honor it brought within the county evidently was sufficient reward. Indeed, the careers of seventeenth-century justices clearly show that for many of them appointment as a "gentleman justice" brought a step upward in social status. Table 1 shows that in Charles County from 1660 to 1692, 25 percent of the justices were ex-servants, and 62.5 percent arrived in the colony without claim to the title of Mr., much less gentleman. Thomas Long of Baltimore County, omitted from the commission in 1686, begged for an explanation that would "take of that scandall, ignominy and reproach as your Pet^r by the occasion afresaid lyes under among his neighbors as a person not worthy to serve but to be discarded from His Lord^{ps} and your Hon^{rs} favour."[72] The man who had been known as James Stoddard, "taylor," but whose success had made him James Stoddard, "gent.," must have been eager to take his seat on the Prince George's County bench in 1699.[73]

The governor appointed the justices, and until 1704 theoretically without advice, but in practice the councillor or Provincial Court justice most familiar with the area probably controlled the selection.[74] In making appointments, little political maneuvering was possible before the eighteenth century because of the shortage of men considered to be qualified and the rapid turnover caused by high mortality. These same considerations led to regular recommissioning of justices unless they proved to be vicious in character.[75] Table 1 shows that in Talbot County, of justices appointed from 1662 to 1692, only one is known to have been dropped from the commission before death for any reason before the revolution of 1689. In Charles, only four men were dropped wtihout good cause during the same period. Kent County shows greater turnover, but not much greater after the 1660s. When the Associators took over the government they sought to keep as many of the Protestant magistrates as possible, and while some refused cooperation, those still living in the 1690s were soon reappointed to office by the royal Governor Francis Nicholson.[76] Justices were not subject to dismissal at the whim of a governor or a councillor. They had security of tenure necessary to develop a sense of public responsibility.

Many of the public services for which the justices were responsible depended upon the conscripted unpaid local officers and jurors drawn from the inhabitants of the county. One of the striking characteristics of seventeenth-century county government was the degree to which participation in these functions was shared by most county householders. While populations were small as well as scattered, wide participation was a necessity if the burdens of office and jury duty were to be spread. Recently freed servants with short-term leases might serve alongside established landowners and share the community recognition that such responsibilities brought.[77] As the century progressed, officeholding and jury service became more and more tied to freehold land tenure at the same time that tenancy was growing. Nevertheless, in several counties about 1700 at least two-thirds of the heads of household owned land or had freehold leases. Studies of three of these counties indicate that even by this date nearly all freeholders, and some tenants as well, participated in local government.[78]

This wide participation may account in part for the rapidity with which law and authority were established in new areas as settlement spread. The need for law and order and other public services supplied incentive for all to cooperate so long as none was saddled with an unfair share or unreasonable power. The social status conferred on humble men compensated somewhat for the burden at the same time that opportunities for service in offices of power provided further upward mobility for men with self-made fortunes. Every man who contributed made his stake in, and support of, community order visible to himself and to others and strengthened the authority of government.

The overthrow of the proprietor in 1689 subjected local government to a severe test. For more than two years the central government was in effect suspended and was only very partially restored during another year before the arrival of a royal governor. Yet during this time county governments functioned without reliance on military force or even unusually repressive use of magistratical powers. The poor were cared for, roads were maintained, taxes were collected, county creditors were paid, criminals were prosecuted, civil disputes were adjudicated. The lives of most inhabitants were not disrupted.

This local order was possible for two reasons. An adequate local organization existed for carrying on these functions, and the county leaders—regardless of political preferences, whether in or out of power—refrained from power struggles among themselves or encouragement of conflict. Both pro- and antiproprietary parties were concerned with the legitimacy of their positions and tried to avoid the violence or bloodshed that could put them at a disadvantage. They encouraged instead the safe routines that would counteract tension and keep the peace. Clearly, the concept of magistracy as a cornerstone of social order was well developed.[79]

Nevertheless, there was not yet a secure or self-aware ruling group in Maryland from which the magistrates were drawn. The justices of the 1680s were mostly immigrants and their social origins were still diverse. As a group, furthermore, their experience as magistrates was limited. Heavy mortality created frequent vacancies on the benches, and justices sitting in July 1689 averaged only seven years of service. Life was short in seventeenth-century Maryland, and most men died before their oldest sons were of age even to manage property, much less inherit a role of leadership.[80] The emergence of hereditary power groups was not even possible before the turn of the century.

Established and workable local institutions must have provided in themselves a stabilizing influence. Everyone knew what was expected of a magistrate or other officer of local government and most people accepted the obligation to contribute the services necessary to enable local government to operate. This framework of powers and duties fostered habits of behavior that enabled county leaders to identify orderly process with both their own and public interest. The development of sound local institutions was a civilizing force in the process of settling a new land.

By 1700 county government in Maryland had acquired the functions and most of the institutional structure that it was to exhibit for the rest of the colonial period. The tobacco inspection acts of the mid–eighteenth century brought new administrative duties to the county courts, but these duties were not new in character.[81] Justices out of court acquired increased jurisdiction, especially over Negro slaves, but most determinations that could lead to imprisonment or heavy fines remained with the full court.[82] Constables were granted some small fees and petit jurors' allowances for verdicts were increased, but profits were not great, given the time contributed.[83] The justices—essentially a committee—the clerks, the sheriffs, and conscripted local officers and jurors continued to enforce the law and provide necessary public services.[84]

A crisis of the royal period, however, somewhat limited the civil jurisdiction of the county justices and might have changed their role out of court. The royal governors had been dismayed at the "extravagant" powers of untrained men to determine many kinds of civil causes, although removal or appeal to the Provincial Court was an available protection to either party. Governor Francis Nicholson had concentrated on finding the ablest men available to serve and then on improving their general performance; but Governor John Seymour (1704–09) attempted to curtail their powers.[85] First, he limited the size of sums that could be litigated in the counties, although not to amounts that excluded any great number of causes. Second, by the use of two county commissions, only one of which granted civil jurisdiction, he empowered only the most experienced or best educated justices to hear civil causes, while maintaining the number of magistrates necessary to serve every neighborhood. Finally, he made the Provincial Court as professional as possible and sent it out on circuit.

Seymour's death in 1709 brought an end to all but one of these experiments. Although the civil jurisdiction of the county courts was not returned to its former level, it was at once increased to £100 sterling and all justices were again empowered to hear civil causes. The Provincial Court ceased to go on circuit and the floor of its jurisdiction was even raised from £6 5s. to £20 sterling, although causes from £6 5s. could still be removed from the lower courts. In 1722 the Assembly passed an act to create assizes, as sessions that included provincial justices on circuit were called. Assizes made access to justices of the higher court more available; but the county courts did not thereby lose jurisdiction. After 1740, furthermore, assize acts were seldom in effect and county court jurisdiction gradually rose from £100 sterling in 1722 to twice that by 1773. In that year the county courts gained powers that made assizes unnecessary: power to try capital felonies, and jurisdiction in all civil causes, including those involving title to land.

Seymour's policy of limiting the number of county magistrates empowered to hear civil causes had had a double purpose that might have produced changes in the county constitution. He had hoped not only to confine these powers to the most able judges but to discourage other justices from attending sessions of court. They were to carry out their functions as neighborhood magistrates but not burden the county with costs of court attendance, and to some degree this was the result. If the policy had continued, the consequences would have been far-reaching. The court made far too many decisions that required knowledge of the neighborhood to make them in the absence of the local justice. Either the judicial and administrative functions of the court would have quickly separated —as finally occurred in the 1790s—or the justices out of court, singly or in groups, would have acquired greatly enlarged powers. As it was, however, most decision-making powers remained with the full court.

The creation of parish vestries after 1692 might also have brought changes in the county government, but most functions necessary were already firmly established in the county courts. The justices lost the power to perform marriages if a minister were available and the keeping of registers of vital information was transferred from the clerk of court to the clerk of the vestry.[86] Otherwise, the parishes and their officers acquired no powers formerly exercised by the county justices.

Over time the vestries acquired some functions supplementary to those of the county courts. From 1696 the vestries could admonish men and women suspected of cohabiting, although proof of fornication in the form of a bastard might be missing, and if the couple refused to separate, punishment in the county court could follow without a trial. The tobacco inspection acts required vestries to nominate the inspectors, and during the French and Indian War the vestries assessed the bachelor tax.[87] All told, however, compared with the vestries of England or Virginia, the governmental powers of Maryland vestries were slight.[88]

Nevertheless, the vestries had potential importance because from 1702 their members were regularly elected. The freeholding parishioners once a year dropped two out of eight and selected two to replace them. In 1730 an act of Assembly required that members be dropped in rotation, thus ensuring that no member served more than four consecutive terms. Vestry concerns admittedly were largely parochial, but they included a limited power—until 1729 subject to confirmation by the county court—to tax all the inhabitants of the parish.[89] Who could vote and who was elected could have significance.

Who voted for vestrymen at the parish meetings supposedly held on Easter Monday each year? Theoretically, all freeholders were

eligible. The parish was an area that included all its inhabitants —
it was not just a congregation of Anglican communicants — and in
law there were no religious restrictions. Presbyterians not only
voted but served on vestries for the first ten years or more, and
this right was upheld in the 1750s.[90] But despite the wording of the
act, it is unlikely that Roman Catholics or Quakers participated in
parish elections. Their attempts to do so would surely have produced
protest and an effort to change the law. Quaker records show that,
instead, Friends persistently refused to pay parish taxes, suffering
consequent attachment of their goods.[91] Possibly some Catholics
did the same, although their more vulnerable position probably
made such defiance impractical.

There is little evidence to show whether Anglican freeholders
took much interest in parish elections. The only lists of voters preserved show a maximum of sixteen freeholders voting in areas that
surely had several times that many. Occasionally no freeholders
appeared.[92] Since taxation by more than ten pounds of tobacco
per poll required Assembly approval, most freeholders may have
counted on their delegates rather than their vestrymen to keep taxes
within reason. Inhabitants probably concerned themselves infrequently otherwise with parish business, which was usually confined
to keeping the church in repair, paying for communion wine, and
selling the parish tobacco.

Who served as vestrymen? A study of vestrymen of two Prince
George's County parishes through 1720 indicates that men of
prominence were usually elected but that middling planters also
served. Thomas Addison, justice and then councillor, was a member
of the Piscataway Parish vestry from 1704 until his death in 1727.
Over one twelve-year period he missed only two meetings. With him
served three middling landowners, two of whom were illiterate. In
neighboring Queen Anne's Parish, burgesses and justices and their
family connections dominated the vestry, but William Ray, an illiterate planter with 300 acres and no known connections with a powerful family, served several terms and was rarely absent. No where
else in Maryland government had such men opportunity — however
theoretical — to sit at a table with justices or a councillor to discuss
policy and have an equal vote.[93]

Whether as time went on parishes continued to recruit planters
below the rank of gentleman is as yet unknown.[94] To the modern

eye the vestry offered political opportunities not to be missed. However, the record of refusals to serve and of absenteeism at vestries across the seventy-four years that followed the act of 1702[95] does not promote the notion that Maryland vestrymen had the same perception, and their constituents are likely to have been equally apathetic. The vestries managed to carry out essential functions, parochial and civil, but the quick demise of parish government in 1776 suggests that Maryland inhabitants set little value on the vestry as an opportunity for local self-rule.

Missing entirely from seventeenth-century local government were the independent statutory commissions for special purposes found in England for expensive projects like swamp drainage. The first such commissions appeared in Maryland in 1723, when the Assembly created boards of trustees in every county empowered to create "free" schools. Since these boards had no power to raise funds from a tax, their success was limited.[96] Beginning in 1768, acts of Assembly began to create similar boards for county almshouses, and these acts provided for financing by local taxation. In consequence, almshouses were soon operating.[97] But it took the drive for public improvements in the nineteenth century to bring other such commissions into being.

Social stability requires mechanisms for settling disagreements, and disagreements that engender real conflict are especially likely to arise over money and taxes. The seventeenth-century justices had power to decide on major outlays and tax the inhabitants to pay for them. Consequently, at the beginning of the eighteenth century, pressure to control this power began to develop in the Assembly, where elected representatives from the counties had a voice. The local delegates came to control Assembly decisions on any local issue that concerned their county and they thus became a force in local government. The losers in this change were the county grand juries, which during the 1690s had shown signs of becoming active spokesmen not afraid to take complaints to the governor and Council. Personal service on the grand jury could give even a small freeholder a chance to make himself heard. But the grand jury could only publicize objections; the delegation could exercise power. Its dependence on voters to keep it in power could make it more responsive than the jury to public pressure.

Two conditions were necessary to allow this rise to power of the county delegation. First the lower house had to acquire greater recognition and procedural sophistication than it had had under the seventeenth-century proprietors, a change that was rapid under the royal governors.[98] Until this occurred, complaints to higher authority were taken to the governor and Council and Provincial Court.[99] Second, and less easy to detect from the limited evidence available, was the growth of opposing local interests capable of organizing politically around issues. Once both conditions existed, men opposed to a policy of the county justices could put pressure on the elected representatives, who could in turn solicit the support of the rest of the lower house for passage of a local law. Other delegations would support this one in return for support on local issues of importance to them. The rule of legislative courtesy could develop and with it entrenchment of the practice of locating in the Assembly the power to make local laws.

How early local political consciousness that reflected more than personal allegiances appeared in the Maryland counties is not easily determined. Presumably, it developed slowly so long as populations were small and the same men tended to dominate all the offices of power. The revolution of 1689 created a province-wide issue that divided leadership, but all sides left the settlement of who should rule to the crown. By the end of 1694 neither the Assembly nor the county benches reflected the divisions the revolution had created. As late as 1700, even the issue of the heavy tax to support the Anglican Church did not affect the election of delegates in Prince George's County, a largely new but expanding area. Here the first sure signs of an internal political life tied to more than personalities appeared in 1710 over county support for a ferry. The justices and grand jury of the court supported the ferry but petitions to the delegates— who included only one justice—induced them to oppose it. One of the earliest examples of the exercise of legislative courtesy followed. The whole lower house backed the local delegation and forced the justices to stop subsidizing the ferry.[100]

About the same time petitions form other counties began to be heard in the Assembly protesting expenditures for courthouses.[101] By 1720 it was usual for county courts to seek legislative authorization in advance for these major outlays, and failure of the Prince George's County court to do so in 1747 led to debate in the *Maryland Gazette*. Against the will of an alleged 600 freeholders, some of whom had signed a remonstrance, the justices had decided to raise 100,000 pounds of tobacco to repair the courthouse in Upper Marlboro on the Western Branch of Patuxent River rather than move the county seat to the budding town of Bladensburg on a tributary of the Potomac. The debate in the *Gazette* faced the issue never raised in the seventeenth century, when the power to raise taxes to pay the "county charge" was granted: was not the power to tax located in the elected Assembly and the administrative power to pass accounts limited to expenditures thus authorized? The Prince George's justices won their immediate battle, but the Assembly of 1748 passed a general law putting a ceiling on expenditures for improvements made without a local act. Fifteen years later a similar law set the maximum that could be paid for the clerk's account. Thus, over the years the autonomy of the courts decreased and control of large expenditures shifted to the elected representatives.[102]

This result must have affected the power structures of the counties, but the research that can go beyond conjecture remains to be done. The controversy over the Prince George's County ferry suggests that as the number of aspirants for power grew, men opposed to the policies of the county justices could elect men of their own views to the delegation. This very fact made membership in the Assembly desirable for county justices, who continued to be well represented. At the same time, any delegate who was not a justice but wanted greater control over county policy probably would have had little difficulty in persuading the governor to appoint him to the bench, unless there was a councillor from the county who opposed him. Not every county was represented on the Council, but any councillor must have had power to veto appointments and legislation for his own county, should he choose to be interested. Interplay and conflict between councillors, delegates, and justices would depend upon local rather than province-wide issues and personalities, and local concerns would usually dominate elections and thus the composition of the lower house. Although this fact may have given provincial politics a parochial cast, it at least permitted some control by voters over local legislation, and especially over heavy taxation.

Demographic and economic developments produced other changes in eighteenth-century local government. Immigrants had dominated the leadership of the seventeenth century and many of them had made rather than inherited the fortunes that gained them offices of power. But soon after 1700, a group of native-born men of wealth and status finally appeared who could inherit these positions. They quickly dominated the Council, Assembly, and county benches, creating an established group to which future aspirants for power would find it necessary to be connected.[103] Men not born to this establishment could enter it, but the social origins of newcomers were higher than in the seventeenth century. The opportunity to start from the bottom, without capital, had greatly diminished, if it had not disappeared.

Prince George's County, newly founded in 1696, can illustrate the change. The majority of justices were immigrants until 1710, and while there were many fewer of obscure origins than had been selected at the founding of earlier counties, most were not born gentlemen. Over the next twenty years, however, only three out of nineteen new justices were not closely connected by marriage or descent with already established families. At least eleven were born in Maryland, and all were sons (eight) or sons-in-law (three) of former justices of the county. Another was a Lee from Virginia, who had married a daughter of Councillor Thomas Brooke.[104] At midcentury the connections were tighter yet. Of twenty-seven men appointed in two commissions issued in 1751, three were immigrants. Of those native born, twenty-one were descended from men who had held office of power fifty or more years before.[105]

This change surely altered the character of local leadership over the eighteenth century, but how is still a matter for conjecture. As justiceships provided less opportunity for upward mobility, they may also have become less valuable to those who were eligible. A mid-eighteenth-century evaluation of the justices commented that many eligible men refused to undertake the trouble.[106] On the other hand, the political opportunities offered justices may have intensified competition for these positions. One result is certain: most justices were men whose expectations from birth included the possibility of appointment to the bench, and in consequence the social distance between rulers and ruled increased. A ruling class, conscious of its role, was coming into being.

Opportunity to participate was constricting also at lower levels of local government. Minor officeholding and jury service were becoming even more closely tied to landowning than before,[107] at the same time that landowners were shrinking as a proportion of the total number of heads of households. A recent estimate of tenancy in Prince George's County finds about half the heads of households leasing their land by the time of the American Revolution.[108] As participation became more restricted, its nuisance value probably rose, and a larger proportion of those eligible may have tried to avoid a turn at troublesome unpaid, or poorly paid, county office.[109] Local government may have lost some of its base in voluntary cooperation of people with common needs.

In seventeenth-century Maryland the English institution of magistracy and the English tradition of obligatory service to the community were quickly transferred, allowing adaptation of reasonably familiar local offices and functions which in themselves encouraged social cooperation. In Maryland this form of stability antedated the emergence of a social class based on inherited wealth and status from which leadership could be drawn. Seventeenth-century justices and sheriffs usually earned appointment by climbing the economic ladder and learned to govern by governing. Among both rulers and ruled the county court as an institution helped establish habits of behavior fundamental to social order.

During the seventeenth century, local conflicts over policy were settled by petitioning the governor and Council to adjudicate them, but shortly after 1700, as population and competition for power grew, increased political consciousness produced a new mechanism. The county delegations in the Assembly gained the power to pass laws for their individual counties. The governor appointed the magistrates but the freeholders elected the burgesses. Thus the eighteenth-century county delegation became a force in local government which supplied a broad-based check on the power of the county magistrates. On the other hand, as the population became predominantly native born, the chance to exercise power at both the county and provincial level became more restricted than before to members of established families. The growth of political consciousness accompanied diminished opportunity for self-made men in a society increasingly based on deference.

The structure of local government established in the colonial period has lasted until very recently in Maryland. Until the 1960s the power to make local laws for most counties still remained in the Assembly, and the rule of legislative courtesy gave this power in effect to the county delegation, with power of veto lodged with the county senator. The structure and functions of colonial local administration had also survived, although judicial and administrative functions had long been separated and professionals operated most county services. County commissioners constituted an executive committee aided by a clerk, an attorney, and a new officer, the treasurer. It had power to license taverns, to administer poor relief (with state aid), to lay out and maintain county roads, to build and maintain county buildings, and to raise taxes to pay for these services. Often the sheriff still ran the jail and was a chief source of police power. Other functionaries and commissions had appeared, especially in urbanized areas, but in most counties the inherited governmental structure was still highly visible.[110]

The long survival of this structure of powers and functions is testimony to its usefulness. It was simple and flexible, and no need for change had been felt when the basis of executive authority had shifted from the governor to the voters, as county offices had become elective over the second quarter of the nineteenth century. In 1915 the Maryland constitution was amended to allow counties to adopt charters with home-rule powers, but no county did so until 1948, and there were only two home-rule counties in 1960.[111] Since then, suburbanization and the reapportionment that followed have created stresses that are transforming county government. But until mid–twentieth century the local institutions inherited from the colonial period provided continuity across centuries of change.

NOTES

1. A good brief overview of both Virginia and Maryland county court development is given in Wesley Frank Craven, *The Southern Colonies in the Seventeenth Century* (Baton Rouge, La., 1949), 200-4, 269-89, 293-94, 302-9. See also Warren M. Billings, "The Growth of Political Institutions in Virginia, 1634 to 1676," *William and Mary Quarterly*, 3rd ser., XXXI (April 1974), 225-42; and Robert Wheeler's essay in this volume.

I have omitted from this essay any discussion of the Maryland militia, the mayor's courts of St. Mary's City or Annapolis, or manorial courts. A brief discussion of the mayor's courts and the manorial courts is provided in C. Ashley Ellefson, "The County Courts and Provincial Court of Maryland, 1733-1763," Ph.D. diss. (University of Maryland, 1963), 11-16. There is little material available to show how the militia actually functioned, beyond what the laws provide. The relative lack of importance that militia appointment carried in local government is indicated by the fact that a civilian might outrank a major or a lieutenant colonel on the county bench.

2. On population, see Russell R. Menard, "Immigrants and Their Increase: The Process of Population Growth in Early Colonial Maryland," in *Law, Society, and Politics in Early Maryland*, Aubrey C. Land, Lois Green Carr, and Edward C. Papenfuse, ed. (Baltimore,

1977), 88-109; and Menard, "Immigration to the Chesapeake Colonies in the Seventeenth Century: A Review Essay," *Maryland Historical Magazine* (hereafter, *MHM*) LXVIII (Fall 1973), 323-29. For what is known of court development before 1658, see William Hand Browne et al., eds., *Archives of Maryland,* 72 vols. (Baltimore, 1883-1972), XLIX, vii-xi; LIII, xi-xii (hereafter, *Md. Archives*); Ellefson, "Courts of Maryland," chapter 1.

3. This paper is based on a study of all Maryland court records before 1710 that remain. The following are published in *Md. Archives:* Provincial Court records (1637-83) in IV, X, XLI, XLIX, LVII, LXV, LXVI, LXVII, LXVIII, LXIX, LXX; records for Kent (1648-76), Talbot (1662-74), and Somerset (1665-68) Counties in LIV; records for Charles County (1658-74) in LIII, LX; and chancery court records (1669-79) in LI. Records for St. Mary's and Calvert Counties are destroyed for the whole colonial period. Seventeenth-century records for Anne Arundel County burned in 1704. The first volume of court proceedings for Prince George's County is printed in Joseph H. Smith and Philip A. Crowl, eds., *Court Records of Prince George's County, Maryland, 1696-1699, American Legal Records,* IX (Washington, D.C., 1964), hereafter, *Court Records PG.* The records still in manuscript are housed at the Hall of Records, Annapolis, Maryland, except as noted.

4. This view of the English tradition is informed by the volumes of Sidney and Beatrice Webb in their series *English Local Government from the Revolution to the Municipal Incorporations Act* (London 1906-1929, reprinted Hamden, Conn., 1963). An excellent summary of their argument is *The Development of English Local Government, 1689-1835* (London, 1963), two chapters reprinted from *Statutory Authorities for Special Purposes* (London, 1922). Excellent discussions of English magistracy of the early seventeenth century are Thomas Garden Barnes, *Somerset, 1625-1640: A County's Government under the "Personal Rule,"* (Cambridge, Mass., 1961), chapter 3; and J. H. Gleason, *The Justices of the Peace in England, 1588-1640: A Later Eirenarcha* (Oxford, 1969).

5. Lois Green Carr, "County Government in Maryland, 1689-1709," Ph.D. diss. (Harvard University, 1968), text, 412-13, 415, 418-23, 504-24; Cyrus H. Karraker, *The Seventeenth Century Sheriff in England and the Chesapeake Colonies, 1607-1689* (Chapel Hill, N.C., 1930); Russell R. Menard, "Major Officeholders in Charles, Somerset, and Talbot Counties, 1676-1689," (hereafter, Menard File) ms., Hall of Records, Annapolis.

6. Acts 1666, c. 2, *Md. Archives,* 11, 130-31, listed as permanent by Acts 1676, c. 2, 550; Acts 1692, c. 56, XIII, 515, listed as in force in Acts 1700, c. 8, XXIV, 105, called for the governor to appoint the coroner and for his oath to be modeled on th at of the English coroner. The act of 1692 expired in 1704, but the governors continued to appoint coroners. See Prince George's County Court Record G, 691; H, 52 (hereafter, PG Ct. Rec.) For an early record of a coroner's inquisition, see *Md. Archives,* LIII, 140-41, 362; for his substitutions for the sheriff, see *Court Records PG,* 44, 315, 384; PG Ct. Rec. B, 255a; C, 120a-21; Talbot County Judgments, 1698, 102 (hereafter, Talb. Judg.) Coroners for every county are listed in September 1689. All but one were also justices (*Md. Archives,* XIII, 241-45). In Prince George's County, 1696-1716, five out of nine coroners were justices. Carr, "County Government," appendix III, table 3; VI, tables 5A and 6, part II. On the coroner, see also *Court Records PG,* xli, xlii.

7. Carr, "County Government," text, 281-85, 490-502; appendix IV; *Court Records PG,* xli-xlii.

8. Alan F. Day, "Lawyers in Colonial Maryland, 1660-1715," *American Journal of Legal History,* XVII (April 1973), 146-65, offers the best discussion of the legal profession in Maryland of this period so far available.

9. For information on constables, see Acts 1649, c. 7, *Md. Archives,* 1, 152; Acts 1661, c. 2, 410-11, revived until 1692; Acts 1692, c. 57, XIII, 515-16; Acts 1700, c. 8, XXIV, 105; Acts 1704, c. 61, XXVI, 343-44; Acts 1715, c. 15, Thomas Bacon, ed., *The Laws of Maryland At Large . . . With Proper Indexes* (Annapolis, Md., 1765), hereafter, Bacon's

Laws. All revivals of temporary laws are indicated in Bacon's *Laws,* which covers legislation through 1763. Citations for legislation beyond 1763 are not provided in this essay unless the law changed before 1776. For examples of constables in performance of their duties, see *Md. Archives,* LX, 350ff, 356, 439, 519; LIV, 273, 299, 323, 453, 540; *Court Records PG,* 22, 393, 462; Baltimore County Court Proceedings, F no. 1, 348 (hereafter, Balt. Ct. Pro.); Talbot County Land Records, AB no. 8, 524 (hereafter, Talb. Land Rec.)

For information on overseers of the highways, see Acts 1666, c. 12, *Md. Archives,* II, 134-35; Acts 1669, c. 13, 219-20; Acts 1671, c. 23, 321-22, revived until 1692; Acts 1692, c. 39, XIII, 486-87; Acts 1696, c. 23, XXXVIII, 95-97; Acts 1699, c. 13, XXII, 475-77; Acts 1704, c. 21, Bacon's *Laws.* For examples of courts ordering roads to be laid out and activities of overseers, see *Md. Archives,* LIV, 272, 299, 323, 648, 652; *Court Records PG,* 250, 282-83, 484, 497; PG Ct. Rec. B, 196a-199a; 216-19, 339, 402; Balt. Ct. Pro. D, 26, 40, 132, 232. Until 1692 the acts allowed the counties to raise taxes to pay for work on the roads, but only Talbot County did so and by 1689 had abandoned the practice (*Md. Archives,* LIV, 445, 481, 544, 579-80; Talb. Judg., 1682-86, 193-4; Land Rec., NN no. 6, 115-16, 170-72, 371-72).

10. Acts 1676, c. 2, *Md. Archives,* VII, 57; Acts 1681, c. 1, 192, revived until 1692; Acts 1692, c. 83, XIII, 557-58, revived until, 1698; Acts 1699, c. 47, XXII, 565; Acts 1704, c. 87, XXVI, 272, revived until 1715; Acts 1715, c. 43, XXX, 280-81; Balt. Ct. Pro. G, 501-2; *Court Records PG,* 5, 113, 300, 323, 395.

11. The first county court jury verdict was recorded March 2, 1656/57 in Kent County; *Md. Archives,* LIV, xx-xxiii, 103. By the 1660s petit juries were being impaneled several times a year in Talbot County (403, 404, 406, 418, 435, 439, 453, 474, 475, 485). Petit jurors were not required to be freeholders until 1699, but the law then passed was not always observed, at least at first. Acts 1699, c. 29, XXII, 511-12; Acts 1704, c. 89, XXVI, 424-26; Acts 1713, c. 11, XXXVIII, 177-79; Acts 1715, c. 37. Bacon's *Laws;* Carr, "County Government," chapter 6, note 143.

12. *Md. Archives,* LIV, 7, 8, 10, 361, 372, 389, 412. After the 1670s, proceedings of coroner's inquests are not recorded.

13. These juries were often called in connection with ejectments heard in the Provincial Court and are to be found in the loose papers called Ejectment Papers, which survive primarily for the eighteenth century. An act of 1699, in force until 1707, provided for proceedings originating in the county court for resurvey of boundaries (Acts 1699, c. 18, *Md. Archives,* XXII, 481-94), and the court records contain many records of juries impaneled under this act: e.g., PG Ct. Rec. B, 2, 5, 48, 78, 231a, 240, 258, 273, 284a, 300, 342, 352c, 387; Charles County Court and Land Record, B no. 2, 236-40 (hereafter, Ch. Ct, and Land Rec.) In 1723 an act that established county land commissions on county court order also called for local juries of inquiry. The act remained in force through the colonial period (Acts 1723, c.8, Bacon's *Laws;* William Kilty, ed., *The Laws of Maryland . . . ,* 2 vols. [Annapolis, Md., 1799], I, hereafter, Kilty's *Laws*).

14. The chancery records contain records of local juries called to determine whether land was escheatable to the proprietor, e.g., *Md. Archives,* LI, 65, 69, 103, 119, 138, 141, 155, 157, 171, 185, 187, 188, 191, 368, 476, 480.

15. Acts beginning in 1669 concerning watermills, acts of 1683 and 1706 for towns, and acts of 1697 allowing courts and vestries to acquire land for courthouses and churches called for condemnation juries. The act that concerned courthouses was repealed in 1704 (Acts 1669, c. 8, ibid., II, 211-14; Acts 1692, c. 70, XIII, 534-36; Acts 1699, c. 40, XXII, 532-33; Acts 1704, c. 16, Bacon's *Laws;* Acts 1683, c. 5, *Md. Archives,* VII, 609-19, revived until 1692; Acts 1706, c. 14, XXVI, 636-45, disallowed, Bacon's *Laws;* Acts 1697, c. 5, *Md. Archives,* XIX, 592-94; Acts 1700, c. 8, XXIX, 107, repealed 1704, Bacon's *Laws;*

Acts 1697, c. 1, *Md. Archives,* XIX, 589–91; Acts 1700, c. 8, XXIV, 107; Acts 1704, c. 38, Bacon's *Laws*).

16. Juries of inquiry to assess damages were not impaneled separately from petit juries until after the mid-1670s. I have not determined exactly when they first appeared. There were seven in Prince George's County, 1696–1709. All members also served on petit juries (*Court Records PG,* 416; PG Ct. Rec. B, 202a, 117, 118, 119, 174, 204; Carr, "County Government," chapter 6, note 150).

17. The first reference in an extant county court record to a grand jury is in Charles County in 1662 (*Md. Archives,* LIII, xix, 250). The first enactment requiring regular im-paneling of grand juries was buried in an act against hogstealing of 1666 (Acts 1666, c. 18, 11, 140–41; Acts 1671, c. 7, 277–78, revived until 1692, c. 32, XIII, 477–78; Acts 1699, c. 29, XXII, 311–12; Acts 1704, c. 89, XXVI, 424–26; Acts 1715, c. 37, Bacon's *Laws*). The act of 1692 was the first to require that grand jurors be freeholders, but through at least 1710 the requirement was not always observed (Carr, "County Government," chapter 6, note 136).

18. For a variety of examples, see *Md. Archives,* LIV, 324, 331, 599, 661; *Court Records PG,* 15, 24–25, 183–84, 256–57, 284–85, 325–26, 350, 393–94, 458, 491, 523; Somerset Judicial Record, 1698–1701, 160 (hereafter, Som. Jud. Rec.), 1696–98, 165.

19. Balt. Ct. Pro., F no. 1, 410–14; *Md. Archives,* XIX, 515–16.

20. Lois Green Carr and David William Jordan, *Maryland's Revolution of Government, 1689–1692,* St. Mary's City Commission publication no. 1 (Ithaca, N.Y., 1974), 6–9; Carroll T. Bond, ed., *Proceedings of the Maryland Court of Appeals, 1695–1729,* Ameri-can Legal Records, I (Washington, D.C., 1933), xvii, xxix–xxxv, xxxviii–xxxix. The Pro-vincial Court in 1660 announced a policy of refusing to hear causes that involved 1,500 pounds of tobacco or less, except on appeal, and in 1676 the Assembly enacted this rule into law (Carr, "County Government," text, 130). For a detailed account of eighteenth-century changes in the floor of Provincial Court jurisdiction in civil causes, see Ellefson, "Courts of Maryland," 85–91. Ellefson points out that later in the eighteenth century councillors once more occasionally sat on the Provincial Court, but they never again domi-nated. Instances of prosecution of justices in the Provincial Court are few. For an example, see Provincial Court Judgments, WT no. 3, 215–17 (hereafter, Prov. Ct. Judg.) Accounts of the development of the Chancery and Prerogative Courts are available in *Md. Archives,* LI, xxxii–lxii; and Elisabeth Hartsook and Gust Skordas, *Land Office and Prerogative Court Records of Maryland,* Hall of Records publication no. 4 (Annapolis, Md., 1946, 81–91.

21. For example, *Md. Archives,* XVIII, 42–43, 59–64, 170–71; V, 476–77, 524–25. 540.

22. Until 1670 all freemen could vote. Some of the early Assemblies included all free-men. The Assembly permanently divided into an upper and lower house about 1660 (New-ton D. Mereness, *Maryland As a Proprietary Province* [New York, 1901], 197–99). From 1676 to 1681 the proprietor struggled with the lower house over whether two or four dele-gates should be called from each county, and from 1681 to 1688 the decision was in his favor. For a recent discussion, see Carr and Jordan, *Maryland's Revolution of Government,* 23–27.

23. Two officers of the central government kept county deputies who were essentially county functionaries. The commissary general (the judge of probate) from 1692 appointed a deputy commissary who granted administrations and after 1694 received inventories and passed accounts for estates valued at up to £50 sterling—later to larger amounts—and by special commission could handle larger estates. His creation saved the estates of those de-ceased major expenses in travel for witnesses to wills, executors, and administrators of estates, while keeping jurisdiction over disputes and responsibility for record-keeping in the central Probate Court. The surveyors general, one for each shore about 1697, appointed

a deputy surveyor in each county who surveyed or resurveyed grants of His Lordship's land. During the royal period, 1692–1715, there were also King's surveyors appointed in the counties to undertake surveys required by judicial proceedings. Under the act for determining uncertain land boundaries, 1699–1707 (see note 13), of the King's surveyors (Donnel McClure Owings, *His Lordship's Patronage: Offices of Profit in Colonial Maryland,* Maryland Historical Society Studies in History, no. 1 [Baltimore, 1953], 81, 84–85; Carr, "County Government," text, 341–44, 376–77, 540–43).

24. The charter is set forth in Francis Newton Thorpe, ed., *The Federal and State Constitutions, Colonial Charters, and Other Organic Laws of the States, Territories, and Colonies Now or Heretofore Forming the United States of America,* 7 vols. (Washington, D.C., 1909), vol. 3 *1677–86.*

25. Joseph H. Smith, "The Foundations of Law in Maryland, 1634–1715," in *Selected Essays: Law and Authority in Colonial America* ed. George Billias (Barre, Mass., 1965), 92–115; Carr and Jordan, *Maryland's Revolution of Government,* 21–29, 206; Carr, "County Government," text, 86–96; George Leakin Souissat, *The English Statutes in Maryland,* The Johns Hopkins University Studies in Historical and Political Science, nos. 11, 12 (Baltimore, 1903).

26. Carr and Jordan, *Maryland's Revolution of Government,* 205–9.

27. *Court Records PG,* xliii–xlv, compares the Maryland commissions of the late 1690s with the English commission. Carr, "County Government," text, 98, 100, 127–43, extends the comparison to earlier and later experiments with the commission. Ellefson, "Courts of Maryland," 43–49, 81–83, also discusses the Maryland commissions.

28. William Lambarde, *Eirenarcha, or of the Office of the Justices of the Peace* (London, 1619), 75–109; Michael Dalton, *The Countrey Justice* (London, 1690), 1–3.

29. Lambarde, *Eirenarcha,* 117–20; Michael Dalton, *The Countrey Justice* (London, 1697), 292–97; see also, Barnes, *Somerset,* 57; S. A. Peyton, ed., *Minutes of Proceedings in Quarter Sessions held for the Parts of Kesteven in the County of Lincoln, 1674–94,* Lincoln Records Society, XXV–XXVI (Lincoln, England, 1931), lxv–lxviii. For Maryland practice, see Carr, "County Government," text, 102–3. Most examples come from the records of Somerset County, where recording practices were exceptionally thorough. See, for instance, Somerset Judicial Records, 1692–93, 31; 1695–96, 103; 1701–02, 60.

30. For Maryland examples, see Talb. Judg., MTW, 49; Balt. Ct. Proc., F no. 1, 246; G no. 1, 176; Ch. Ct. and Land Rec., P no. 1, 188–89; R no. 1, 44–45, 163, 165; Som. Jud. Rec., 1687–89, 29; 1693–94, 108–09; 1695–96, 9, 11–12; 1698–1701, 11–12; 1701–02, 65–66, 135, 169–70; 1707–11, 128–29; PG Ct. Rec. A, ff. 78, 85, 59, 234–35, 356, 401–4, 405, 430; B, ff. 58, 93; Kent County Court Proceedings 1, 792, 795; Dorchester County Land Record no. 4 1/2, 108, 123.

Seventeenth-century English law and practice in contempt is murky. See John C. Fox, "The Summary Process to Punish Contempt," *Law Quarterly Review,* XXV (July 1909), 238–54, (October 1909), 354–70; "The Nature of Contempt," ibid., XXXVII (April 1921), 191–202; "The Writ of Attachment," ibid., XL (January 1924), 43–60; William Hawkins, *A Treatise of the Pleas of the Crown; or a System of the Principle Matters Relating to that Subject, Digested under their Proper Heads,* (hereafter, Hawkins) 3rd ed., 2 vols. (London, 1739), I, 58; II, 141; and Thomas G. Barnes, ed., *Somerset Assize Orders, 1629–1640,* Somerset Record Society, LXV (Frome, England, 1959), xxix–xxx.

31. Acts 1661, c. 2, *Md. Archives,* 1, 410–12, revived until 1692; Acts 1692, c. 57, XIII, 515–18; Acts 1699, c. 29, XXII, 511–12; Acts 1704, c. 89, XXVI, 424–26; Acts 1715, c. 37, XXX, 308–31. Examples abound in the court proceedings.

32. Carr, "County Government," text 110–15, 432–33. Dalton, *The Countrey Justice* (1690), 22–26, 261–63, lists all the powers of English justices late in the seventeenth century. Ellefson, "Courts of Maryland," 174–76, lists all the powers of the single Maryland justice, 1733–63.

33. Hawkins, 11, 82, 84–85, 103, offers a clear discussion of these powers to make preliminary inquiries and their history in English practice. See also William Sheppard, *The Faithful Councellor: or the Marrow of the Law in English,* 2nd ed., 2 vols., (London, 1653), 1, 284, 297. This was a book found in Maryland seventeenth-century inventories. For use of these powers in Maryland, see Carr, "County Government," text, 101-3, 198-204. A detailed account of a preliminary inquiry appears in *Calendar of Maryland State Papers, no. 1, The Black Books,* Hall of Records Commission publication no. 1 (Annapolis, Md., 1943), no. 41; see also nos. 49, 50, 51, and 52.

34. Acts 1694, c. 30, *Md. Archives,* XXXVIII, 26; Acts 1696, c. 21, 93–94; Acts 1697, c. 2, 101; Ellefson, "Courts of Maryland," 79–80. For these inferior English courts, see William Greenwood, *Boyaeythpicon, or a Practical Demonstration of County-Judicatures . . .,* 5th ed. (London, 1675), 4–6, 14–26, 38, 53–54, 74 (second numbering); and Karraker, *The Seventeenth Century Sheriff,* 37–52. Jurisdiction granted to single Maryland justices was in causes to 200 pounds of tobacco or 20s. sterling, increased in 1715 to 400 pounds of tobacco or 40s. sterling.

35. Acts for *supersedeas* are in Acts 1676, c. 13, *Md. Archives,* II, 537–38, revived until 1692; Acts 1692, c. 10, XIII, 447–48; Acts 1699, c. 39, XXII, 528–30; Acts 1704, c. 37, XXVI, 298–301; and Acts 1715, c. 29, Bacon's *Laws.* Acts for probate of accounts are in Acts 1671, c. 25, *Md. Archives,* II, 323–24, revived until 1692; Acts 1692, c. 59, XIII, 519–20; Acts 1699, c. 8, XXII, 466–68; Acts 1704, c. 49, XXVI, 324–25; and Acts 1715, c. 33, Bacon's *Laws.* For other powers, see Carr, "County Government," 125–27.

36. See references in note 35.

37. Civil actions in the court of the single justice were not recorded; hence the difficulty in determining who exercised this jurisdiction.

38. Russell R. Menard, "Economy and Society in Early Colonial Maryland," Ph.D. diss. (University of Iowa, 1974), table 5-1, demonstrates that at a minimum 70 percent of the people listed in the Maryland headrights came as servants or had their way paid by another.

39. Of the thirteen justices appointed in Charles County at its founding, 1658-61, five were illiterate and only four can be proved capable of signing their names. Five were ex-servants. All owned land, but, although they died with varying amounts of personal estate, ranging from £70 to £1,006 (over the years 1660-86), when appointed none was much removed in status from the small planters of his neighborhood. At the same time none of obvious superiority was being overlooked. These data receive excellent discussion in Menard, "Early Colonial Maryland," chapter 5. Carr," County Government," chapter 7, shows that during the first thirteen years of Prince George's County, 1696-1709, twenty-three of the twenty-seven justices appointed were the wealthiest available. In one instance, inherited rank received precedence over sheer wealth. In three other instances, the men appointed were the wealthiest at the moment in their areas. None identified as having major mercantile wealth failed to be appointed.

40. For example, from 1679 to 1789, Henry Jowles, son of John Jowles, Esq., of Surrey, England, sat in Calvert County with Richard Marsham, an ex-servant. In the mid-1690s, Kenelm Cheseldyne, son of the Reverend Kenelm Cheseldyne of Blaxham, Lincolnshire, sat on the St. Mary's County bench with Philip Lynes, an ex-servant. Carr and Jordan, *Maryland's Revolution of Government,* 242-43, 266-68 (Jowles and Cheseldyne); Carr, "County Government in Maryland," appendix 8A under William Barton (Marsham); Menard File (Lynes), described in table 1. Table 1 indicates that justices who arrived in Maryland without claim to a title of deference must often have outnumbered those who had arrived with such a claim.

41. Henry Ridgley of Anne Arundel County, Randall Hanson of Charles, and Francis Hutchins of Calvert (*Md. Archives,* XX, 107; Prince George's County Land Record A, 21; C, 46a, hereafter, PG Land Rec.) Eleven of the justices of the 1680s were illiterate (see

Menard File). Five were still sitting in 1689. Of the justices appointed in Charles County, 1660–92, 23 percent were illiterate.

42. Lorena S. Walsh and Russell R. Menard, "Death in the Chesapeake: Two Life Tables for Men in Early Colonial Maryland," *MHM*, LXIX (Summer 1974). 211–27. Preliminary results from a study of Maryland inventories, "Social Stratification in Maryland, 1658–1705," being conducted by P. M. G. Harris, Menard, and Carr under the auspices of the St. Mary's City Commission and with funds from the National Science Foundation (GS-32272), show that at least 72 percent of the 1,735 men who left inventories in four Maryland counties during these years died without children or before any of their children were of age to care for property.

43. For discussions of the commission, see Ellefson, "Courts of Maryland," 43–49, 81–83; *Court Records PG*, xliii–xlv; and Carr, "County Government," text, 127–39, 142, 477–78. For examples of commissions, see *Md. Archives*, III, 422–24, 554–55; *Court Records PG*, 1–2, 186–87, 519–20; and Som. Jud. Rec., 1687–89, 1–3. In 1733 the proprietor reverted to the pre-1689 practice by naming all councillors to county commissions, as was always done in England in commissioning the justices of quarter sessions, but with one exception councillors did not sit. The exception was Daniel Dulaney, who often attended Frederick County Court. (Aubrey C. Land, "Lord Baltimore and the Maryland County Courts," *Maryland Law Review*, XX, (Spring 1960), 138–40; Ellefson, "Courts of Maryland," 161.)

44. However, George Talbot sat in Cecil County in 1684 and Vincent Low appeared frequently in Talbot County, 1685–88 (Cecil County Judgments, 1683–92, 4–5; Talb. Land Rec., NN no. 6, 97, 117, 147, 172, 175, 207, 223, 228, 298, 306, 307).

45. Acts 1674, c. 16, *Md. Archives*, II, 413–14, listed as a permanent act in Acts 1676, c. 2, 550, repealed in 1692.

46. Acts 1663, c. 19, ibid., I, 496–97; Acts 1669, c. 16, II, 222; Acts 1674, c. 8, 397–98; Acts 1684, c. 5, XIII, 172–73; Acts 1692, c. 65, 528–29; Acts 1700, c. 8, XXIV, 105; Acts 1704, c. 63, XXVI, 346; Acts 1708, c. 12, XXVII, 367–68; Acts 1715, c. 14, Bacon's *Laws*.

47. C. 3, *Md. Archives*, VII, 201–3; Acts 1692, c. 34, XIII, 479–81, revived until 1698; Acts 1699, c. 2, XXII, 553–55. Acts 1704, c. 25, XXVI, 266–68, amended the law to allow county court trial only on the first offense but to permit the Provincial Court to apply the county court penalty on the second offense. Before then the Provincial Court had applied these penalties when a jury had found that the value of the stolen goods was less than 1,001 pounds of tobacco (see, e.g., Prov. Ct. Judge., WT no. 3, 424–27; see also, Carr and Jordan, *Maryland's Revolution of Government*, appendix C, 298–301).

48. Joseph H. Smith interprets the act of 1681 as making the jurisdiction exclusive to the county court (*Court Records PG*, xlviii). Ellefson finds that after 1704, at least, jurisdiction was concurrent ("Courts of Maryland," 441).

49. Carr and Jordan, *Maryland's Revolution of Government*, 7–9, 298–301.

50. For changes in jurisdiction, see note 83. The policy of the Provincial Court that it would not hear causes under 1,500 pounds of tobacco was announced in 1660 and enacted into law in 1676 (*Md. Archives*, III, 422–23; Acts 1676, c. 13, 11, 538).

51. Carr and Jordan, *Maryland's Revolution of Government*, 298–301; Carr, "County Government," text, 182–83.

52. All surviving court proceedings provide ample evidence that the court exercised the powers granted, sometimes before they were enacted into law.

53. Acts 1654, c. 30, c. 39, *Md. Archives*, I, 348–49, 352–53; Acts 1658, c. 6, 373–74; Acts 1661, c. 10, 409–510; Acts 1662, c. 4, 441–42, revived until 1674; Acts 1662, c. 18, 451–52; Acts 1662, c. 20, 453–54, revived until 1676; Acts 1664, c. 8, 489, repealed 1676, Acts 1664, c. 24, 500–501; Acts 1666, c. 22, c. 24, II, 146–47, 147–48, revived until 1671;

Acts 1671, c. 19, c. 31, 298-99, 335-36, revived until 1676; Acts 1674, c. 7, 396-97, revived until 1692; Acts 1676, c. 7, 523-28, revived until 1692; Acts 1692, c. 15, c. 79, XIII, 451-57, 546-48, revived until 1699; Acts 1697/8, c. 12, XXXVIII, 117-18; Acts 1699, c. 43, XXII, 546-53, revived until 1704; Acts 1704, c. 53, XXVI, 257-62, revived until 1715; Acts 1715, c. 44, Bacon's *Laws.*

54. Acts 1678, c. 5, *Md. Archives,* VII, 65-68, revived until 1692; Acts 1688, c. 3, XIII, 213-15; Acts 1692, c. 46, c. 66, 488-91, 545-46; Acts 1694, c. 21, XXXVIII, 13-15, revived until 1695; Acts 1695, c. 5, 44-48; Acts 1697/8, c. 8, 116-17; Acts 1699, c. 35, XXII, 518-22; Acts 1704, c. 40, XXVI, 304-8. This law expired in 1708 over a quarrel about whether the Assembly could grant fees for ordinary licenses to the county courts and no new law passed until 1717, c. 1, XXXVI, 503-7. Courts granted licenses in the interim. See Carr, "County Government," text, 322 and annotation; Newton D. Mereness, *Maryland As a Proprietary Province* (New York, 1901), 355-60.

55. Acts 1671, c. 8, *Md. Archives,* II, 279-81, revived until 1692; Acts 1692, c. 45, XIII, 491-93; Acts 1700, c. 8, XXIV, 105; Acts 1704, c. 71, XXVI, 354; Acts 1715, c. 10, Bacon's *Laws.*

56. Acts 1658, c. 8, *Md. Archives,* I, 374-75; Acts 1663, c. 16, 493-95; Acts 1671, c. 27, II, 325-30; Acts 1681, c. 2, VII, 195-201, revived until 1692; Acts 1688, c. 4, XIII, 215-17; Acts 1692, c. 3, c. 47, 498-500; Acts 1699, c. 41, XXII, 533-44; Acts 1704, c. 20, XXVI, 324-49; Acts 1715, c. 39, Bacon's *Laws.* For a detailed discussion of the jurisdiction of the court over orphans and their guardians, see Lois Green Carr, "The Development of the Maryland Orphans' Court, 1658-1715," in Land, et al., *Law, Society, and Politics in Early Maryland,* 41-61.

57. There was no explicit legislative authorization for dispensing poor relief. Evidently it was considered to be covered by the act authorizing the county courts to raise taxes to pay the county charge, discussed below.

58. Roads were covered by acts listed in note 9. Bridges and ferries were covered only by the county levy act discussed below.

59. See references in note 45.

60. In 1711 the Assembly began to insist that clerks served during good behavior and that the court could dismiss a clerk and give temporary appointment to another if necessary. However, in 1754 Lord Baltimore reasserted his right to dismiss a clerk at pleasure. The Constitution of 1776 put appointment in the hands of the chief justice of the county court. (*Md. Archives,* XXIX, 64; Mereness, *Maryland as a Proprietary Province,* 189.)

61. Carr, "County Government," text, 445-46, 603-4.

62. *Md. Archives,* XIX, 39, 412; Acts 1694, c. 26, XXXVIII, 21; Acts 1696, c. 15, 86-87.

63. C. 3, *Md. Archives,* II, 273.

64. Evidence of these expenditures appears in the county levy accounts, usually recorded with the proceedings of the November court. A separate record survives for Baltimore County, 1699-1706, ms. in the Maryland Historical Society, Baltimore.

65. See, for example, Balt. Ct. Pro. G no. 1, 364, 392, 573; *Md. Archives,* XIX, 515-16.

66. Acts 1671, c. 3, *Md. Archives,* II, 273; Acts 1704, c. 34, Bacon, *Laws.*

67. See, for example, *Md. Archives,* V, 476-77; 524-25; 540; XVII, 42-43, 59-61, 170-71; VIII, 32-35, 49; XX, 106-11, 133, 189-91, 287, 339, 420, 454, 472, 507-8, 515-16, 524; XXIII, 61, 105, 153, 205, 215, 223, 380, 468-69.

68. Acts 1692, c. 25, *Md. Archives,* XIII, 468-69; Acts 1697, c. 10, XXXVIII, 108; Acts 1699, c. 26, XXII, 509; Acts 1704, c. 15, XXVI, 227, revived 1707, 1710, Bacon, *Laws;* Acts 1713, c. 1, *Md. Archives,* XXXVIII, 170; Acts 1715, cc. 46, Bacon, *Laws.*

69. In Prince George's County, 1696-1729, for example, forty-six men served as justices. Of these, only seven were ever sheriffs. One sheriff was never a justice. See Carr,

"County Government," appendix, tables 5B, 6 (part I), 8A; Commission Book, 1726–86, ms. Before 1689 sheriffs' terms were often longer than three years and the office was less available.

70. Carr and Jordan, *Maryland's Revolution of Government*, 38–40, lists all councillors, 1666–89; David William Jordan, "The Royal Period of Colonial Maryland, 1689–1715," Ph.D. diss. (Princeton University, 1966), appendix A, lists councillors, 1692–1715. Compare these lists with officeholders listed in Owings, *His Lordship's Patronage*.

71. Jordan, "Royal Period of Colonial Maryland," covers these changes in detail.

72. *Md. Archives*, V, 540–41.

73. PG Land Rec. A, 154–56, PG Ct. Rec. A, 443.

74. Local nominations can be found before 1689 but not often. Nicholson openly relied on councillors and Provincial Court justices. From 1699, royal instructions to the royal governors required that they consult the Council. (*Md. Archives*, V, 525; XIII, 23–24; XX, 386; XXIII, 129, 174, 259; Leonard Woods Labaree, ed., *Royal Instructions to British Colonial Governors, 1670–1776* [New York, 1935], I, no. 512.)

75. See, for example, *Md. Archives*, V, 565; Ch. Ct. and Land Rec., A no. 2, 5, 250, 259; B no. 2, 242–43, 248.

76. Carr and Jordan, *Maryland's Revolution of Government*, 214.

77. For example, Som. Jud. Rec., DT 7, 48, 144–48, 196; AZ 8, 156. See also Russell R. Menard, "From Servant to Freeholder: Status Mobility and Property Accumulation in Seventeenth-Century Maryland," *William and Mary Quarterly*, 3rd ser., XXX, (January 1973), 42–43.

78. Carr and Jordan, *Maryland's Revolution of Government*, 181–85.

79. Carr and Jordan, *Maryland's Revolution of Government*, chapters 2–4.

80. Ibid., 186–87; see also note 42 above. Billings, "The Growth of Political Institutions in Virginia," 238–39, finds much greater longevity among Virginia justices but less developed sense of public responsibility than I have found, differences that require exploration.

81. A useful summary of these laws can be found in Vertrees, J. Wyckoff, *Tobacco Regulation in Colonial Maryland* (Baltimore, 1936).

82. In 1715 the single justice acquired power to order whippings for servants on complaint of the master up to thirty-nine lashes (Bacon's *Laws*, c. 44); and from 1748, he could fine those who harbored runaway servants or slaves (c. 19). From 1717 he had power to try Negroes accused of thefts and misdemeanors otherwise triable in the county courts and punish by whippings to forty lashes (c. 13); and from 1723 he could order cropping of ears of Negroes who resisted a constable (c. 15). From 1719 the single justice could put any nonhouseholder freeman in custody until he found a householder who would be responsible for his taxes (c. 12), and in 1768 the justice acquired power to return a vagrant to his home county or sentence him to a workhouse (c. 29). In 1723 exclusive jurisdiction to hear complaints against men who refused to provide labor for work on the roads was given to the single justice with power to fine (c. 17). From 1752 to 1760, he could hear and determine bastardy cases, subject to appeal to the county court (Acts 1752, c. 2, *Md. Archives*, L, 79–81, expired 1760, Bacon's *Laws*). Other criminal or administrative jurisdiction granted was minor. From 1716 a justice could fine those who failed to attend election courts (c. 11). From 1728 he could fine men who hunted without permission on enclosed lands (c. 7), and from 1730, men who hunted deer out of season (c. 17). Beginning in 1748, a justice could fine a county clerk for not keeping office hours (c. 7), and from 1753, those who failed to report discovery of a lost boat within ten days (c. 10). Single justices also fined for various neglects under the tobacco inspection acts (see Acts 1763, c. 18). The civil jurisdiction of the single justice also was extended. From 1715 he could take special bail and charge a fee (two justices were required if the action was in the Provincial Court) (c. 28), and from 1729 he could issue attachments in actions within his civil

jurisdiction (c. 8), which was increased in 1853 to 50s. (c. 12, *Md. Archives,* L, 291-92), although modified in 1763 by a right of appeal to the county court in causes brought for more than 33s. sterling (c. 21). For a more complete list of powers of single justices in the eighteenth century, see Ellefson, "Courts of Maryland," 174-77. Except as noted, all references to laws are Bacon's *Laws.*

83. Acts 1719, c. 3, c. 12, Bacon's *Laws.*

84. I have examined the court proceedings for Queen Anne's County (Eastern Shore), 1751-59, 1770, and Prince George's County (Western Shore), 1755-57, 1771-73, to determine whether the activities and organization of the county courts had changed materially since 1710. Apart from the duties required under the tobacco inspection acts, the main change before 1773 was an increase in criminal jurisdiction granted in 1737, which gave the courts power to try and condemn slaves for major felonies if the county court met before the next assize (Acts 1737, c. 7, *Md. Archives,* XL, 92-94; Acts 1751, c. 14, Bacon's *Laws*).

D. Alan Williams has argued that in Virginia in the eighteenth century, fees for constables and other petty offices were sufficient to encourage planters to seek them ("The Small Farmer in Eighteenth-Century Virginia Politics," *Agricultural History,* XLIII (1969), 97-101). I found no evidence of such a development in my sample, which on this point I extended to the years 1720-30 and 1750-75.

85. The following discussion is based on Carr, "County Government," text, 135-43, 192, 309-10, 545-52; and Ellefson, "Courts of Maryland," 74-95, 116-46. For examples of the commissions issued during Seymour's administration and immediately after, see PG Ct. Rec. C, 170a; D, 89, 232, 316; E. 18.

86. Acts 1695, c. 1, *Md. Archives,* XXXVIII, 37-41; Acts 1700, c. 1, XXIV, 92; Acts 1704, c. 2, XXVI, 355.

87. Gerald E. Hartdagen, "The Vestries and Morals in Colonial Maryland," *MHM,* LXIII (December 1968), 360-78; Hartdagen, "The Vestry as a Unit of Local Government," *MHM,* LXVII (Winter 1972), 363-88; Carr, "County Government," text, 528-39. I am in disagreement with Professor Hartdagen's view that the vestry's role in local government was significant.

88. For English vestries, see Sydney and Beatrice Webb, *English Local Government,* vol. 1, *The Parish and the County* (London, 1906); for those of Virginia, see William Seiler's essay in this volume.

89. Gerald E. Hartdagen, "The Anglican Vestry in Colonial Maryland: A Study in Corporate Responsibility," *Historical Magazine of the Protestant Episcopal Church,* XL (September 1971), 317-18; Hartdagen, "The Anglican Vestry in Colonial Maryland: Organizational Structure and Problems," ibid., XXXVIII (December 1969), 351-53.

90. Carr, "County Government," text, 669-70; chapter 7, note 175; appendix 6, tables 4B, 7B, 7C.

91. Kenneth Carroll, *Quakerism on the Western Shore* (Baltimore, 1970), 62-65.

92. Hartdagen, "The Anglican Vestry in Colonial Maryland: Organizational Structure and Problems," 352-53.

93. Carr, "County Government," text, 668-76; appendix 6, tables 7A, 7B, 7C.

94. For a discussion of other aspects of vestry membership, see Hartdagen, "The Anglican Vestry in Colonial Maryland: Organizational Structure and Problems," 354-55.

95. Ibid., 358-60.

96. Acts 1723, c. 19, Bacon's *Laws.* Little information about these schools has yet been found.

97. Acts 1768, c. 29, Kilty's *Laws;* Acts 1771, c. 18, Acts 1773, c. 9, c. 18, c. 30; Acts 1774, c. 16, *ibid.* These acts contain references to a number of almshouses (or workhouses) finished or nearly finished.

98. Carr and Jordan, *Maryland's Revolution of Government,* 206-7.

99. For examples, see *Md. Archives*, V, 476-77, 524-25, 540; XVII, 42-43, 58-64, 170-71; VIII, 32-35, 49; Som. Jud. Rec., 1687-89, 99-101.

100. Carr and Jordan, *Maryland's Revolution of Government*, 184; *Md. Archives*, XXVII, 525; XXIX, 58; PG Ct. Rec. G, 37a, 39, 129, 168, 285-86.

101. Morris L. Radoff, *The County Courthouses and Records of Maryland, Part One; The Courthouses*, Hall of Records Commission publication no. 12 (Annapolis, Md., 1960), 21-23, 61-69, 106-8, 117-18, 137-38; Acts 1710, c. 7, *Md. Archives*, XXVII, 160-61, 164.

102. *Maryland Gazette*, January 20, February 10, March 16, 23 (supplement), April 13, 20, 27, May 4, 11 (supplement), 18 (postscript), 25, June 4 (extraordinary appendix,) 1747; Acts 1748, c. 20, Bacon's *Laws;* Acts 1763, c. 19, ibid.

103. This change in the Council and the Assembly is documented in David W. Jordan, "Political Stability and the Emergence of a Native Elite in Maryland, 1660-1715," in *Essays on the Chesapeake in the Seventeenth Century*, ed. Thad W. Tate and David Ammerman, (Chapel Hill, N.C., forthcoming); "Maryland's Privy Council, 1637-1715," in Land et al., *Law, Society, and Politics in Early Maryland*, 65-87.

104. Carr, "County Government," text, 614-43 (esp. table 9, 617-20), 696-97; appendix 6, table 5B.

105. Unpublished research by the author.

106. Brief Answers to the Queries relative to the Government of Maryland . . . . November 17, 1763, Portfolio II, no. 7b, ms., Hall of Records, Annapolis, Md.

107. Unpublished research in the records of Somerset County, Russell R. Menard, University of Minnesota; and in those of Prince George's County, Allan Kulikoff, Institute of Early American History and Culture.

108. Edward C. Papenfuse, Jr., "Planter Behavior and Economic Opportunity in a Staple Economy," *Agricultural History*, XLVI (April 1972), 301-2.

109. Since this essay was written, Allan Kulikoff has studied the political participation of heads of households on a list of taxables for Prince George's County taken in 1733 and found that landowners who were settled in the community still participated broadly in conscripted local office. He expects to find less in the 1770s.

110. Morris L. Radoff, comp., *Maryland Manual, 1959-60* (Annapolis, Md., 1960), 301-55. The author prepared this and the preceding edition of the *Manual* and organized the county section to reflect the structure of county government.

111. Ibid.

The County Court
in Colonial Virginia

ROBERT WHEELER

Local government in Virginia was based on the county, the main geographic and political unit. The county court, because of its position as the middleman between a weak and remote central government
and local inhabitants, was given broad judicial and administrative
power. Since it controlled a relatively small population, the local
bench was responsive to community needs. The justices who made
up the court were the upper portion of an integrated social, economic, and political elite who added a personal paternalistic flavor
to county government. As the colonial period developed, these men
strengthened their authority in comparison to the two other levels
of government; the colony and the parish. By the end of the seventeenth century the basic system had been established and modified;
later expansion was a response to the economic and social matura-
tion of the colony. Throughout the seventeenth and eighteenth cen-

turies the county court was the principal bulwark of local government in Virginia and the principal institution responsible for broadening political participation in the colony.

Beneath the surface simplicity of local government in Virginia lies an extremely complex system. In terms of jurisdiction and duties the relationship among the three levels of government — parish, county, and colony — was never clearly spelled out. Therefore, functions of the three levels of government frequently overlapped. Moreover, no formal lines were drawn between the judicial and administrative functions of the local court, and no clear differences were drawn among the various judicial duties it performed.

Originally local courts were established in the colony as a matter of convenience and a recognition of the physical distances that separated settlers in Virginia. The first courts, created by an ordinance of Governor Argoll Yeardly in 1619 and confirmed by a statute passed five years later, were "monthly courts" which met in the most remote areas of the colony "for punishing petty offences."[1] Although over the next four decades the governor and the General Assembly defined the roles of the local courts more precisely, the essential elements of the system were embodied in an order of March 20, 1629, to the Elizabeth City Court. The commissioners, the justices of the court, were instructed to determine all suits that did not exceed one hundred pounds of tobacco, to conserve the peace, to enforce all laws and inflict appropriate punishments except when the case involved loss of life or limb, and to keep records of all their proceedings.[2] All of these jurisdictional guidelines, particularly those prohibiting the court from considering cases of mutilation or death and restricting the value of suits it could try, were maintained throughout the colonial period.

The most important single event in the development of local government occurred in 1634, when the central government divided the colony into eight shires (later to be called counties), and required each shire to have a court, regardless of its distance from Jamestown. For the remainder of the colonial period, with each new political division a new court was established. By 1782 there were seventy-two counties and courts in Virginia.[3]

Because the original motivation for founding local courts was judicial, their relationship to inferior and superior courts was an integral part of the system. Counties were divided into parishes, administered by parish vestries and their officers, the churchwardens. The vestries, responsible for maintaining the moral character of parish residents, prosecuted cases of adultery, fornication, failure to attend church, and other offenses, provided for the poor, and collected taxes to support the churches and ministers. Since the vestry had no criminal jurisdiction, representatives of the parish (normally the churchwardens or occasionally the minister) presented alleged offenders to the local court for adjudication. The county court could order the vestry to perform certain duties—such as requiring the parish to confirm the boundaries of all tracts within it—in accordance with laws passed by the Assembly.[4]

Above the county court were both the General Court, comprised of the governor and his councillors, and the Assembly. As long as an appellant posted bond for twice the value of the suit, cases could be appealed from the county court to the General Court if either litigant was dissatisfied with the local decision and if the suit was valued at above £10. sterling. Even though the local panel often investigated the facts of a case before passing it on, the General Court had original jurisdiction over loss of life or limb.[5] The higher court normally tried cases of murder, arson, treason, mutiny, piracy, rape, and those which involved large amounts of tobacco.[6] Early in the seventeenth century, appeals could be made either to the General Court or the Assembly, depending on which group met first. By 1647 cases had to go to the General Court first, unless there was a question of law or if the judgment of a local court was presumed biased.[7] Very few cases seem to have gone to the Assembly. The system which had evolved was effective. "I am confident," wrote John Hammond in 1656, "more speedy justice and with smaller charge is not in any place to be found."[8]

By the mid-seventeenth century, the outline of local government had been established. The next 125 years can be separated into two periods: from 1650 to 1700, local government was modified and expanded to meet new situations created by increasing specialization of judicial and administrative functions of government; from 1701 to 1776 the local government was further refined in response to economic and social trends and the power of and participation in county government was strengthened considerably when compared to parochial or colonial levels.

The governor, with the advice of the Council, picked members of the county court from "the most able, honest, and judicious persons of the county."[9] However, the governor's power of appointment was limited, since he selected from a list of nominations made by the county court itself. Thus, throughout the colonial period the local benches were essentially self-perpetuating. The number of appointments varied from county to county but normally at least eight men sat at one time on the monthly sessions.[10] To insure that each court had some members who were comparatively well-versed in legal matters, the governor also designated three or four justices to be part of the quorum; at least one member of the quorum had to be present for the court to make decisions. Court sessions were held monthly during the seventeenth and eighteenth centuries, except for a short period after 1643, when they met bimonthly.[11]

Justice was personal in Virginia. The scale of life allowed a great deal of face-to-face contact among county residents. It was likely, therefore, that when people came to court they were not strangers, but were known to a number of men on the court. In the seventeenth century, the most prominent members of county society accepted a place on the county court out of a sense of responsibility to the community. In keeping with their sense of duty, the justices received no compensation for their service. An analysis of members of the Lancaster County Court from 1650 to 1670 indicates the justices owned at least twice as much land as the average householder, controlled nearly half of the labor force in the county, and were major creditors in the community.[12] It is likely that these planters were precisely the men in the community whose stature insured that their opinions would be sought in personal as well as official matters. In a local society with an integrated social, economic, and political leadership, it must have come as no surprise to the residents that these men were selected to govern.

The duties of a justice could be a considerable burden, particularly if there were no other justices in the neighborhood to share the work load. In 1693, Henry Tooker, a member of the Surry County bench, refused to take the oath of office for the year because "the trouble was very great upon him, there being no other justice in the parish where he dwells."[13] His obstinacy did not save him in the end for he did serve on the court. There were undoubtedly many justices who faced similar problems.

Local government in Virginia went beyond the natural leadership and involved many other residents as participants in the process. Petty jury duty was one way heads of households became personally involved. In most cases decisions were made by the justices themselves, but some litigants exercised their right to a jury trial, which had been granted to them in 1643.[14] At each court session the sheriff selected twelve of the "most able men of the county" to be a standing jury to act if they were needed. Jurors decided all matters of fact, not law, and during deliberations were sequestered without "food or relief" until a decision was reached. Normally, they were not used in debt cases; they were, however, frequently called in suits of trespass, assault and battery, slander, and complex land disputes.[15]

Another way in which citizens became involved was through service on the grand jury which investigated all breaches of the penal code and met twice each year to make presentments to the court.[16] In effect, the grandjurymen acted as local informants who confirmed or denied rumors, especially those dealing with the codified standards of morality. Most of those accused of violating the law by this body had been absent from church, or were adulterers, fornicators, common swearers, or drunkards. But the grand jury could embarrass (few fines were imposed) parish vestries, churchwardens, and even the county court itself for not carrying out their respective duties.[19] This moral and political watchdog was used sparingly at first. The Assembly noted that it was "generally neglected," and passed an act in 1677 which required each county court to appoint a grand jury each year or to be heavily fined for negligence, further stipulating that two hundred pounds of tobacco was to be paid by each person refusing to serve as a grand juror. Throughout the remainder of the colonial period, these juries met regularly and made their presentments. Many of the duties they performed had initially been under the jurisdiction of the parish vestry, and while this act did not prohibit the vestry from acting, it appears that as the century progressed, the grand jury became the main body in the county responsible for enforcing public morals. This diffusion of local authority further reinforced the personal nature of justice.

The duties of the justices extended beyond presiding over the sessions. John Hammond emphasized the availability of the magistrates: "Justice [in Virginia] is duly and daily administered, hardly can any travaile two miles together, but they will find a justice, which hath power himself to hear and determine mean differences, to secure and bind over notorious offenders."[20] By the second half of the seventeenth century, justices of the peace had a wide-ranging jurisdiction. In addition to deciding cases of less than 20s. or two hundred pounds of tobacco, a justice could have criminals arrested and held for the next session of the court. However, even in minor matters, the justice's decisions on debt cases could be appealed to the bench, which had final jurisdiction in all cases.[21] Much of Virginia was still a frontier during this period and men who were heavily in debt frequently left the county to escape punishment or imprisonment; in order to insure that creditors received some satisfaction, a justice could seize the property of those who were suspected of having absconded.[22]

Besides their judicial responsibilities, individual justices of the peace had a host of administrative duties which included accepting wolves' heads as proof of claim to bounty, judging the disputed quality of tobacco, swearing appraisers of estates, and appointing fenceviewers to ensure that stray animals did not destroy crops.[23] In at least one county, Surry, the local justice also selected constables for one-year terms.[24]

The paternalism of local government under the individual justice is apparent in a series of laws which protected servants. Before midcentury, a mistreated servant could complain to the nearest magistrate who might summon the master and try to work out a settlement. Just after Bacon's Rebellion in 1677, the Assembly, realizing masters were taking advantage of their servants by renegotiating indentures before they expired, ordered that no master could make a new contract with his servant unless it was approved by at least one justice.[25] Another law that served to maintain order on the local level was the requirement that strangers living in a household for more than nine months be brought before a justice of the peace to be identified, particularly for tax purposes.[26]

All these responsibilities of the justices kept them in almost daily contact with their neighbors. The individual justice probably knew the particulars of nearly every case that came from his local neighborhood to the court. If a resident had any complaint he would first go to the nearest justice either for resolution or to take the proper oaths and give testimony required in a court session; in this way the justices could keep minor issues from coming before the full body or suggest the proper way to bring the issue to the bench.

To facilitate the judicial process, it became rather routine practice for ad hoc courts, comprised of several members of the court, to sit and thereby serve as intermediate bodies between full court sessions and the judicial actions of a single justice. Occasionally, when cases became too complicated to solve in court, three commissioners were delegated to investigate the issue and report back to the court, which normally confirmed their findings.[27] Adjudication was possible in suits under 1,000 pounds of tobacco if at least two justices of the peace were present, and one was a member of the quorum. And to simplify judicial procedures, residents could come before two or more magistrates and admit their indebtedness.[28] In general, justices were granted control over those actions and appointments which they could administer more efficiently than the entire court; because they knew the local area in which they lived and served, they added a distinctly neighborly flavor to Virginia local government.

In the early history of most Virginia counties, the justices sometimes had to assert the primacy of their position by punishing residents who did not treat them with the proper respect. However, after the first decade or so their position was established and seldom challenged. In order to enforce proper decorum, the procedure of demanding silence and asking the crier to call for the plaintiff and the defendant to answer was followed in each court. The colonist who came into court for the first of many visits must have been impressed with this official air which was visually reinforced by the wooden railing or bar separating the seated justices from those who had business at court.[29]

In its judicial capacity, the court tried both criminal and civil cases. While in law its jurisdiction was restricted, in practice nearly all actions were first heard in the county court. From 1642 to the end of the colonial period the justices had control over all cases under 1,600 pounds of tobacco or approximately £10. sterling, but they also decided most cases of greater value, even though these actions were under the original jurisdiction of the General Court.[30] Similarly, the preliminary investigation, arrest and hearing of suspected capital criminals took place on the county level.[31] Only if the justices thought there was reason to believe the accused was guilty would they refer the case to the superior court; if there was not sufficient evidence the accused would be set free. The function of the court in these specific instances was to relieve the burden on the General Court.

Two major changes in the last half of the seventeenth century expanded the power of the court. The first was a 1662 statute which allowed county courts to make bylaws "because small inconveniences happen in the respective counties and parishes which cannot be concluded in general law."[32] The statute was modified in the late 1670s by requiring two elected residents of each parish to sit with the justices when they made these bylaws.[33] However, the Commission of Trade and Plantations did not approve, for in 1683, it ordered the repeal of all laws which allowed local courts to make bylaws and suggested that a new law be passed requiring approval of any local bylaws by the governor and Council. The regulations recorded in some county order books indicate the courts did not use this provision to expand their power, but only to refine it.[34] Since the justices used their power sparingly, the new law was apparently not needed, for one was not passed.[35] Since they passed regulations only on procedural matters the bylaw power was not an important one.

The second change increased the jurisdiction of local government. Until 1692, no group of local residents could try anyone in cases of loss of life or limb. But because of the increasing number of slaves in the colony who were committing capital crimes, the governor was empowered by the Assembly to issue specific commissions of oyer and terminer to such persons "as he shall think fit" (normally justices of the peace and other prominent residents) to try slaves.[36] These "commissions" heard evidence without juries and could order the execution of convicted slaves. In addition to the precedent in the English legal system, the creation of these special courts gave local magistrates the authority to punish slaves without altering their jurisdiction over white colonists.

The normal judicial business of the local bench included a wide variety of cases. By the mid-1660s it performed all the functions separated in the mother country into common pleas, King's bench, exchequer, chancery, church, and admiralty courts.[37] The largest number of suits brought to the court were concerned with debt. Decisions in these cases were often made as a matter of record for the creditor, since many debtors either acknowledged their debt or simply did not appear to defend themselves. Numerous conflicts of interest resulted in debt cases because the magistrates were often plaintiffs. Order books are filled with the constant departure from the courtroom and return of justices who were currently involved in suits before the session.[38] Favorable decisions far outnumbered unfavorable ones when a court member was a party in the action; since most decisions merely recorded debts, this pattern does not necessarily indicate bias on the part of the court. The court order books, therefore, provided an official register of indebtedness. Few of these cases were ever actually tried.

The probate of wills and the transfer of property were constant and important problems in the colony. After 1645, the local bench performed the functions of a probate court, administering and registering wills and approving and recording appraisals of inventories and accounts.[39] Great care was also taken to insure that orphans' estates were kept intact. A portion of one session each year was set aside to appoint guardians who had posted security, review the estate to make certain the overseer was managing it properly, and also to investigate the treatment and education of the children involved.[40] If the guardian or master, in instances where the orphan had been apprenticed, was abusing his position, he could be forced to give more security for good behavior or be removed altogether.[41] Clearly there is more than a hint of paternalism in these regulations, for the courts took this responsibility seriously. The Surry court required guardians to bring the child as well as the accounts to court to insure good treatment.[42] Moreover, an orphan who was fourteen years of age could select his own guardian as long as the justices gave their approval. The concern for dependent children went beyond official duties and demonstrates the personal nature of government in colonial Virginia.

Regardless of the final decision, there are constant reminders in the statutes that the main issue in any deliberation was to decide who was right.[43] Therefore, judgments were not to be postponed or information rejected because the proper form had not been followed. Extension of this began in 1645 when local benches were authorized to set aside time in their schedules for equity or chancery cases.[44] These suits generally involved damages in either criminal or civil cases and were undertaken to moderate a strict interpretation of the law.[45] In both of these ways, elimination of some questions of form and mitigation of strict legalistic interpretations, the emphasis was on judiciousness.

The county court in its position as the key unit in local government also assumed broad administrative as well as judicial powers. These ranged from regulating the local economy by licensing and fixing rates which tavern-keepers, millers, and ferry operators could charge, to, when convenience demanded, appointing someone to supply food and drink on court days. As settlement moved away from the rivers toward the interior of the three great necks of the Virginia Tidewater, and as land transportation became more important, the local bench appointed officers to open and maintain roads and bridges within the county, thereby bringing the inhabitants into greater contact with each other.

The court set aside two meetings a year specifically for financial matters. Perhaps the most important annual gathering was the levy court held at the end of the year. All residents seeking compensation for services rendered to the county during the previous year — from those who kept the courthouse clean and supplied with candles to the greatest charge on nearly all lists, reimbursing burgesses for their expenses — were considered along with bounties and officers' salaries.[46] When the list was complete, the court would divide the total debt by the number of "tithables" (all white males over fifteen and all black males and females over fourteen)[47] in the area and fix the county tax. Each household head had to pay this tax as well as the colonial levy, which already would have been determined by the assembly. In the seventeenth century, the burden of these combined taxes was, on occasion, heavy, but the largest proportion of the tax load stemmed from the levy fixed by the parish to support its services and expenses.[48] In order to remunerate local residents for service performed for the colony, an annual court of claims was held to judge the validity of these requests and to send them to the Assembly. The court, therefore, controlled county taxation, channeled requests to the Assembly, and through its officers, collected public funds. It also ensured that no one withheld names from the list of tithables by punishing those who attempted to cheat. An examination of the lists of county debts again shows the justices as major creditors, especially since virtually all of them were burgesses and because they frequently provided credit to build and maintain prisons, ferries, and other public property.[49]

Another important administrative function of the court was its role as the major recording agency of the colony. Each year, normally just before the tithable lists were drawn up in June, residents would bring in servants and slaves to have their ages determined.

If they were very young, the master would not have to pay taxes on their labor for several years, so it was to his benefit to buy young workers and have the court officially confirm their ages. After the lists were assembled, a copy was placed on the church door in each parish; thus anyone who did not report the proper number of tithables could be easily discovered and fined for this neglect.[50]

Records of virtually all land transactions were handled by the local court. Even though the governor and colonial secretary issued patents under the headright system, the local body, partially because they possessed a neighborly knowledge of the applicant, granted land certificates to those who supplied a list of people they had transported into the colony. In the first ten or fifteen years of a county's existence, these original deeds served as a seventeenth-century stock market, for they were more often "assigned" to some creditor than sold.[51] These assignments were registered with the courts. Deeds, leases, mortgages, and many other documents, all found their way into seventeenth- and eighteenth-century court record books. In order to reduce the number of land disputes which inevitably occurred, the court ordered all boundaries in the county confirmed at regular intervals. When a disagreement arose, the magistrate resolved the matter, often with the help of a jury.

In its administrative capacity the court recorded marriage licenses, and using its judicial powers, the court could force spouses to live together or grant one of them separate maintenance.[52] Another delegated responsibility was the function the court played in carrying out orders of the governor, Council, and the General Court. From time to time the governor would ask for lists of all officers in the county or an enumeration of all those eligible for militia duty. In its judicial role, the bench often implemented legal decisions of the General Court, such as collecting fines, and accepting bonds for good behavior from those found guilty of slander in the superior court.[53]

The court took both its judicial and administrative roles for granted and there appeared to be little confusion at the local level. In fact, there is no distinct division of duties in the order books themselves for lists of recorded deeds, verdicts in debt, and slander cases, the disposition of presentments of the grand jury, and appointments characteristically appear one after another on the pages of one session of the court.

Although the system was superficially simple, the increasing jurisdiction of the court necessitated the aid of an increasing number of officers. The most active subordinates, the sheriff and the court clerk, had slightly ambiguous positions with respect to the court, since they were appointed by the governor from recommendations of the magistrates.[54] For most of the colonial period, the sheriff's office was rotated on an annual or biennial basis among members of the court.[55] A justice serving as sheriff did not sit on the court, for his role was split between colonial and local jurisdiction. As a representative of the governor, he collected public, county, and land taxes (in the form of quitrents), paid local creditors, and passed the remainder on to the governor. His responsibility included supervising and certifying the elections of burgesses and also the transportation of prisoners to the capital in cases involving loss of life or limb.[56] On the county level, the sheriff was the chief police officer of the court responsible for issuing warrants, making arrests, executing writs, and by a system of bonds assuring the appearance of defendants, witnesses, and juries at court sessions. Other police duties included running the county jail and presiding over the physical punishment ordered by the court to those who were unable to pay fines.[57]

The position of sheriff was one of the few profitable local offices available. Before the justice was sworn in as sheriff he had to provide security for his performance and conceivably could lose money if he were very incompetent. The county paid fees for performing each service and a ten percent commission was collected for directing the county levy.[58] Probably most men accepted the responsibility of the office and welcomed the compensation they received, but the rotation among the justices of the peace was a relief to those who were undoubtedly burdened by its numerous duties.

In the seventeenth century, the county clerk was part of the literate elite. In Virginia he was appointed by the governor and responsible to the secretary of state in the colony.[59] Keeping minutes of court decisions and copying all appropriate documents were part of the official duties of the office. The clerk also issued licenses for marriages and ordinaries and certificates for headrights on the instruction of the court. The increasing complexity of the legal system in Virginia can be measured, in part, by the long list of fees the clerk received for making copies of his records.[60] By the 1680s twenty-seven different rates were fixed for various services. This local scribe was an important part of local government since he knew all the issues before the court and also was familiar with the form and content of the statutes. According to Robert Beverly, in the 1680s clerks began to enter reasons for decisions into the record; they pretended "to set precedents of inviolable form to be observed in all future proceedings"; but Governor Thomas Culpepper ordered that all judgments should be entered without reasons, and the procedure was dropped.[61] In any case, the clerk's advice was undoubtedly valuable to county residents.

Each county had two other officers who performed quite specific duties. When any suspicious death occurred in the county, a coroner would call an inquest to determine if foul play were involved.[62] The importance of land necessitated the appointment of a county surveyor, who determined the precise boundaries of disputed lands and laid out patented tracts; later in the century he also supplied the owner with a plat of the land and kept a record of all surveys.[63] The position of surveyor was probably more functional in the western areas of the colony. Both coroners and surveyors received fees for their work, but these posts seem to have been used infrequently during much of the century.

By far the largest group of subordinate officers were court-appointed constables who served annual terms and received no compensation. In at least one county they were selected from a group of middling or even poor householders who were long-term residents of the area.[64] Since the constable helped the sheriff perform his duties, the office gave many average residents a taste of involvement in the political system. The constable kept the peace in his precinct (a geographic division which was a matter of convenience), executed orders of the sheriff, and insured that court orders were obeyed. He could detain suspects, and was an important part of sounding the "hue and cry" used to tell other residents of escaped servants or slaves.[65]

Surveyors of highways were drawn from middling planters who had experience as constables. These men generally were wealthier than those who served only as constables and were appointed to keep roads and bridges open and passable. More substantial members of the community were selected because their status allowed them to recruit householders within their jurisdiction to perform necessary labor to carry out their instructions with minimal conflict.[66]

As the numbers and duties of local officers grew, the relationship

between county and colonial government changed in the last half
of the seventeenth century. The procedure for judicial appeal was
altered because of the increasing interaction between the colonial
government and the mother country. Before 1680, appeals from
the county court went to the General Court and then on to the
Assembly. A dispute arose between the Assembly and the General
Court in the 1680s. The Assembly objected to the procedure which
allowed councillors who had already judged the case in the General
Court to sit on the Assembly committee which made the final decision. Lord Culpepper, the colonial governor, was disturbed by the
implications of the burgesses' position and received a ruling from
England which stated that all appeals from the General Court had to
go to the King in Council rather than to the Assembly.[67] A com-
promise between the House of Burgesses and the governor allowed
appeals under three hundred pounds sterling to be heard by the
Burgesses; but in effect, the ruling made the General Court the court
of last resort in the colony.[68] Therefore, after 1683 all appeals went
from the county to the General Court.

Another change expanded rather than restricted local government
by establishing a formal method of bringing local grievances to the
attention of the Assembly. Prior to Bacon's Rebellion there was no
such opportunity, and residents had to rely on their burgesses to
represent them. After the rebellion an annual meeting of the court
was scheduled to collect and consolidate community protests.[69] Although the grievances involved some local problems, such as vagrancy or hog-stealing, county residents used these appeals to pressure
the Assembly to define problems and to seek their legal resolution
since laws would be passed if the issue raised was a general one.
Opening up the entire legal system to local petitions of grievance,
did serve to expand the concept of responsive government in the
colony.

By the end of the seventeenth century the county court had reinforced its place at the center of government in Virginia. The progression of jurisdiction from the vestry to county court to General
Court was established, but the central judicial and administrative
position of the county unit was obvious. Virtually all official business was filtered through the local magistrates and other court
officers. Local benches were the focal point of political interaction for the colonists and, as such, they were more prominent than
any other body. Under their guidance local residents who served as

jurors or as minor officers, became more involved both numerically and experientially with local government.

There were those who criticized the system of local government in the colony. Hartwell, Blair, and Chilton, three royal informants, wrote in 1697 that the major problem in Virginia was that "all the courts of England [are] in one" and "the same men judges in all."[70] Undoubtedly, there were minor abuses created by the overlapping roles of the local court; but, in general, the bench seemed concerned with rendering a just decision rather than one which benefited a particular group in the community.[71] The unity of judicial and administrative roles embodied in the local courts, while confusing to those familiar with the English system (like Hartwell, Blair, and Chilton), made for more efficient government in Virginia. In effect, the magistrates brought to the case before them more than legal background and probably the resident had a greater chance of receiving equitable treatment under this sytem.

There were few basic changes in local government after the turn of the eighteenth century because the system had by this time been clarified and perfected over a sixty-six-year period. Specialization and expansion took place throughout the remainder of the colonial period as new roles appeared and were incorporated into the structure thereby increasing participation.

A comparison of seventeenth- and eighteenth-century court order books indicates that the governmental differences between the two periods parallel social and economic change. Simply in terms of the number and variety of cases, the eighteenth-century records show tremendous expansion. Whereas in the earlier century a court session might consider twenty to fifty cases in one or two days, by the eighteenth century a three-day session of seventy-five cases or more was not unusual. The nature of the cases was also much more specific. Whereas earlier records listed cases in order without any particular designations, later books recorded plaintiffs, and defendants, and often indicated the type of case: information, trespass, assault and battery, petition, debt, and chancery.[72] Increasingly, suits were continued over many court sessions to allow both parties time to make appropriate rebuttals. Another indication of the growing complexity was the appearance of a variety of writs which defined specific types of action.[73]

The two major revisions of Virginia's laws in 1705 and 1748 add further evidence of this increasing complexity. Specific rules for plaintiffs and defendants, case rules, and a form for oaths, were all precisely defined.[74] By midcentury, the distinction between common law and chancery suits was explicitly made and elaborate rules for each set up.[75] Some provisions limited the use of juries to cases above £5 and allowed those under that amount to be determined by petition under common law. In chancery suits, appeals were prohibited if the suit was less than ten pounds sterling, except when land was involved.[76]

Local magistrates seem to have taken these changes as a warning of the additional burden the office brought. Many men refused to sit on the court and many who were justices wished to be relieved because of the pressure of private business.[77] The popularity of the local magistracy apparently had declined in the second half of the colonial period, and the increasing weight of official duties must have been partially responsible. This decline in popularity opened up positions to those who would not have had the opportunity in the seventeenth century. Proportionally more men gained experience in the court in the eighteenth century than in the seventeenth and the base for the selection of officers was necessarily broadened.[78]

The complexity of legal matters after 1700 made the presence of lawyers more common at court sessions. There were representatives of litigants before this time, and some, like William Fitzhugh, were learned and prominent, but most courts had seen few lawyers in the seventeenth century.[79] Possibly the lack of lawyers had made residents more disposed to bring even minor cases to court and it also may have made government more personal because the justices and officers of the court were consulted rather than a trained counsel. The content of the case, rather than its form, had been more important in Virginia for the same reason. In the seventeenth century, if someone could not attend court, a power of attorney would authorize a friend, usually not a lawyer, to represent the party in court as a matter of convenience. In the eighteenth century, however, often neither party appeared in person, both having legal counsel. In an effort to control a growing profession, but one which had always been suspect in the colony, lawyers were required to obtain licenses to practice.[80] Furthermore, each county had another lawyer, the King's attorney, who represented the governor and the colony, particularly in suits where part of the fine would go to the colonial government.

Social and cultural changes in the eighteenth century caused an expansion of the jurisdiction of the justices and the court. For example, a number of new statutes were passed to regulate the increasing number of slaves who were brought into court. Single justices were to report unauthorized meetings of slaves; any two justices could list "outlying" slaves, post their names on parish doors, and order them killed on sight if they did not return to their masters.[81] Masters of "incorrigible runaway" slaves could bring proof of their obstinacy into court and receive permission to maim the slave as long as the punishment did not "touch life." Robert "King" Carter, perhaps the wealthiest man in the colony, and a man who owned several hundred slaves, received permission on several occasions to dismember runaways.[82] Another indication of the importance of controlling slaves was the increase in the number of commissions of oyer and terminer issued by the Governor. In order to avoid unnecessary expense, an act of 1765 acknowledged the continuing power of local government. By this statute each county court received a blanket commission of oyer and terminer to try, and acquit or execute any slave accused of committing a capital offense. Any four justices, including one member of the quorum, could take oaths and proceed without the help of a jury.[83] As the number and concentration of slaves grew in eighteenth-century Virginia, local government expanded with the help of new powers to deal with the ensuing problem.

Economic regulations, previously a negligible function of local government, also became necessary in the eighteenth century. Virginia had suffered for over a century because the quality of its produce was never efficiently controlled. Finally, in 1730 an elaborate inspection system was enacted for the staple crop, tobacco, and the court and its officers became integral parts of this new program, which was eventually expanded to other crops.[84]

Tobacco warehouses were constructed in each county under the direction of the court, and three men "reputed to be skillful in tobacco" were appointed by the governor and Council to inspect all hogsheads and issue notes to the planter. Inspectors were required to keep records of the weight of each owner's tobacco, the mark he used to identify his hogsheads, and the vessel he shipped it in.[85] As the system developed, the court was given more power; it began to nominate inspectors, review their books annually, and supervise the construction of public wharves.[86] Individual justices, with the help of the sheriff or constable were to investigate exportation of uninspected tobacco or any shipped in bulk, destroy it, and fine the violator.[87] If creditors refused to accept approved tobacco, three justices "nearest to the warehouse" were summoned, sworn, and instructed to evaluate its quality; a majority could either order it to be burnt or taken in satisfaction of a debt.[88] Rather than causing a decline in the power of the county court, these new duties increased its importance.

Regulation worked so well in the colony that after 1742 the courts themselves appointed inspectors of beef, pork, turpentine, pitch, and tar, to ensure the quality of the products and to certify the weight of the containers.[89] Statutory provisions were included to ensure that only inspected products were exported and, again, the court assumed responsibility.[90] As a further precaution against contamination of cattle, drovers had to report to a justice and swear the cattle did not have a contagious disease. The magistrate would then appoint two viewers to inspect the cattle, and if they were free from disease, the justice would issue a bill of health which had to be produced on demand.[91] In part, these duties simply expanded the role of the court in regulating the economy, but they also indicated the increasing importance of economic factors, the continued authority of local government, and the participation by local residents.

Economic differentiation in the social order altered the qualifications of the jurors and reflected a more differentiated society. The vague instruction of the seventeenth century to select for jury duty only "the most able men in the county," was given more precision in the eighteenth century. Residents with estates valued above a specific amount were selected. By 1748 the sheriff summoned freeholders with visible estates of at least £100 to try breaches of the peace, treason, felonies, violations of the penal code, or cases involving land. No person who had an estate of less than £50 could sit on any jury.[92] A procedural change somewhat altered the functioning of the grand jury in that presentments for violations of the moral code were now made by individual members rather than the entire jury. In other words, each grand juror was responsible for policing his neighborhood and reporting to the court.

As the position of justice became less desirable for some prominent members of the community, other offices also became more burdensome. Duties and fees continued to increase, especially for the sheriff and the clerk. In order to be certain some justice would accept the office of sheriff, the Assembly required each justice to serve at least one year or else be heavily fined.[93] The complexity of court cases and the increasing use of writs caused the clerk to perform many new functions. The list of fees for his office, which numbered twenty-seven in the 1680s, reached nearly one hundred by 1745.[94] Fines were imposed on many minor officers to insure that they complied with the new duties. Inducements had not been necessary to get constables to serve in the seventeenth century, but in the eighteenth, as an inducement to perform the more onerous duties, such as tobacco inspections, the Assembly ordered them to be free from paying taxes for as long as they remained constables.[95] As a result, fewer men stayed in office for longer periods of time. In one county constables were drawn from a group of lower-middling planters, while surveyors of highways continued to be selected from a slightly wealthier group. In the eighteenth century, there was virtually no overlapping of these two offices; those men who served in one, generally did not serve in the other.[96] These new laws did not mean that government was less efficient in the late colonial period, but that the complexity and time involved had increased as a system created for a simpler time became overburdened.

Local government in colonial Virginia was conducted in a personal, face-to-face manner, and based on an implicit model of concentric circles. The neighborhood was the smallest. A local justice, the current grand juror, and a member of the parish vestry were all available within a few miles for consultation and complaint throughout the seventeenth and eighteenth centuries. A slightly larger series of circles, defined loosely by precincts, included constables and surveyors of highways, members of the community who had assumed responsibility for a limited time. Probably most planters served at one time or another in one of these capacities. The next larger unit was the parish. Even though its jurisdictional significance declined in the eighteenth century, vestrymen, churchwardens, the minister and custodian watched over the church and residents' morals. The largest and most important circle encompassed each county. Local magistrates, the sheriff, the clerk, surveyors, coroners and, in the eighteenth century, inspectors of tobacco and other commodities, all operated at the county level and exercised strong decision-making powers. Obviously the last circle was the colony itself, encompassing the governor, General Court, and the Assembly.

Using this model, it is possible to describe the impact of the major alterations in local government. As the focal point of the local area changed from a scattered group of landholdings to a more compact settlement with a rudimentary communication system, so too did the focal point of Virginia. Many duties assigned to the General Court, plus many parish duties, devolved to the county court. The movement from seventeenth- to eighteenth-century local government can be characterized by a centrifugal force which blurred the distinct identity of the precinct and the parish, while it increased both the power of the county court, and the time it spent in the daily business of governing. By the end of the colonial period, the county court was not less, but more powerful than it had been.

Possibly one of the many reasons for the increasing political awareness of many eighteenth-century Virginians was that they were experiencing increasing involvement at the local level. Even though the duties of the bench seem to have become more bothersome, the county had little trouble finding men to sit on the court. In fact, in Lancaster County, residents competed vigorously for court appointments, and large numbers of men, on occasion most members of the bench, were candidates for the House of Burgesses. The reason for these changes stemmed from the increase in the number of men in the county who qualified by wealth for the posts, and who thought they deserved the position because of their social position. Democratic elements are difficult to locate. These developments, coupled with the addition of many new officers and inspectors, increased political involvement. This increase in involvement undoubtedly made residents more interested in local and, potentially, in colonial matters.

NOTES

1. William W. Hening, ed., *The Statutes-at-Large . . . of Virginia* (1619-1792) (New York, 1823), I, 125 (1623/4); Philip A. Bruce, *Institutional History of Virginia in the Seventeenth Century,* 2 vols., (New York, 1910), I, 484. For a more complete analysis of local government see Bruce, *Institutional History;* Oliver P. Chitwood, *Justice in Colonial Virginia,* Johns Hopkins University Series in History and Political Science (Baltimore, 1905), XXIII, nos. 7, 8; Wesley F. Craven, *The Southern Colonies in the Seventeenth Century,*

1607–1689 (Baton Rouge, La., 1949); Charles S. Sydnor, *Gentlemen Freeholders: Political Practices in Washington's Virginia* (Chapel Hill, N.C., 1952); Bernard Bailyn, "Politics and Social Structure in Virginia," in James M. Smith, ed., *Seventeenth-Century America: Essays in Colonial History* (Chapel Hill, N.C. 1959), 90–115; Percey S. Flippin, *The Royal Government in Virginia, 1624–1775* (New York, 1919); and Albert O. Porter, *County Government in Virginia: A legislative history, 1607–1904* (New York, 1947).

2. Hening, *Statutes at Large*, I, 132–33 (1628/9).

3. Ibid., 224 (1634); Chitwood, *Justice*, 75.

4. Hening, *Statutes at Large*, I, 240–43 (1642/43); see also I, 126 (1623/4), 155 (1631/2), 160 (1632), 399–400 (1642/43), 432–33 (1657/8); II, 52 (1661/2) 101–2 (1662); Beverley Fleet, ed., *Virginia Colonial Abstracts*, 34 vols. (Baltimore, 1961), vol. 32, *Accomacke County, 1637–1640*, 28 (1634/5); Bruce, *Institutional History*, I, 55–92; William Seiler, "The Anglican Parish in Virginia," in James M. Smith, ed., *Seventeenth-Century America*, 119–42.

5. Hening, *Statutes at Large*, I, 304 (1645), 334 (1646), 345 (1647), 477 (1657/8); Bruce, *Institutional History*, I, 647–89.

6. Bruce, *Institutional History*, I, 667.

7. Hening, *Statutes at Large*, I, 345 (1647).

8. John Hammond, *Leah and Rachel* (London, 1656), in Peter Force, comp., *Tracts and Other Papers Relating Principally to the Origins, Settlement, and Progress of the Colonies in North America*, 4 vols. (Washington, D.C., 1836–46), III, no. 14, 16.

9. Hening, *Statutes at Large*, II, 69 (1661/2).

10. Ibid., I, 132 (1628/9); II, 21 (1660/1); Chitwood, *Justice*, 76–77.

11. The quorum was defined as early as 1623/4 as the most prominent members of the court, the commanders. See Hening, *Statutes at Large*, I, 125 (1623/4), 133 (1628/9). For the function of the members of the quorum, see I, 87–88 (1661/2), 359 (1676, Bacon's *Laws*). Prior to 1643 the courts were called monthly courts, see I, 125 (1623/4), 272–73 (1642/3); then the name was changed to county courts. By the 1660s meetings were held monthly (II, 69–71 [1661/2]).

12. The justices of the Lancaster County Court from 1649 to 1653 owned almost six laborers while the rest of the householders averaged three and had patented 1,960 acres versus 960 acres for other residents. Debts owed to their estates at death indicate their control of credit. See Robert A. Wheeler, "Lancaster County, Virginia, 1650–1750: The Evolution of a Southern Tidewater community," Ph.D. diss. (Brown University, 1972), 26–27, 50–52.

13. Surry County, *Orders, 1691–1713*, 64 (1693); see also 222 (1701).

14. Hening, *Statutes at large*, I, 273 (1642/3).

15. Ibid., I, 303 (1645), 314 (1645/6); II, 73–74 (1661/2). For examples of the types of cases see Surry County, *Orders, 1671–1691*, 150 (1677), 162 (1677/8), and 251 (1679).

16. Hening, *Statutes at Large*, I, 304 (1645); II, 74 (1661/2), 103 (1661/2); III, 71–75 (1691), 137–40 (1696). All household heads were eligible for jury duty but most courts seem to have selected from a group of long-term residents who occupied the middle of the socioeconomic scale. See Lancaster County, *Orders, 1713–1721*, 299–300 (1718).

17. See, for example, Surry County, *Orders, 1671–1691*, 102 (1675), 344 (1681), and 498 (1685).

18. Hening, *Statutes at Large*, II, 407–8 (1677).

19. Force, *Tracts*, III, no. 14, 15.

20. Ibid.

21. For jurisdictional limitations see Hening, *Statutes at Large*, I, 335 (1646), 435 (1657/8), 455 (1657/8), and 458 (1657/8). For an example of a rare appeal from the

judgment of a single justice whose decision was upheld by the court, see Surry County, *Orders, 1671–1691,* 464 (1684).

22. Hening, *Statutes at Large,* II, 214 (1665).

23. Ibid., I, 259 (1642/3), 328 (1646), 332 (1646), 458 (1657/8); II, 87 (1661/2), 100–1 (1661/2), 268 (1668); Craven, *Southern Colonies,* 285–86.

24. Surry County, *Orders, 1671–1691,* 252 (1679).

25. Hening, *Statutes at Large,* I, 254–55 (1642/3); II, 117–18 (1661/2), 338 (1676/7).

26. Ibid., II, 405 (1676/7).

27. See, for example, Surry County, *Orders, 1671–1691,* 92 (1675).

28. Hening, *Statutes at Large,* I, 435 (1657/8), 455 (1657/8).

29. Ibid., II, 72 (1661/2); Bruce, *Institutional History,* I, 525–28.

30. Hening, *Statutes at Large,* I, 270–72 (1642/3), 345–46 (1647), 398–99 (1655/6); III, 287–302 (1705); VI, 325–50 (1753).

31. Bruce, *Institutional History,* I, 667–68.

32. Hening, *Statutes at Large,* II, 171–72 (1662); Craven, *Southern Colonies,* 294.

33. Hening, *Statutes at Large,* II, 441–42 (1679).

34. Chitwood, *Justice,* 92, note 77.

35. Surry County, *Orders, 1671–1691,* 53 (1674), 104 (1675), 200 (1678).

36. Hening, *Statutes at Large,* II, 102–3 (1962).

37. Henry Hartwell, James Blair, and Edward Chilton, *The Present State of Virginia and the College* (1697), ed. Hunter D. Farish (Williamsburg, 1940), 44.

38. See any court order book.

39. Hening, *Statutes at Large,* I, 302–03 (1645).

40. Ibid., I, 260 (1642/3), 416–17 (1656); II, 92–94 (1661/2), 295–96 (1672).

41. Ibid., II, 94 (1661/2).

42. Surry County, *Orders, 1671–1691,* 498 (1685); *Orders, 1691–1713,* 58 (1692).

43. Surry County, *Orders, 1671–1691,* 500 (1685/6).

44. Hening, *Statutes at Large,* I, 303–4 (1645).

45. Thomas Blount, *Nomo-Lexicon: A Law Dictionary (1670)* (Los Angeles, 1970). Maritime cases were also considered (see Hening, *Statutes at Large,* I, 466–67 [1657/8]).

46. Fleet, *Virginia Abstracts,* vol. 10 *Charles City County, Orders, 1655–1658,* 22 (1655); vol. 13, *Charles City County, Orders, 1664–1665, Fragments, 1650–1696,* 29 (1662).

47. Hening, *Statutes at Large,* I, 361–62 (1649), 454–55 (1657/8); II, 84 (1661/2), 170 (1662), 296 (1672), 478–80 (1680); III, 258–61 (1705).

48. William Seiler, "Anglican Parish," 137.

49. See note 45.

50. Hening, *Statutes at Large,* III, 258–61 (1705), which summarizes developments in the seventeenth century.

51. In Lancaster County most original patents were quickly assigned to pay debts. Between 1657 and 1669, 55,000 acres were assigned (Wheeler, "Lancaster County," 38).

52. Hening, *Statutes at Large,* I, 243 (1642/3), 252 (1642/3), 332 (1646); II, 28 (1660/1); Surry County, *Orders, 1671–1691,* 496 (1685).

53. See, for example, Surry County, *Orders, 1671–1691,* 43–51 (1674); 77 (1674); 353 (1681).

54. Hening, *Statutes at Large,* I, 392 (1655/6).

55. Ibid., II, 21 (1660/61), 78 (1661/2).

56. Ibid., I, 259 (1642/3), 264–65 (162/3), 284 (1644), 299–300 (1645), 444 (1657/8).

57. Hening, *Statutes at Large,* I, 264–65 (1642/3), 266 (1642/3), 284 (1644), 295–97 (1644/5); Cyrus H. Karraker, *The Seventeenth Century Sheriff: A Comparative Study of the Sheriff in England and the Chesapeake Colonies; 1607–1689* (Philadelphia, 1930), passim. Craven, *Southern Colonies,* 281–85.

58. Hening, *Statutes at Large,* I, 266 (1644); Karraker, *Seventeenth-Century Sheriff,* 130ff.

59. Hening, *Statutes at Large,* I, 305 (1645).

60. Hening, *Statutes at Large,* II, 485–86 (1680); see also I, 266 (1642/3), 295 (1644/5); II, 143–46 (1661/2).

61. Robert Beverley, *The History and Present State of Virginia* (1705), ed. David F. Hawke (Indianapolis, 1971), 50.

62. Hening, *Statutes at Large,* II, 419 (1677).

63. Ibid., I, 125 (1623/4), 335 (1646), 404 (1655), 452 (1657/8); II, 235 (1666).

64. In Lancaster County from 1657 to 1669 men in the lower half of the socioeconomic scale who were constables lived in the county longer (six years) than the average householder (Wheeler, "Lancaster County," 44).

65. Hening, *Statutes at Large,* II, 277–79 (1670); Bruce, *Institutional History,* I, 602–3.

66. In Lancaster County from 1657 to 1669 surveyors of highways were middling householders who paid taxes on 4.5 tithables and had lived in the county 8.6 years (Wheeler, "Lancaster County," 44). For regulatory laws, see Hening, *Statutes at Large,* I, 436 (1657/8); II, 103 (1661/2).

67. Hartwell, Blair, and Chilton, *Present State,* 26–27; Beverley, *History,* 49.

68. Craven, *Southern Colonies,* 397; Bruce, *Institutional History,* I, 693–95.

69. See, for example, Lancaster County, *Orders, III, 1686–1696,* 135 (1695); and R. H. McIlwaine, ed., *Journals of the House of Burgesses 1702–1712,* 157–58 (1702).

70. Hartwell, Blair, and Chilton, *Present State,* 28.

71. Hartwell, Blair, and Chilton, *Present State,* 28.

72. Surry County, *Orders, 1741–1744,* 1–10 (1741), for example.

73. Writs such as *scire facias, dedimus, mittamus,* and *assumpsit* appear more frequently.

74. Hening, *Statutes at Large,* III, 302 (1705), 319 (1705), 382–401 (1705).

75. Ibid., V, 348–50 (1748), 408–32 (1748), 489–508 (1748), especially 496–508.

76. Ibid., V, 498–501 (1749), 505 (1748).

77. See, for example, Lancaster County, *Orders, VIII, 1721–1729,* 51 (1721).

78. In Lancaster County from 1720 to 1750 more men served fewer years than in any previous period (Wheeler, "Lancaster County," 137).

79. Bruce, *Institutional History.*

80. Hening, *Statutes at Large,* V, 345–50 (1748).

81. Ibid., IV, 130 (1723); V, 477 (1748).

82. Ibid., IV, 132 (1723); Lancaster County, *Orders, V, 1702–1713,* 233 (1708).

83. Hening, *Statutes at Large,* VIII, 137–39 (1765).

84. Ibid., IV, 247–71 (1730).

85. Ibid., IV, 251 (1730), 259 (1730), 268–69 (1730), 384 (1734).

86. Ibid., IV, 481 (1736); V, 124–60 (1742); VI, 154–93 (1748).

87. Ibid., V, 145–60 (1742); VI, 184 (1748).

88. Ibid., IV, 390–93 (1734); VI, 186–87 (1748).

89. Ibid., V, 164 (1742).

90. Ibid., V, 164–68 (1742); VI, 146–51 (1748); VII, 570–75 (1762); VIII, 143–45 (1765).

91. Ibid., VIII, 245–47 (1766).

92. Ibid., V, 525–26 (1748).

93. Ibid., III, 499–502 (1710); IV, 84–86 (1720); V, 515 (1748); VIII, 524 (1772).

94. Ibid., V, 331–36 (1745); see also, III, 442–46 (1705); IV, 64–72 (1718), 344–48 (1732), 412–17 (1734), 496–501 (1736).

95. Ibid., IV, 170 (1726); VI, 51–53 (1748).

96. Wheeler, "Lancaster County, " 135.

The Anglican Church:
A Basic Institution
of Local Government
in Colonial Virginia

WILLIAM H. SEILER

One of the basic English institutions transferred to the New World was the Church of England. The Anglican faith came with the first settlers to Virginia in 1607 and was endorsed as the state church by the first General Assembly in 1619.[1] An alliance of politics and religion in an established church was the usual institutional arrangement of time, as tests for treason and heresy were interwoven to determine the loyalty of the subject. In such a system a person could live within a unified social structure, comfortable in the promise that institutional responsibility would maintain civil order and encourage the proper faithfulness leading to eternal salvation.[2]

Enough people—the number varies from place to place and time to time—living in a given area join together in developing some kind of institutional structure to promote their common objectives and provide general services. The parish as a unit of the Anglican state church existed as a useful historical example of local government from English experience, and it met the practical necessity of performing needed functions in the sparsely populated, rural, tidewater area of early Virginia settlements. Here, in these isolated Anglican parishes, colonial adjustments built a Virginia church with dedication to self-governing controls.

Four important elements dominated the organization of the colonial church in Virginia: the adaptations required by the lack of a resident bishop, an essential appointment if the clerical organization of an episcopal church was to be completed; the role of the colony governor as the representative of the King, the supreme governor of the Church of England; the action of the Assembly, particularly the House of Burgesses, as primary determinant of the broad outlines of ecclesiastical policy; and the distinct entrenchment of local control in the parishes, particularly in their governing boards, the vestries.

There never was a resident bishop in Virginia. During the early years, there was no clear relationship of the colonial church with any particular bishop in England, although the assumption prevailed that the English plantations in North America were within the purview of the bishop of London, who had been a member of the original Virginia Company.[3] Finally, Bishop Henry Compton, who assumed the See of London in 1675, successfully sought jurisdiction over the Virginia clergy, and this limited control was recognized in the instructions issued to the royal governors from 1679 to the American Revolution.[4]

An official known as a commissary became the bishop of London's representative in the colony after 1689. Representing "the bishop in the outplaces of the diocese,"[5] there nevertheless were severe limitations on his Virginia functions, including the inability to confirm, ordain, or consecrate ministers, restricting him essentially to overseeing the clergy as individuals. The most notable of the commissaries in Virginia was Dr. James Blair, who received the first appointment in 1689 and filled the office until his death in 1743.[6] Blair's influence within the colony, during the more than half-century he served as commissary, was more directly related to his family associations through marriage, his personal aggressiveness, his presidency of the College of William and Mary, and the position he filled on the Council, rather than to any considerable authority in his office. Other men who followed in the commissary's office never achieved Blair's stature.

The royal governor, as the King's agent, was the principal colonial representative of the English ecclesiastical government. In his office, as lay ordinary, were vested such important episcopal functions as issuing licenses for marriages, probating wills, receiving the ministers' orders upon their arrival in the colony, recommending them to parish assignments, and inducting clergymen into their livings—a source of dispute with the parish vestries.

Throughout the colonial era a succession of governors either advanced or depressed the church depending upon the individual's personal interest and professional competence. Generally speaking, this essentially secular executive had to attend to other matters of higher priority than the affairs of the church. Probably the most important consideration in assessing the governor's role is the fact that there was no continuity in the office during the early years of settlement. From the beginning of royal control in 1624 until Governor Berkeley was removed in 1652, Virginia had seven different governors or acting governors in eleven administrations. Later, when substantial figures such as Andros, Nicholson, Spotswood, and Gooch came to office, they found local self-government entrenched in the parishes, which by ordeal or conciliation they learned to respect.

English authorities, having forfeited control by failure to complete the church organization, defaulted to the House of Burgesses the responsibility of serving as the primary determinant of colonial ecclesiastical policy. The legislature established new parishes and consolidated others, defined their boundaries, fixed the salaries of ministers, resolved complaints concerning dissolution of vestries, and provided for the collection of parish taxes. It exercised those duties that would have been fulfilled in England by an established diocesan organization or ecclesiastical synod.[7]

Forced by the developments of the first century of colonial growth to concentrate attention upon effectual methods of preserving the faith and answering the demands of local government functions, the parish became, in the words of Herbert L. Osgood in his classic study of seventeenth-century America, "a mark of the exclusive supremacy of Anglicanism in Virginia."[8]

As the colony steadily increased in population and territorial expansion occurred, new parishes were formed, often by division of large ones, while smaller ones were merged where the decreasing number of parishioners could no longer support costs of maintaining a minister and other parochial responsibilities.[9] Many of the new parishes formed the nucleus of new counties, usually established shortly thereafter.[10]

The Virginia parish was modeled upon its English example, which was "merely the base of a more or less elaborate hierarchy of government," and it did not become an autonomous or independent entity in ecclesiastical or civil affairs.[11] In Virginia, however, absence of a resident bishop and firm diocesan control throughout the colonial period meant no rigid adherence to the hierarchical structure. Freedom of action became a working principle in the development of the Virginia parish and brought about the predominance of the laity in determining church policy.[12]

The vestry was the governing body for the administration of ecclesiastical affairs in the local parish and, because of the church-state connection, it also had the administrative responsibility for a number of civil duties. The vestry was the only permanent group within the institutional framework of the church that dealt continually with the affairs of the parishioners in their daily lives. It became the strongest single factor in the development of the Anglican Church in colonial Virginia.

Origins of the Virginia vestry system can be found as early as 1610–11 in the "Laws Divine, Morall and Martial &c." proclaimed by Sir Thomas Dale when "foure of the most religious and better disposed" men were to assist the minister.[13] In 1632 a law specified that churchwardens were to be chosen yearly at Easter and were annually to accompany the minister to Jamestown to make necessary church reports. In the same year another law specified that a committee in each parish was responsible for construction and repair of church buildings. This board, in conjunction with the churchwardens, obviously represented a transitional step to formal recognition of the parish vestry.[14]

The first use of the term *vestry* in an extant official record can be found in the minutes of the Accomack County Court, September 14, 1635, where it was ordered to erect a parsonage. The court, determining that "there have heretofore been no formal vestry nor vestrymen," appointed eleven men to serve in that capacity.[15] It appears this authority stemmed from an act of Assembly,[16] now disappeared, authorizing such a body, or the adaptation of the English vestry system to the colonial scene prior to legislative enactment.

A legislative act directing a vestry to be established in each parish may have been enacted at the time counties were organized in 1634. An act of 1642 referred to an act of 1636 ordering this.[17] A serious revision of the laws in March 1643 included detailed church legislation, and in it "the most sufficient and selected men," the minister, and two or more churchwardens were to comprise the parish vestry.[18] They were responsible for tax levies and assessments and for church repair, and the churchwardens were also responsible for presentments at a yearly meeting of the county court "of such misdemeanors as to their knowledge have been committed the year before . . . namely, swearing, prophaning God's name, and his holy Sabboths, abuseing his holy word and commandments, contemning his holy sacraments or anything belonging to his service or worship. . . . [and of] any person or persons of what degree or condition soever shall abuse themselves with the high & foule offences of adultery, whoredome or fornication or with the loathesome sinne of drunkenness in the abuse of God's creatures."[19]

After the Restoration, in 1661, the Assembly directed that the number of vestrymen not exceed twelve, and the following year, in a revision of the laws of the colony, provision was made for the specific designation of twelve men for the vestry of each parish. In this act of 1662 the minister was designated the presiding officer, and the vestry was to choose two of its number to serve as churchwardens for one year.[20] Almost one hundred years later, in 1757, the Assembly got around officially to recognizing the quorum by law at seven, with a majority vote of this number sufficient for contractual obligations.[21] A careful survey of the vestry books shows that meetings of the vestries attended by the full membership were rare, but they were generally attended by more than seven members during the colonial era.

In 1645 the democratic principle of election of vestrymen was approved by the Assembly when an act was passed allowing "the major part of the parishioners . . . to make choice of such men as by pluralities of voices shall be fitt."[22] Freemen, following the suffrage requirements for the burgesses, thus elected vestrymen. Then came the period of the Commonwealth and Protectorate in England, when Anglicanism was in retreat before the forces of Oliver Cromwell. What was the response in Virginia? The House of Burgesses delegated control to the parishes, grounding the church more firmly than ever on a local basis.[23]

After the Restoration, in the 1662 revision of the laws, confirmation was given in the vestry legislation to what is probably the most influential of all provisos: co-optation by the members. This meant that "in case of the death of any vestry man, or his departure out of the parish, . . . the said minister and vestry make choice of another to supply his roome."[24] The Assembly, in granting this right of the membership to perpetuate itself and its views through appointment rather than election, encouraged permanence of leadership, valuable for stability during a time of stress. Later it authorized the corporate existence of the vestries, like the county courts.[25] As restrictive as it may appear, this principle of co-optation distinctly continued the idea of colonial self-government in its local expression. The procedure continued for the remainder of the colonial period, excepting an abortive attempt at the time of Bacon's Rebellion in 1676 to reinstate election by parishioners, and when a special act required an election, as mentioned below.[26]

Intellect, wealth, and social position became associated with vestry membership, as with membership on the county court and in the House of Burgesses and Council. Self-perpetuation of vestrymen was a part of the emerging pattern of control by affluent tidewater planters. They were burgesses and county justices. Many of these vestrymen served a long time. In the vestry book of Kingston Parish, Gloucester County, as an example, the names of Dudley, Armistead, Cary, Hayes, Tabb, Gwynn, Billops (Billups), and Throckmorton appear regularly. George Dudley, later captain, served thirty-four years (1721–1754, 1757–1758). John Hayes served at least eighteen years (1740–1758), and Captain Thomas Hayes at least twenty-nine years (1740–1769). Charles Debnam (Dednom, Debrum) was vestryman from 1740 until his death in 1760. Hugh Gwynn and Gwynn Reade served twenty-one and seven years respectively. The Armisteads were represented by Colonel Henry Armistead, William, John, William of Hesse, Captain Francis, and George. Captain Thomas Smith regularly attended from 1760 through the last entry in the vestry book in 1796, a period of thirty-six years; Thomas Junior served at least thirteen years, and was a vestryman in 1796 when the record closed.[27] This was characteristic of the personnel and their length of service in the tidewater vestries, and of the interrelationships of families of influence who dominated their membership.

Although the number of vestrymen in each parish was set at twelve in the act of 1662, this number was exceeded from time to time, and there was no firm limitation on two churchwardens in some of the parishes. Christ Church Parish at one time had six churchwardens and eighteen vestrymen, and later fluctuated between two and three churchwardens until two became a definite commitment after 1728.[28] The increased number of vestrymen serving in some of the parishes during the latter part of the seventeenth and early part of the eighteenth centuries was the result of consolidating old parishes and forming new ones. In merging parishes, there was a tendency to combine vestries, allowing the greater number to serve until the membership declined by attrition to twelve. In forming new parishes, there was acceptance in most cases during this period of allowing vestrymen in the older parish to serve in either the old or new one depending upon location, then electing members to fill the ranks in each case to twelve. After 1744, with only one exception, Hening's *Statutes* show that the Assembly followed the policy of ordering the dissolution of vestries and totally new elections when consolidating and creating parishes.[29] As parishes generally preceded counties, when political and judicial organization of counties was initiated, vestrymen could be identified as local officials with experience in church government, and thus eligible for service in new secular county offices.

Many elections were held as new parishes were formed to match the expanding colonial development. Also, long use of co-optation and consequent failure to hold regular elections led to abuses, of course, and in the quarter-century before the Revolution there were frequent petitions to the Assembly requesting dissolution of specific vestries and new elections. In 1748 a bill dissolving all vestries and ordering new elections was prepared by a specially appointed committee, but it did not get beyond the first reading.[30] Numerous reasons were given for dissolution: disputes between two factions of the vestry, either over the minister or the building or repair of churches; reflection in local parish arguments of wider colonial disputes; complaints concerning tax levies in the later years, including especially irritation with the sheriffs over their collection of parish and other taxes; frequent allegations leveled against the vestries as "the twelve old men," who should be replaced because of infirmities.

Heavy influx of dissenters into the western areas in the eighteenth century did not bring much disruption in the beginning, as most of the affairs of these counties were dominated by them. Criticism increased, however, and in 1759 a blanket act removed all vestrymen who were members of dissenting churches, although section 5 of the act left open a wide door of accommodation in those places where dissenters were in complete control. It furnished an exception in those cases where "the number of vestrymen, who are not dissenters, in any parish, shall be less then seven, . . . such vestry shall continue as at present until the matter shall be represented to the General Assembly."[31] Disestablishment of the church would solve this issue. During the later years of the colonial period, the Assembly was very responsive to the petitions by inhabitants requesting redress of their grievances.[32] Significantly, one is impressed that in ordering new elections, there is an almost constant notation in the act that once the new vestry is elected, co-optation will prevail once again.

Throughout the long decades of the colonial era, the Anglican parishes represented the distinct entrenchment of local control of the Church of England in Virginia, and the vestries as their governing boards fulfilled the leadership role in directing parochial functions — religious and secular.

One of the important ecclesiastical duties of the vestry was employing the minister. In England, the right to present (nominate) a clergyman to a parish belonged to the patron, the owner of the advowson. Then, the bishop confirmed the selection by admitting him to the benefice (collation) and inducting the rector. If no nomination was made within six months, the bishop had the power to collate a minister to the parish and induct him, induction assuring permanent tenure except for proved charges of moral laxity or dereliction of duty. In Virginia, it was a different matter. With no bishop in the colony, the right of induction was vested in the governor. A number of contests occurred over presentation, collation, and induction, displaying confrontations between the governor pressing the royal authority against the parish vestry defending the principle of colonial self-governance.

Who had the right to select the minister? After the dissolution of the Virginia Company in 1624, it was claimed by the governor and Council, but custom put it in the parish. In 1643 the Assembly specifically granted permission to the vestries "to elect and make choyce of their ministers."[33] In 1662 this vestry right was re-enacted,[34] giving the representatives of the parish laity the same control as held by the English patron. This right of nomination was zealously defended throughout the colonial era.

The vestries, facing a critical shortage of ministers in the seventeenth century and lacking previous knowledge of candidates, adopted the practice of engaging ministers on a year-to-year basis.[35] Commissary Blair said this was referred to "by a name coarse enough, viz. Hiring the Ministers."[36] The supply of ministers improved in the eighteenth century[37] and included greater numbers of men born in the colony,[38] although they still had to endure a long ocean voyage to England for confirmation and ordination. Annual employment of ministers by the vestries was the dominant method during the colonial era.

Collation and induction by the governor were to cause contention in Virginia. Prior to 1680, however, the scarcity of ministers deferred these issues. Usually, a new parson arriving in the colony would offer his certificate of ordination to the governor,[39] and the governor would send the clergyman with a letter of recommendation to a vacant parish, where he was received on a year's appointment. Later, this matter of collation and induction was entangled in the related issues of clerical salaries and internal politics and played a part in the removal from office of Governor Edmund Andros in 1698.

In 1699 Commissary Blair formulated an extensive plan for the church in Virginia, including careful attention to the status of the clergy. It extended to eighteen months the period for a parish to obtain a minister, and increased the total time to three and one-half years before the governor should act. It was never implemented.[40]

When Francis Nicholson succeeded Andros as governor, appreciative of his predecessor's difficulties and a few of his own unfortunate early experiences in reference to presentment, collation, and induction, he agreed to send the entire question to the King's attorney general in England for an opinion. Sir Edward Northey returned his consequential reply in 1703, upholding the vestry's right to present within six months, but the governor, as ordinary, could act after that time, and that he "shall and may collate a Clerk to such Church by lapse, and his collatee shall hold the Ch[ur]ch for his life."[41]

On March 3, 1704, Governor Nicholson referred this opinion to the Council, which promptly sent it to the vestries for their comments.[42] Forty-six parishes returned replies, and it was obvious that the great majority would brook no interference from the governor. This clearly signaled the entrenchment of the vestry positions as defenders of local control within an important colonial institution.[43] Only two parishes reported ministers already inducted, and four did comply by presenting their incumbents to the governor for induction. Six vestries pertinently remarked that it was a matter for the General Assembly to handle and not the attorney general in England; others pointed out that Sir Edward knew the English situation, but that he was not acquainted with colonial problems. Nineteen of the parishes reported that they were well satisfied with their ministers but that they would not offer them for induction. After the overwhelming number of negative replies was received, Nicholson tabled the entire proposition. Blair gave up his attempts, and soon was in league with the governor's opponents in engineering his removal.

Later, in 1718, Governor Spotswood renewed the issue of collation by the governor in parishes "as often as any of them shall happen to be void," with the design of increasing the crown's prerogative in this matter as he had promoted it in others.[44] This time, as he had done in the later stages of his contest with Nicholson, Commissary Blair supported the vestries in their opposition to the governor. When Spotswood was dismissed as governor in 1722, ecclesiastical disputes over parish territorial organization and collation of ministers were important items in the total list of objections to his administration.[45]

The governor's claim to collation and induction as constituent parts of the crown's prerogative in the colony did not disappear with Spotswood's removal, but it never again served as the focus of disruptive cleavage. A careful analysis of parochial reports of 1724 found the average length of ministerial service to be twenty-one years. Only five were inducted, the rest serving on annual agreements with their vestries. As Brydon remarked, "Certainly the lack of induction did not prevent the long tenure of curés shown in these reports."[46] Governor Gooch, for example, left office after twenty-two congenial years without promoting induction, and after agreeing with the Burgesses in an act of 1748 to extend from six to twelve months the time the vestries could present a minister.[47]

Even with the extended period of time for presentation for induction, the vestries evidently did not do so. As William Kay, a minister in conflict with his vestry pointed out in 1752, he did not think that more than three clergymen were inducted in the colony.[48] Kay won his case for salary and damages and helped to reassert that in "practical operation, although an incumbent minister who was not instituted as rector might have his incumbency terminated at the end of any year by order of the vestry, he could, in the meantime, exercise all the spiritual rights of the rectorship, both in his ministry to the people and in his possession and use of the church buildings, as well as the glebe."[49] When Robert Dinwiddie came to the governor's office in 1751, he was alarmed at "the exorbitant Power of the Vestries," and wrote to the bishop of London in 1755 about his "Concern that the Prerogative of the Crown, and Your Lordship's Jurisdiction, should be so much invaded," but he decided there was nothing he could do about it.[50]

Vestry opposition to crown prerogative over the presentation of their ministers was finally resolved in the contest over the American episcopate in the years immediately preceding the Revolution. A successful campaign to establish the episcopate would have meant denial of a continuous colonial development of parochial autonomy, especially through active intervention by a bishop in the appointment and tenure of ministers. Actually, in Virginia, where the church was most firmly established, an American episcopacy was opposed, and, further, excepting a small clique, there was little clerical support for it.[51]

Parish vestries supervised at the local level many institutional duties assigned to the state church. In addition to employing the minister, it was a basic vestry function to determine the tax for all church-state purposes within the territorial limits of the parish. This levy, like the county and other public levies, was a poll tax assessed on the basis of tithables.[52] As the taxing agency, it got a response from the recipients usually associated with this type of activity.

The vestry was originally ordered to meet sometime between October and December, "when the Tobacco is ready," to calculate the debts of the parish, determine the total amount needed to defray expenses and the amount per tithable, and provide for the collection of the tobacco. Actually, this time was not observed very carefully, and by 1765, recognizing that the early spring was the more common time, the Assembly said that all levies should be determined annually before April 10.[53]

The collection of the parish levy was originally assigned to the churchwardens, and there is evidence that the English custom of granting them the assistance of two sidesmen was followed for a time.[54] References to these sidesmen are few; there was instead a greater use of more than two churchwardens. After the middle of the seventeenth century, collection of the parish levy was often turned over to the sheriff (sometimes he was a churchwarden), who combined it with his legally assigned collections of the quitrents, county, and public levies.[55] A careful reading of the vestry books will show, however, that there was no uniformity in this practice, and the churchwardens in many areas continued to collect the parish tax. In 1708 in Petsworth Parish the minister himself was the collector of the parish levy.[56]

The allowance for collecting the tobacco taxes was a substantial sum and worth the effort. By the act of 1696 the fee was set at 5 percent of the levy, and was increased to 10 percent in 1727, with an additional amount allowable if remoteness made it difficult to get the tobacco to the landing for shipment. Before 1748 there was a wide range of percentage payments regardless of the law; after legislation in that year that set the fee at 6 percent, all vestries seem to have conformed to the new figure. Public notice of the levy was made in each church by the minister, and the collectors had to give bond to the clerk of the vestry for the amount to be collected.[57]

The announcement of the levy corresponded to the use of the church during the earlier colonial era as a weekly disseminator of official notices, government proclamations, and publications of laws and orders. With compulsory attendance at services, it was an even better place than the county court for these purposes. In 1736, with the establishment of the *Virginia Gazette,* the announcement function began to decline. The churchyard on a Sunday was a center of activities for an essentially separated, rural population, and there was no necessity to hurry from the churchyard after service. Business affairs could share time with gossip and family news, and Philip Vickers Fithian in the later eighteenth century recalled the "rings of Beaux chatting before & after Sermon on Gallantry" and the "assembling in crowds after Service to dine and bargain."[58]

The major continuing expenditure in the parish budgets was the minister's salary. The goal during most of the colonial period was to approximate a salary equivalent to £80 sterling, as stated in the act of 1662 setting the tobacco allowance at 13,333 pounds.[59] In 1696 there was an increase to 16,000 pounds, although it was a hollow victory for the clergy because dropping former additional allowances for cask and collection allowed a net advance of only 651 pounds.[60] By 1748 the amount was 17,280 pounds by law, the equivalent of about £100 sterling in the years approaching the Revolution. In the legislation of 1748 a glebe of 200 acres was also prescribed at the expense of the parish, and was to include "one convenient mansion house, kitchen, barn, stable, dairy, meat house, cornhouses, and garden."[61] Often it was less, by agreement, and in some cases there was no glebe at all. In other parishes, allotments were given in lieu of a glebe. Lack of arrangements for adequate support indicated a general parsimony which kept those parishes longest vacant in times of short ministerial supply.

Payments above the minimum occurred for a variety of reasons, including rewards for the special talents of the clergyman in fulfilling the many demands of his parochial office. He was entitled to perquisites for marriages, churchings, burials, and funeral sermons.[62] At the time of the great debate of 1696 on the subject of clergy salaries, the value of the additional perquisites varied between the £5 claimed by the clergy, who wanted more salary allowance, and the £15 calculated by the Assembly, which was more interested in checking a salary increase. Many ministers received additional amounts of tobacco for services rendered in neighboring parishes as supply pastors, with records of as much as 10,000 pounds extra in one year.[63] Income accruing from all sources in a more substantial eighteenth-century tidewater parish could have approximated as much as £150 or perhaps a total of £175.

With salary payments allocated in fixed tobacco amounts, fluctuations in the price of tobacco seriously affected the take-home pay of the ministers. Also, the quality of tobacco within the parish was important in determining the value. "Sweetscented" tobacco was more popular than "Oronoco" up to 1724, and ministers serving "SS" parishes therefore fared better than those serving "O" parishes, as they were designated in government reports, with an average difference from £35 to £40.[64] Students of colonial history are familiar with the prominent association of tobacco prices, the salaries of the Virginia clergy, and the prominent role of Patrick Henry as they contributed to the celebrated "Parson's Cause" of 1763, which served as one of the dramatic incidents in the prelude to revolution. If the Rev. James Maury had received allowance on his claim appropriate to the spiraling tobacco prices, he would have received £250 in damages instead of one penny.[65]

In summary, from the parochial view, the pastor's salary was a substantial part of the budget. For the Virginia Anglican clergy it meant that most were above the great majority of the small land-holders in the socioeconomic scale, but appreciably below the affluent planters who were the leading members of their vestries. This is not to deny the enterprising preacher who extended his landholdings by adopting the necessary methods of an acquisitive society, or the clergyman who married into one of the more promi-nent families, with Commissary James Blair a foremost example, thus achieving social status and economic rewards.

Two of the four extant vestry books for the latter part of the seventeenth century show that the average annual parish levy was about forty-five pounds of tobacco per tithable.[66] This was a larger amount than that prescribed for either the public or county levies, with the total coming to about one hundred pounds per tithable.

Three representative levies in St. Paul's Parish, Hanover County, for the eighteenth century show:[67]

Year	Total Levy in Lbs. Tobac.	Tithables	Lbs. per Tithable
1715	23,692.5	729	32.5
1731	37,920	1,185	32
1756	67,680	2,115	32

This represents a stable, enviable consistency in rate as population and the total levy increased. Significantly, although the major con-tinuing expenditure in the parish budgets was the minister's salary, another trend in parish expenses is illustrated in this example. In 1715, the minister's salary amounted to 67.5 percent of the total budget; in 1731, it came to 46.9 percent; and by 1756 it was 25.5 percent. On the other hand, parish responsibility for secular affairs, particularly the care of the poor, steadily accelerated. Charity to the poor was a religious duty. It was deemed a local problem, a parochial problem. In 1715, 1,227.5 pounds of tobacco for this purpose represented 5.1 percent of the total levy; in 1731, it had increased to 8.4 percent; and by 1756 the 13,160 pounds represented 19.4 per-cent of the total. With the disestablishment of the church in the eighteenth century at the time of the Revolution, this became a secular function of the overseers of the poor.[68]

A number of circumstances contributed to the poverty of an individual. The vestry made arrangements for the care of the indigent blind, sick, infirm, and insane, and burial costs were assumed for those unable to pay them. There were many destitute widows included in the vestry's responsibilities. The parish often gave a money or tobacco allotment to some parishioner for the care of a poor person, and in other cases barrels of corn and supplies of wheat, port, and salt, were allotted for the poor, along with other sundries, including bedding, shoes, clothing, and even livestock. Some women in the parish took care of several charity cases and received the allotments due each of them for their subsistence.

Churchwardens were given authority under an act of 1727, renewed in 1748, to remove children from poor parents "to prevent the evil consequences attending the neglect or inability of poor people to bring up their children in an honest and orderly course of life." If the county court justices approved the removal, the churchwardens were allowed to bind the children as apprentices, as was also arranged for orphans upon court order.[69]

By 1755 an important innovation occurred in the handling of poor reflief. An act in that year recognized that there were far more poor people, and "for the prevention of great mischiefs arising from such numbers of unemployed poor," all parish vestries were allowed (not ordered) to build, purchase, or rent one or more houses and land up to one hundred acres, to serve as workhouses for the poor. Two or more parishes were permitted to join in this enterprise, and there were several instances of attempts to do so. Churchwardens could assign persons to these workhouses, and cut off any subsistence if they refused to go. Interestingly, inmates of the workhouses were required to wear an identifying shoulder patch, "cut either in blue, red, or green cloth," identifying their parish association. Refusal to wear the patch meant denial of all further relief until compliance, or five lashes for each offense.[70] There seems to be no diminution in individual allocations in the parish records, and there is no real evidence as to the effectiveness of the workhouses or the stigma of the patch, but there is evidence that a number of parish vestries earnestly put this program into operation.[71]

Large expenditures occurred periodically for church buildings and glebe lands, as well as for more modest chapels of ease to serve settlers living in areas remote from the main church. In some cases, vestry houses were constructed for the use of vestry meetings and for storing church supplies.[72] It was the responsibility of the vestry to provide the necessary accessories "for the decent and orderly performance of Divine Service," usually called the "ornaments" of the church.[73] Sextons were appointed by the vestrymen or churchwardens to take care of buildings, churchyard, vestry houses, and to see that the church "ornaments" were delivered for the services. Often the selection of the sexton was a way to assist what otherwise might be a charity case, and in several parishes the widow of the sexton was continued as "sextonness," with the tobacco wages paid for her duties augmented by another grant "for her relief."[74] In other parishes the duties of clerk of the vestry and sexton were combined.[75]

What was the vestry's responsibility in identifying and prosecuting those parishioners engaged in sinful activities? Churchwardens were to make presentments to the county courts for offenses against the moral law, and this gave vestrymen a vital influence on the colonial mores. By the later years of the eighteenth century the grand juries were probably more active than the churchwardens in presentments for immoral violations, but throughout the colonial period it was an essential duty of the laymen representatives of the established church. The fact that these vestry presentations were to secular rather than ecclesiastical courts, as in England, was further evidence of the separate organization developed in Virginia.

The most frequently cited indictments were for drunkenness, bastardy, adultery and fornication, profanity, slander, and absences from church services. There were several kinds of punishment for those found guilty as charged. As one author astutely observed, "They reflected the harshness, the grasping quality of pioneer life. That which life gave most abundantly to the individual, colonial punishment sought to take from him. From the man of wealth it took some form of money; from the servant and slave, bodily strength; and from the woman, dignity. Furthermore, these punitive measures might deter potential malefactors—or so the legislators hoped."[76] Fines collected for convictions were given to the churchwardens for the support of the poor.

To check intemperate use of liquor among a population generally described as liberal in its drinking habits, colonial laws pressed checks upon excessive public drunkenness. It has been argued that prosecution on this charge was strict and efficient,[77] and certainly the vestry books record many instances of presentments in this category. Five shillings, or fifty pounds of tobacco, was a standard penalty, and if the offender had no money, chattels, or property of any kind upon which an attachment could be made, ten lashes "on his bare back well laid on" was the penalty prescribed by law.[78] Numerous presentments of the same individual as a "Common Drunkard" brought increased penalties.[79]

Bastardy was one of the most frequent charges for moral iniquity, with an increased number of cases occurring after the importation of indentured servant women. Coming for the most part from the lower classes in England, these women found the terms of their contract, the nature of their employment, and the associations imposed on them by their housing and social life combining to encourage a promiscuousness with which they may likely have been familiar. There is ample record in the vestry books of the costs to the parish of supporting illegitimate children. A petition to the Assembly in 1696 from Gloucester County asked relief from this drain on the taxpayers, but the Assembly held that sufficient accommodation prevailed both for prosecution of offenders and support of the bastards.[80] In 1748 the Burgesses passed a resolution affirming Stafford County's plea that persons purchasing white women servants should provide for the illegitimate children of those servants "without burthening the several Parishes with that charge."[81] The churchwardens quickly made arrangements to see that a bastard was bound out, to avoid charges to the parish. This indenture continued until thirty years of age, and, of course, the money or tobacco received for the contract went for the use of the parish poor. In 1765 this indenture was reduced until the level of twenty-one years for males and eighteen years for females was reached.[82]

The commandment in the Decalogue pertaining to adultery was rigidly upheld in the early years of the colony, but a more lenient atmosphere on punishment of this break with the moral code began in the eighteenth century. Those guilty of profanity and "malitious and envious slandering and backbiting"[83] were subject to penalties similar to those for other moral offenses: fines, flogging, the ducking stool, and public repentance.

Absence from church services brought severe punishments in the early years, but was modified to a 1s. fine per absence by an act of 1632. Then in the Restoration era, as part of a renewed emphasis on the state-church relationship, the fine was increased in 1662 to fifty pounds of tobacco (or 5s.). After the Toleration Act was accepted in Virginia, the Assembly set the standard penalty for the duration of the colonial period: for any person twenty-one years of age or over who was absent one month or more from church services, the fine was 5s. or fifty pounds of tobacco, and dissenters were required to attend their own services at least once in two months.[84]

One of the most important secular duties of the vestry was supervision of land processioning.[85] In an agrarian society, land and the laws regulating its distribution and safeguarding its possession were of paramount importance. In Virginia an equivocal and vacillating land policy, along with the inaccuracy of many surveys, produced innumerable law suits which distended the court calendars to the great expense and confusion of the colonists. Attempting to remedy the situation, the Assembly in 1662 passed an act declaring that the boundaries of lands held within the colony should be determined by land processioning by view of the inhabitants. Once every four years, on the order of the county courts, the vestries of the established church were to divide the parishes into precincts, and the freeholders of adjoining lands were to examine and renew the boundary marks. This practice was not widely followed during the seventeenth century, partly because of the indefinite terms of the statute. In 1705 and 1710, however, acts giving more detailed instructions for land processioning were passed, and throughout the greater part of the eighteenth century this ancient English procedure was an integral part of the colony's land policy.

After 1705 the vestry books disclose a scrupulous adherence to the law in enforcing land processioning activities. These books were frequently used for recording the returns, in many cases taking up considerable portions of them. These records now furnish the main sources of information, excepting Hening's *Statutes,* for this phase of the Virginia colonial land policy. The number of processioners and precincts varied from parish to parish depending on population and the claimed or settled land within it. In October 1785, upon the disestablishment of the Church of England in Virginia, the duty of processioning was removed from the parish vestries and assigned to the overssers of the poor, still under the direction of the county courts.

The same legislative session that ordered land processioning in 1662 also ordered the county courts to appoint annually surveyors of highways. Each parish vestry, upon request of the surveyor, was to furnish sufficient workmen from tithables in the parish to clear roads and make and repair bridges. This duty of the vestries cotinued throughout the colonial period, although no specific mention is made of its in the statutes following 1705.[86]

An important civil duty of the vestry was undertaken between 1723 and 1730, when the vestries received the responsibility of appointing two persons in each precinct to determine the names of those tending tobacco plants and to count the plants. It was an attempt by the Assembly to remedy the frauds resulting from the repeal in 1717 of the tobacco law of 1713, and to cope with three years of low prices. The act of 1723 restricted the number of tobacco plants per inhabitant, and gave the examiners the right to destroy all plants in excess of the approved number. Fines were to be levied on vestries that did not comply, and the vestry books show a close attention to this duty. Many of the tobacco examiners were those who served as land processioners. This participation in significant crop control legislation made the vestries a part of one of the most important colonial economic measures.[87]

Multiple duties of the vestries reflected the events, momentous and influential, pedestrian and routine, that were a part of the Anglican Church as a basic institution of local government in colonial Virginia. Here was the expression of the state church alliance of religious and secular affairs. Absence of a resident bishop and firm diocesan control meant that the governor, the Assembly, and the parish created necessary adaptations for the preservation of the Virginia church, especially the distinct entrenchment of local control in the parishes, particularly in their governing boards, the vestries.

It is helpful to remember that impediments on transportation and communication dictated a different pace of life than became the mode in a later day, and that a limited number of people were one's neighbors and weekly associates during a lifetime spent in a small area. These things contributed to the necessity of a vital parochial institutional structure to promote common objectives and provide general services. In the parish, people attended to their religious responsibilities, worshipping in their church or at a chapel of ease, exchanging comments in the churchyard on Sunday, receiving governmental notices from the parson's lectern or, if able to read, getting them firsthand from the church door. They looked to their churchwardens to uphold the moral law by presenting to the county court those guilty of offenses against it. The vestrymen, possessing influential status, selected the minister, defending this right against those governors who sought to advance their own control of this matter as a right of royal prerogative. They provided for the church buildings and property. They administered secular assignments ranging from land processioning to care of the poor. Laying the parish levy encumbered them with the heavy duty of assessing substantial taxes. Vestrymen contributed to their dominance of parochial affairs by choosing replacements (co-optation) for members in the event of death, resignation, or removal from the parish. This brought a continuity of leadership emphasizing local control, particularly in the tidewater area by affluent planters.

In the quarter-century before the American Revolution, there were increasingly complex changes in the society of Virginia and the American colonies. More and more duties of the parish vestries were taken over by the county courts. Many elections were ordered by the House of Burgesses as population increase and territorial expansion occurred, as well as those elections ordered because of internal parochial difficulties. Separation of church and state, for example, became a prevailing demand, often pressed by greater numbers of dissenters moving into the colony, especially into the frontier counties, and it was answered in Virginia by the disestablishment of the Anglican Church in 1784. The dedication to self-governance, locked in the institutional structure of the Virginia church, was reflected in the secular litany offered for American independence.

For over a century and a half the Church of England was a basic institution in the Virginia colony. Distinctive, local characteristics became prominent in the structure and practice of the Virginia church as an ocean of distance and time separated it from direct association with both the substance and forms of the church in the mother country. Here, reliance upon self-government and independent action emerged from the impetus of necessity and soon became the process of daily operation. Nothing so completely realized the unique institutional development of the Church of

England in colonial Virginia as the influence of local attitudes and actions expressed in the Anglican parish and its vestry.

NOTES

1. J. P. Kennedy and H. R. McIlwaine, eds., *Journals of the House of Burgesses of Virginia, 1619–1776,* 13 vols. (Richmond, 1905-15), I *1619–1658/59,* 13; 36; see also Francis L. Hawks, *Contributions to the Ecclesiastical History of the United States of America,* 2 vols. (New York, 1836-39), I, 35–36. The basic reference on the Anglican Church in colonial Virginia is George MacLaren Brydon, *Virginia's Mother Church and the Political Conditions under Which It Grew,* 2 vols. (Richmond, 1947-52). Good accounts in general histories may be found in Wesley Frank Craven, *The Southern Colonies in the Seventeenth Century, 1607–1689* (Baton Rouge, La., 1949); and Daniel J. Boorstin, *The Americans: The Colonial Experience* (New York, 1958).

2. Perry Miller, "The Religious Impulse in the Founding of Virginia," *William and Mary Quarterly* hereafter, *(W & M Q),* 3rd ser., V (1948), 498; VI (1949), 27–28, 32–33; Evarts B. Greene, *Religion and the State* (New York, 1941), 8–9.

3. Arthur Lyon Cross, *The Anglican Epicopate and the American Colonies* (New York, 1902), 4; William W. Hening, ed., *The Statutes-at-Large . . . of Virginia, 1619–1792,* 13 vols. (Richmond, 1809-23), I, 57ff. for the charters; Susan M. Kingsbury, ed., *Records of the Virginia Company of London,* 4 vols. (Washington, D.C., 1906-35), I, 34; III, 583; see also William H. Seiler, "The Church of England as the Established Church in Seventeenth-Century Virginia," *Journal of Southern History* (hereafter, *JSH*), XV (1949), 499–502.

4. Leonard W. Labaree, ed., *Royal Instructions to British Colonial Governors, 1670–1776,* 2 vols. (New York, 1935), II, 489–90; Henry Hartwell, James Blair, and Edward Chilton, *The Present State of Virginia and the College,* ed. Hunter D. Farish (Williamsburg, Va., 1940), 67. It is important to note that collating to benefices, granting licenses for marriages, and the probating of wills, usually English bishopric functions, remained the authority of the governor.

5. Hawks, *Ecclesiastical History,* I, 73.

6. Parke Rouse, Jr., *James Blair of Virginia* (Chapel Hill, N.C., 1971); Brydon, *Virginia's Mother Church,* I, chapters 19, 20.

7. G. M. Brydon, "The Origin of the Rights of the Laity in the American Episcopal Church," *Historical Magazine of the Protestant Episcopal Church* (hereafter, *Hist. Mag. Prot. Episcopal Ch.*), XI (1942), 318.

8. Herbert L. Osgood, *The American Colonies in the Seventeenth Century,* 3 vols. (New York, 1904–06), III, 82.

9. A thorough documentation of colonial parish boundaries may be found in three studies on this subject for the entire history of the Protestant Episcopal Church of Virginia by Charles Francis Cocke, all published as bulletins (14, 22, and 28) by the Virginia State Library, Richmond: *Parish Lines, Diocese of Southwestern Virginia* (1960), *Parish Lines, Diocese of Southern Virginia* (1964), and *Parish Lines, Diocese of Virginia* (1967).

10. In ten of thirteen tidewater counties established between 1701 and 1776, parish organization preceded the counties.

11. Sidney and Beatrice Webb, *English Local Government from the Revolution to the Municipal Corporations Act,* vol 1, (London, 1906), *The Parish and the County* 4, 5–6, 40–51; for the ecclesiastical origins and development of the English parish, ibid., 37–39, note 6; A. R. Powys, *The English Parish Church* (London, 1930), 1.

12. G. M. Brydon, "The Origins of the Rights of the Laity in the American Episcopal

Church," *Hist. Mag. Prot. Episcopal Ch.*, XII (1943), 313; see Boorstin, *The Americans*, 123–39.

13. [W. Strachey], comp., *Lawes, Divine, Moral and Martiall*, in *Tracts Relating to . . . the Colonies in North America*, ed. Peter Force, 4 vols. (Washington, D.C. 1836–46), III, no. 2, 11.

14. Hening, *Statutes at Large*, I, 155–56, 185. The earliest extant court record in Virginia refers to churchwardens, when a court held at Accomack Plantation, January 7, 1633, issued an order to them for "power to distrayne upon goods and Chattels of . . . inhabitantes" who did not contribute corn and tobacco toward the payment of the minister (Susie M. Ames, ed., *County Court Records of Accomack-Northampton, Virginia, 1632–1640* [Washington, D.C. 1954], 1).

15. Ames, *Court Records*, 39.

16. Brydon, *Virginia's Mother Church*, I, 93.

17. *Virginia Magazine of History and Biography* (hereafter, *VMHB*), I (1893), 50ff. Both the acts of 1636 and 1642 were unknown to Hening at the time of his compilation of the Virginia colonial statutes.

18. Hening, *Statutes at Large*, I, 239–82, passim.

19. Ibid., I, 240–41.

20. Ibid., II, 25, 44–45.

21. Ibid., VII, 132; for example, St. Paul's Parish, Hanover County, in 1773 postponed final action because only five vestrymen were present. Less than a month later seven attended and inspected and approved the earlier proceedings. (C. G. Chamberlayne, ed., *The Vestry Book of St. Paul's Parish, Hanover County, Virginia, 1706–1786* [Richmond, 1940], 508, 509; see also Vestry Book, Upper Parish, Nansemond County, 1744–1793 [ms., photocopy, Virginia State Library], 15.)

22. Hening, *Statutes at Large*, I, 290–91.

23. Ibid., I, 433.

24. Ibid., II, 45. Although resignation of a vestryman meant his replacement by co-optation, this reason was not formally recognized until 1757 (ibid., VII, 132).

25. Ibid., III, 296; H. R. McIlwain, ed., *Executive Journals of the Council of Colonial Virginia*, 5 vols. (Richmond, 1925–30), II, 98.

26. In 1676, with the legislature under Bacon's control, an act was passed providing for the election once every three years of twelve vestrymen by the freeholders and freemen of every parish "if they see fit" (Hening, *Statutes at Large*, II, 356). The act was repealed later in the year with the collapse of the rebellion (ibid., II, 380).

27. The information on the Kingston Parish vestrymen is in William H. Seiler, "The Anglican Parish Vestry in Colonial Virginia," *JSH*, XXII (1956), 315–16; other examples are ibid., 315n; and see the account about Petsoe Parish, Gloucester County, in the seventeenth century in Seiler, "The Anglican Parish in Virginia," in *Seventeenth-Century America*, ed. James Morton Smith (Chapel Hill, N.C., 1959), 119–21.

28. G. C. Chamberlayne, ed., *The Vestry Book of Christ Church Parish, Middlesex County, Virginia, 1663–1767* (Richmond, 1927), passim.

29. Hening, *Statutes at Large*, V, 260, 268, 384; VI, 257; VII, 141, 150, 413–14, 416–17, 421, 429, 614, 618; VIII, 43, 206, 397, 399, 403, 426, 604. The exception was in 1755 when the vestry of Nottoway Parish, Amelia County, was continued and St. Patrick's, Prince Edward, was ordered to elect twelve vestrymen (ibid., VI, 504).

30. *Journals, House of Burgesses, 1742–1749*, 334.

31. Hening, *Statutes at Large*, VII, 302–3.

32. For examples, see Seiler, "Anglican Parish Vestry," 318–19. "In the three decades before the revolution, fifty-seven parishes held at least eighty-five vestry elections" (Joan

Rezner Gundersen, "The Myth of the Independent Virginia Vestry," *Hist. Mag. Prot. Episcopal Ch.*, XLIV [1975], 137).

33. Hening, *Statutes at Large*, I, 241–42.

34. Ibid., II, 46.

35. By 1662 there were only ten ministers in the forty-five to forty-eight parishes. R[oger] G[reen], *Virginia's Cure* (London, 1662), in *Tracts*, ed. Force, III, no. 14, 9, reports about fifty parishes, but it appears that there were between forty-five and forty-eight at this time. By 1680 the number had improved to thirty-five clergymen; by 1702 there were thirty-seven ministers and fifty-one parishes. List of 1680 in *VMHB*, I (1894), 242–44, with corrections in *W & M Q*, 2nd ser., XVII (1937), 466–68; and the list of 1702 in *VMHB*, I (1894), 373–77, where Accomack and Kingston Parishes, omitted from this list, were probably vacant.

36. Hartwell, Blair, and Chilton, *Present State of Virginia*, 67.

37. Governor Spotswood reported in 1717 only two parishes without a minister, and one other supplied by a neighboring pastor (R. A. Brock, ed., *The Official Letters of Alexander Spotswood . . . 1710–1722*, 2 vols. [Richmond, 1882–85], II, 254). Commissary Blair reported no vacancies in 1737, "unless it be a new parish or two, that are not yet quite ready for them" (*W & M Q*, 2nd ser., XX [1940], 128). Governor Gooch reported no vacant parishes in 1749 (ibid., 220). In 1774 on the eve of the Revolution, only five parishes were vacant in the list of ninety-five, and, significantly, in terms of personnel supply in the eastern tidewater heart of Anglicanism, only one parish in that area out of sixty in thirty-six counties was vacant (Purdie and Dixon, *Virginia Almanac for 1774*, list reprinted in *W & M Q*, 1st ser., V [1896], 200–203); Westover Parish, Charles City County, was vacant, but it had been filled 1758–73 by William Davis, and was again filled circa 1776 by James Ogilvie (Edward Lewis Goodwin, *The Colonial Church in Virginia* [Milwaukee, 1927], 323). Ministers were in ninety-two of ninety-five parishes in 1776 (*VMHB*, XLI (1932), 11–12).

38. By 1776, forty-four of seventy-one clergymen in the colony whose birthplaces have been determined were born in the colonies, of whom thirty-eight were born in Virginia (G. M. Brydon, "New Light upon the History of the Church in Colonial Virginia," *Hist. Mag. Prot. Episcopal Ch.*, X [1941], 26; see also *VMHB*, XLI [1933], 12). This suggests that a lack of native clergymen did not hamper the eighteenth-century Virginia church as reported in Herbert L. Osgood, *The American Colonies in the Eighteenth Century*, 4 vols. (New York, 1924), III, 104.

39. From 1662 to 1688 the certificate was required from any bishop in England; after 1688 from the bishop of London (Hening, *Statutes at Large*, II, 46; *Executive Journals, Council*, I, 515).

40. A good summary of the entire document may be found in Rouse, *Blair of Virginia*, 143–48.

41. William Stevens Perry, ed., *Historical Collections Relating to the American Colonial Church*, 3 vols. (Hartford, 1870–73), I, 128; see also R. T. Barton, ed., *Virginia Colonial Decisions*, 2 vols. (Boston, 1909), II, B2–B3.

42. *Executive Journals, Council*, II, 353.

43. P.R.O., London, C.O. 5, vol. 1314, part 2, 63; extracts from these parochial replies of 1704 have been published in Brydon, *Virginia's Mother Church*, I, appendix VIII, 517–34, where it is stated that forty-seven parishes reported. North Farnham reported twice.

44. *VMHB*, XX (1912), 343.

45. Discussion of events concerning Governor Spotswood and the church may be found in Leonidas Dodson, *Alexander Spotswood, Governor of Colonial Virginia, 1710–1722* (Philadelphia, 1932), 189–201.

46. Brydon, *Virginia's Mother Church*, I, 377. For a discussion of the activities of Anglican clergymen in the Virginia parishes, see Seiler, "Anglican Parish," 129-33.

47. Hening, *Statutes at Large*, VI, 90.

48. Perry, *Historical Collections*, 390.

49. Brydon, *Virginia's Mother Church*, I, 100-101; II, 265.

50. Thomas Dawson to bishop of London, July 28, 1754, *W & M Q*, 2nd ser., XX (1940), 528, 533; Governor Dinwiddie to bishop of London, August 11, 1755, in *The Official Records of Robert Dinwiddie*, ed. R. A. Brock, 2 vols. (Richmond, 1883-84), II, 162.

51. Cross, *Anglican Episcopate*, 226-40, discusses opposition in Virginia to the episcopate; see also Brydon, *Virginia's Mother Church*, II, 347-64; and Carl Bridenbaugh, *Mitre and Sceptre: Transatlantic Faiths, Ideas, Personalities, and Politics, 1689-1775* (New York, 1962), 316-23.

52. Definition of those who were tithables at different times in the colonial period may be found in Hening, *Statutes at Large*, I, 128, 281 (1624); I, 144 (1629); I, 255 (1649); II, 84 (1661); II, 170 (1662); II, 479-80 (1680). In 1705 the definition was substantially set for the remainder of the colonial period: all male persons sixteen or above, all Negro, mulatto, Indian women, sixteen or above, "not being free," except that in all cases the county courts or vestries could exempt for reasons of charity (ibid., III, 258-59; IV, 133 [1723]; VIII, 393 [1769]). See also Hugh Jones, *The Present State of Virginia*, ed. Richard L. Morton (Chapel Hill, N.C., 1956), 221n.

53. Hening, *Statutes at Large*, VIII, 103; Hartwell, Blair, and Chilton, *Present State of Virginia*, 54.

54. Hening, *Statutes at Large*, I, 155, 160, 180, 240, 241.

55. Philip Alexander Bruce, *Institutional History of Virginia in the Seventeenth Century*, 2 vols. (New York, 1910), I, 92-93; P. S. Flippin, *The Royal Government in Virginia, 1624-1775* (New York, 1919), 312-17; Albert Ogden Porter, *County Government in Virginia: A Legislative History, 1607-1904* (New York, 1947), 35, 36, 39, 93.

56. Chamberlayne, ed., *Vestry Book, Petsworth Parish, Gloucester, 1677-1703*, 95.

57. Hening, *Statutes at Large*, III, 152; IV, 205; VI, 89.

58. Hunter Dickinson Farish, ed., *Journal and Letters of Philip Vickers Fithian, 1773-1774: A Plantation Tutor of the Old Dominion* (Williamsburg, Va., 1957), 100.

59. Hening, *Statutes at Large*, II, 45.

60. Ibid., III 151-53; see Commissary Blair's comments on this at later date in Perry, *Historical Collections*, I, 12-13; see also Bruce, *Institutional History*, I, 157-58; and Brydon, *Virginia's Mother Church*, I, 314.

61. Hening, *Statutes at Large*, VI, 88-90; on ministerial salaries, see Brydon, *Virginia's Mother Church*, I, 13-19; II, 238-39.

62. Examples may be found in Hening, *Statutes at Large*, I, 243; II, 54, 55; and Perry, *Historical Collections*, I, 282.

63. E.g., John Span, minister of St. Stephen's Parish, Northumberland County, 1712-22 (Goodwin, *Colonial Church*, 308; Bishop [William] Meade, *Old Churches, Ministers, and Families of Virginia*, 2 vols. [Philadelphia, 1857], II, 393, 467), also served in Wicomico Parish from 1712 to 1720 as a supply pastor, receiving 400 pounds of tobacco per sermon. He received the 10,000 pounds in 1713 and again in 1715. (*Vestry Book, Wicomico Parish, Northumberland County, 1703-1795* [ms., photocopy, Virginia State Library], 10ff., passim.)

64. Arthur Pierce Middleton, *Tobacco Coast: A Maritime History of Chesapeake Bay in the Colonial Era* (Newport News, Va., 1953), 98.

65. There are some human sidelights not often mentioned in connection with this famous Two-Penny Act and court case that gave Patrick Henry such an accelerated leap to

prominence. In the same year that the Rev. Mr. Maury got one penny in damages, the Fredericksville Parish vestry, which had refused to grant him the larger market price for his salary, ordered the garden of his glebe repaired at the expense of the parish, continued to grant his annual salary as their minister until his death in 1770, and then "unanimously received" Matthew Maury, his son, as their new pastor. (*Vestry Book, Fredericksville Parish, Louisa County, 1742–1787* [ms., photocopy, Virginia State Library], November 21, 1763; February 8, 1770.)

66. C. G. Chamberlayne, ed., *Vestry Book, St. Peter's Parish, New Kent and James City Counties, 1684–1786,* 7–66 passim, gives the levy from 1686 to 1699, with an average annual per tithable assessment of 42.1 pounds of tobacco; C. G. Chamberlayne, ed., *The Vestry Book of Petsworth Parish, Gloucester County, Virginia, 1677–1793* (Richmond, 1933) [the parish was originally known as Petsoe], 2–55 passim, gives the levy from 1676 to 1699, with an average annual per tithable assessment of 58.8 pounds of tobacco. During the last two decades before the Revolution, the county rate was probably higher than the parish. See Seiler, "Anglican Parish," 137, 137n.

67. Chamberlayne, ed., *Vestry Book, St. Paul's Parish, Hanover, 1706–1786,* for the dates mentioned.

68. Hening, *Statutes at Large,* XII, 29–30.

69. Ibid., IV, 212–13; VI, 32; *Vestry Book, Christ Church Parish, Lancaster County, 1739–1783* (ms., photocopy, Virginia State Library), November 20, 1752; C. G. Chamberlayne, ed., *Vestry Book, Blisland [Blissland] Parish, New Kent and James City Counties Virginia, 1721–1786* (Richmond, 1935), 16; good examples of these indenture contracts may be found in C. G. Chamberlayne, ed., *Vestry Book, Petsworth Parish, Gloucester, 1677–1793,* by consulting the topical index under "Binding Out" and "Indenture."

70. Hening, *Statutes at Large,* VI, 475–78; H. R. McIlwaine, ed., *Legislative Journals of the Council of Colonial Virginia,* 3 vols. (Richmond, 1918-19), III, 1140, 1141. There is a possibility that legislation was passed authorizing workhouses for the poor before 1755, perhaps in 1749 (*Journals, House of Burgesses, 1742–1749,* 330, 374, 376, 400). The texts of acts passed in that year are not included in Hening. In 1752 Upper Parish, Nansemond County, was allowed to sell some land bequeathed to the parish for glebes, the money to be used for new glebe land and partly for "erecting a house for the reception of the poor of the parish." Hening, *Statutes at Large,* VI, 268. This house was constructed and the parish poor ordered to it in 1754 (Wilmer L. Hall, ed., *The Vestry Book of the Upper Parish, Nansemond County, Virginia, 1743–1793* [Richmond, 1949], October 14, 1752; March 25, November 14, 1754; Hening, *Statutes at Large,* VI, 519).

71. C. G. Chamberlayne, ed., *The Vestry Book of Stratton Major Parish, King and Queen County, Virginia, 1729–1783* (Richmond, 1931), 157, 159, 195; Chamberlayne, ed., *Vestry Book, Blissland Parish, New Kent and James City, 1721–1786,* 147, 154, 196, 197; Chamberlayne, ed., *Vestry Book, Christ Church Parish, Lancaster,* November 22, 1764; November 23, 1767; November 6, 1769; November 19, 1770; and passim; *Vestry Book, Elizabeth River Parish, Norfolk County, 1749–1761* (ms., photocopy, Library of the College of William and Mary), October 20, 1753; December 17, 1756 (the other workhouse had burned down "by accident"); Chamberlayne, ed., *Vestry Book, Wicomico Parish, Northumberland, 1703–1795,* 80; Chamberlayne, ed., *Vestry Book, Petsworth Parish, Gloucester, 1677–1793,* 326, 329, 355.

72. For descriptions of vestry houses, see *Vestry Book, Truro Parish,* February 19, 1750, February 23, 1767, in Philip Slaughter, *History of Truro Parish in Virginia,* ed. E. L. Goodwin (Philadelphia, 1908); *Vestry Book, Shelburne Parish, Loudoun County, 1771–1805* (ms., photocopy, Virginia State Library), November 30, 1772; Chamberlayne, ed., *Vestry Book, Blissland Parish, New Kent and James City, 1721–1786,* October 8, 1750; Chamberlayne, ed., *Vestry Book, Wicomico Parish, Northumberland, 1703–1795,*

October 24, 1774; November 18, 1772; in the latter entry the conversion of the new part of the old church was ordered for this purpose; C. G., Chamberlayne, ed., *Vestry Book, Kingston Parish, Gloucester, 1679–1796,* November 5, 1759; November 29, 1760; *Vestry Book, St. Mark's Parish, Culpepper County, 1730–1753* (ms., photocopy, Virginia state Library), October 9, 1733; Chamberlayne, ed., *Vestry Book, St. Paul's Parish, Hanover, 1706–1766,* May 19, 1747; October 22, 1772.

73. Brydon, *Virginia's Mother Church,* I, 383–85.

74. Chamberlayne, ed., *Vestry Book, St. Peter's Parish, New Kent and James City, 1684–1786,* 306, 310, 314, 316; Chamberlayne, ed., *Vestry Book, St. Paul's Parish, Hanover, 1706–1786,* 98ff., 112ff., 161, 336, 365, 369, 372, 395; Chamberlayne, ed., *The Vestry Book of Kingston Parish, Mathews County, Virginia (until May 1, 1791, Gloucester County), 1679–1796* (Richmond, 1929), 20–23.

75. R. A. Brock, ed., *The Vestry Book of Henrico Parish, Henrico County, Virginia, 1730–1773* (Richmond, 1874), passim; Chamberlayne, ed., *Vestry Book, St. Peter's Parish, New Kent and James City, 1684–1786,* 31ff.

76. Susie May Ames, *Studies of the Virginia Eastern Shore in the Seventeenth Century* (Richmond, 1940), 197.

77. Bruce, *Institutional History,* I, 38–42.

78. Ibid., I, 39; Hening, *Statutes at Large,* III, 170, 360; *Essex County Orders, 1745–1747* (Virginia State Library), 66; *Princess Anne County Orders, 1717–1728* (Virginia State Library), 320; *County Court Records,* passim.

79. *Northumberland County Orders, 1767–1770* (Virginia State Library), 438. An early act specified that any man three times convicted of drunkenness was not allowed to hold public office (Hening, *Statutes at Large,* I, 433).

80. *Journals, House of Burgesses, 1695–1702,* 64.

81. Ibid., *1742–1749,* 265.

82. Hening, *Statutes at Large,* VIII, 134–35.

83. Ibid., II, 51.

84. Ibid., I, 180; II, 48; III, 170–71, 360–61.

85. The information on land processioning is adapted from William H. Seiler, "Land Processioning in Colonial Virginia," *W & M Q,* 3rd ser., VI (1949), 416–36.

86. Hening, *Statutes at Large,* II, 103; examples concerning assignments by the vestries to work on highways and bridges may be found in Chamberlayne, ed., *Vestry Book, St. Peter's Parish, New Kent and James City, 1684–1786,* 9, 14, 38–39; and in Chamberlayne, ed., *Vestry Book, St. Paul's Parish, Hanover, 1706–1786,* 3, 18, 23.

87. Hening, *Statutes at Large,* IV, 134, 197, 241; *VMHB,* XX (1912), 158–78; *Journals, House of Burgesses, 1712–1726,* xlix, *1727–1740,* xviii, 50; examples showing compliance of the vestry with the tobacco counting acts may be found in the vestry books, e.g., Chamberlayne, ed., *Vestry Book, St. Paul's Parish, Hanover, 1706–1786,* 109–11, 122, 126; Chamberlayne, ed., *Vestry Book, St. Peter's Parish, New Kent and James City, 1684–1786,* 9–11, 15, 25–26, 33–34, 37.

The Responsible Gentry
of Colonial South Carolina:
A Study in Local Government,
1670-1770

RICHARD WATERHOUSE

In the pre-Revolutionary period, Charles Town, the only urban center of consequence south of Philadelphia, possessed many of the characteristics of a city-state.[1] In fulfilling its role as the port through which passed the major share of South Carolina's imports and exports, it dominated the colony's economic life. Moreover, since not only the colony's merchants but also the more substantial planters lived at least for the greater part of the year in Charles Town, it inevitably became the hub of the colony's social activity.[2] Finally, as the location of the governor's residence and the place of meeting for the Assembly, the Council, and the Courts of General Sessions and Common Pleas, Charles Town was the center of the colony's administrative, judicial, and political life. This dominance—economic, social, and political—was made still more nearly complete because the institutions that formed the backbone of local government in

Massachusetts and Virginia, namely, the town meeting and the county court, were never permanently established in South Carolina.

Institutions of local government did exist, however, in South Carolina in the form of vestries and road commissions. Moreover, justices of the peace and commissioners for particular projects, appointed by the governor and Assembly respectively, performed a number of duties at the local level. Historians have generally assumed not only that these institutions of local government were essentially insignificant, but have also argued that the planter and merchant members of the colony's elite were so preoccupied with the social pleasures to be found in Charles Town that they had little time to involve themselves in the administration of government at the local, or for that matter the central, level.[3]

Yet in the eighteenth century strong institutions of local government were the basis of political power and at the heart of political culture both in England and in most of the American colonies.[4] In this context it is unlikely that the South Carolina elite, sharing so many of the political attitudes and assumptions of, for example, the Virginia planters, were indifferent to the value of local government or to their responsibility as the accepted leaders of their society to provide government at the local level.[5] The elite were in fact, and such is the contention of this essay, very willing to serve as members of church vestries and road commissions, and, less frequently, as justices of the peace, and they performed the duties attached to these offices very effectively. They thereby acknowledged their social responsibilities, especially to the parish-based communities of the hinterland in which their plantations were located, and demonstrated their conviction that as members of the colony's elite, they possessed both the right and the duty to provide effective government at the local level.

The county courts in Virginia dispensed justice in cases of common and criminal law and equity, but also performed many administrative tasks, such as fixing tax rates, licensing taverns, determining the prices of certain goods and services, building and maintaining roads and bridges, and appointing specified county officers. In colonial South Carolina, however, no county court system was permanently established before 1769, and justices of the peace performed only minor legal and administrative duties.

Justices of the peace were appointed in South Carolina from the earliest times. Those nominated were appointed by the governor with the advice of the Council. Although justices possessed only relatively minor legal powers, they did have authority to determine all cases of debt involving up to £20 current money (South Carolina currency).[6] In 1746 the Assembly passed a law entrusting all debt cases involving £75 current money or less to two justices and three freeholders sitting as a court; however, this act was soon disallowed by the Privy Council.[7] Justices of the peace also had authority to levy fines on those who sold grain and bread at falsely declared weights.[8] In cases where one man's cattle caused damage on another's plantation, a justice could assess damages against the owner of the cattle, providing the assessed charges totaled £20 current money or less.[9] The justices also granted licenses to tavern keepers and peddlers and delivered vagrants to the South Carolina regiment's recruiting officer.[10] Their authority in dealing with offences against the law committed by blacks was far more extensive: two justices and three freeholders could try any blacks accused of a capital crime and pronounce the death sentence on those found guilty.[11]

County courts existed only briefly in South Carolina. In 1721 a county court was established in each Granville, Colleton, and Craven Counties, with two precinct courts installed in Berkeley County. Both the county and the precinct courts were designed to be courts of pleas, assize, and jail delivery, although the establishing act of 1721 provided that cases involving life and limb or debts of more than £25 sterling were still to be determined by the Court of General Sessions and Common Pleas meeting in Charles Town.[12] To what extent the county and precinct courts ever functioned in the 1720s is uncertain, but in 1731 the Assembly, acting on the advice of Governor Robert Johnson who was seeking the support of the Charles Town merchants, passed a law that allowed the plaintiff in any civil suit to choose the site of the trial; because most of South Carolina's creditors were merchants they invariably preferred the Charles Town Court of Common Pleas. This act effectively destroyed the county and precinct courts and, although the laws that had authorized their establishment remained on the books, the courts themselves in fact ceased to function.[13]

In Virginia, the county courts, with justices acting as their judges, exercised considerable authority in local affairs, and a man's ap-

pointment to the office of justice added considerably to his prestige.[14] It would seem from the claim of William Simpson, who wrote
a manual for South Carolina's justices, that the same was true in
this colony; he stated that the justices in South Carolina included
"the most sufficient persons" in each county, and certainly many
of South Carolina's wealthiest citizens were justices of the peace.[15]
Yet many of those nominated as justices, especially those living
in the areas most distant from Charles Town, were men of modest
economic circumstances. In 1737 the grand jury of the province
noted that "many are in the Commission of the Peace, who have
not so much as a Freehold or pay Five Pounds per Annum towards
the support of the Government"[16] Governor James Glen complained
in 1749 that so little regard was held for the office that it was difficult to persuade men to accept appointment as justices.[17] The lack
of power attached to the office seems to have accounted for its lack
of appeal. One of the objections to the act of 1747 allowing justices
to determine cases of debt involving more than £20 current money
was simply that many of the colony's justices were incompetent to
determine such cases.[18] Not only, in the grand jury's words, had the
office "become contemptible," but the justices did not always perform the duties required of them.[19] In cases brought before justices
of the peace that involved matters beyond their jurisdiction, they
were authorized to examine offenders and bind them over to the
next session of the Court of General Sessions. It was the duty of
justices to attend this court and report to it their proceedings involving informations, examination, and recognizances. Their failure
to make these reports on at least one occasion prompted the chief
justice, Robert Wright, to declare that in future those justices who
neglected this duty would be fined.[20]

It is likely that men of wealth and status declined to accept appointment as justices of the peace because of the restricted legal
authority attached to the office, more so than that the powers delegated to the justices remained limited because of the unavailability
of men of status and wealth (especially in the areas outside Charles
Town) to carry out the duties that were traditionally assigned, for
example, in Virginia and England, to the office. The fact was, as I
argue below, that men of wealth and status dominated both the
town and country vestries. The failure of the South Carolina Assembly to delegate more than minor powers to the justices resulted from

the fact that, at least before 1760, the colony's population remained confined to the low country, and the relative closeness of most inhabitants to Charles Town made for ease of access to the Courts of Common Pleas and General Sessions which met there: the establishment of courty courts with judicial powers comparable to those of Virginia was therefore unnecessary.

In the absence of strong county courts the most important institution of local government in colonial South Carolina was the parish vestry. Altogether, the South Carolina Assembly established a total of twenty-three parishes in the colony between 1706 and 1770. These parishes encompassed all the low country extending from the Atlantic coast to the fall line, as well as the greater part of the lower back country, stretching beyond the pine forests into the piedmont. However, no parishes were established in the western piedmont of the back country before the Revolution. The vestry minutes for ten of these parishes are extant, including those located in both the urban and rural low country as well as in the lower back country.

The first ten parishes were established in South Carolina by an act of 1706. For each parish there were to be two churchwardens and a vestry consisting of seven vestrymen, all of whom were required to be freeholders of or owners of taxable property in the parish and members of the Church of England. Elections of vestrymen were held annually, and all freeholders and persons holding taxable property in the parish were entitled to vote.[21] Although the act of 1706 limited the powers of the vestry to the maintenance of churches, parsonages, and glebes, the vestries in later years exercised jurisdiction over a much broader area of local affairs. Initially, care of the poor had been administered by the commissioners appointed by the Assembly, but a 1712 act transferred this authority to the vestries.[22] By this act immediate responsibility for raising the poor tax as well as for distributing the proceeds rested with the churchwardens, while overall supervision of caring for the poor was exercised by the vestry. In 1712 the Assembly passed a law establishing a free school in Charles Town and empowering the vestries in the country parishes to build parish schools with funds drawn from the public treasury, and to employ schoolmasters.[23] Although not legally authorized to do so, the vestries also occasionally exercised police and judicial authority. For example, in 1728 the St.

Helena's Parish vestry voted to prosecute those inhabitants of Beaufort owning lots in the town who had failed to conform to a law requiring them to build on those lots within a specified time.[24] Also, the vestry of Prince Frederick's once acted as a jury of inquest into the death of a servant;[25] and in 1772 the St. Philip's vestrymen, after investigating the conduct of people who had attended a funeral, voted to present the offenders for prosecution in the Court of General Sessions.[26]

The churchwardens performed duties in areas in which the vestrymen had no authority. Their most important function was to supervise the conduct of elections to the Assembly. The elections were always held at the various parish churches, and the churchwardens ensured that the correct voting procedures were followed, counted the votes, and gave formal notice of the winners. In addition to these responsibilities the churchwardens enforced the laws relating to the sabbath and safeguarded the firearms of all who entered the churches.[27]

The parishes for which vestry minutes are extant include St. John's Berkeley, St. John's Colleton, Christ Church, St. Stephen's, St. Helena's, Prince Frederick's, St. Mathew's, St. David's, St. Michael's, and St. Philip's. Certain of these parishes had characteristics in common. St. John's Berkeley, St. John's Colleton, and Christ Church, the country parishes among them closest to Charles Town, encompassed some of the colony's earliest settled areas. These parishes, too, were more densely populated than the other country parishes listed. St. Stephen's, St. Helena's, and Prince Frederick's enclosed areas further removed from Charles Town, areas which although they were settled at about the same time as the first three parishes in the case of St. Stephen's and St. Helena's or slightly later in the case of Prince Frederick's, nevertheless contained a relatively smaller number of settlers, at least during the early decades of the eighteenth century.[28] The area of the lower back country that in 1768 was included within the boundaries of St. Mathew's and St. David's remained sparsely settled until the 1750s. Most of those who lived in these parishes, therefore, were newcomers to the area and in many cases to the colony itself. Moreover, whereas large plantations worked by gangs of black slaves were typical of the low country parishes, small farms worked by their owners were characteristic of the lower back country parishes. St. Philip's and St. Michael's were of course distinguished by the fact that they were the two Charles Town parishes. The parishes can usefully be grouped in terms of their shared characteristics as reflected by an analysis of vestry and churchwarden membership for all years up to and including 1770. In St. Mathew's and St. David's, both formed in 1768, the membership of the vestries is examined up to 1776.

St. John's Berkeley and Christ Church Parishes were among the colony's original parishes, both established in 1706.[29] St. John's Colleton was originally part of St. Paul's Parish, but in 1734 the sea islands formerly included within the boundaries of St. Paul's were declared to constitute a separate parish and named St. John's Colleton.[30] In the first decades of the eighteenth century not only was St. John's Berkeley one of the colony's most populous parishes but also one of the most prosperous. Tax returns for 1720 indicate that at this time the inhabitants of only two other parishes owned more land, and the residents of only three other parishes owned more slaves, than those of St. John's Berkeley (see table 1). In later years, as the soil in the parish began to wear out, many residents moved into the colony's less settled parishes.[31] As a result, by 1769 the St. John's residents ranked sixth in terms of land and eighth in terms of slaves owned (see table 2). The Christ Church planters were never as prosperous as those of St. John's Berkeley. Indeed, throughout the colonial period the inhabitants of Christ Church owed less land and fewer slaves than the residents of most of the colony's parishes. As was the case in St. John's Berkeley, soil exhaustion in Christ Church led to an outward movement of people to the extent that in 1741, the parish's minister, Levi Durand, claimed that there were only ten families of "easy circumstances" in the whole parish.[32] By contrast, the planters of St. John's Colleton, whose land was especially suitable for rice-growing, remained prosperous throughout the entire colonial period.

Some men of modest means were elected to the offices of vestryman and churchwarden in these same three parishes, but throughout the period before 1770 the majority of those elected to these positions were wealthy (see table 3).[33] Moreover, especially in St. John's Berkeley and St. John's Colleton and to a lesser extent in Christ Church, it was the old settled families that dominated vestry membership. For example, in St. John's Berkeley Parish, six families that had arrived in the colony before 1700, the Broughtons, Cordes, Harles-

TABLE 1.
Wealth of Parish Residents, 1720.

Parish	Slaves	Land Acreage	Acres per Slave
St. Andrew's	2,493	197,168¾	79.09
St. James Goose Creek	2,027	153,267½	75.61
St. Paul's	1,634	187,976	115.04
St. John's (Berkeley)	1,439	181,375	126.04
St. Philip's (Charles Town)	1,390	64,265	46.23
St. Thomas and St. Dennis	942	74,580	79.17
Christ Church	637	57,580	90.39
St. James Santee	584	117,274	200.81
St. George's	536	37,457	69.88
St. Bartholomew's	144	30,559	212.22
St. Helena's	42	51,817	1233.74
Total	11,868	1,163,319¼[a]	—

Source: South Carolina Archives, Transcripts of Records in the British Public Record Office Relating to South Carolina, IX, 22–23.

a. In the original the total number of acres was listed as 1,163,239¼. This error was first discovered by Converse D. Clowse, *Economic Beginnings in South Carolina, 1670–1730* (Columbia, S.C., 1971), p. 225n.

tons, Keiths, Lejaus, and Ravenels served 146 of the total 236 terms served on the vestry in the period from 1731 to 1770. In St. John's Colleton, those who were members of families that had settled in the colony before 1700 were elected to 82 percent of all terms served as vestrymen and 71 percent of all terms served as churchwardens.[34] This is not to suggest that later settled families were altogether excluded from vestry membership in these or other early settled parishes.[35] Because many of Christ Church's first settled families moved to the later settled parishes in search of virgin land, they failed to dominate vestry membership to the same extent as their counterparts had in St. John's Berkeley and St. John's Colleton. Their departure opened the way for the election to church office of greater numbers of newcomers.[36]

This evidence suggests an important conclusion: in the first settled parishes there was a strong sense of commitment to the parish society, particularly among the longer established and wealthier families. Such families dominated vestry membership, especially of St. John's Berkeley and St. John's Colleton, as a result of their willingness to serve multiple terms. Even those who owned houses in Charles Town and listed that town as their place of residence chose

TABLE 2.
Wealth of Parish Residents, 1769.

Parish	Slaves[a]	Land Acreage[a]	Acres per Slave
St. Michael's and St.			
Philip's (Charles Town)	26,695	938,124	35.14
St. Bartholomew's	5,494	138,217	25.16
St. Paul's	4,919	114,409	23.26
Prince Frederick's	3,772	160,863	42.65
Prince George's	3,366	153,378	45.57
St. John's Colleton	3,321	64,331	19.37
St. George's	2,880	87,022	30.22
St. John's Berkeley	2,680	102,164	38.12
St. Andrew's	2,640	65,398	24.77
St. James Santee	2,543	85,897	33.78
St. Helena's	2,467	60,871	24.67
Prince William's	2,103	56,829	27.02
St. Luke's	2,091	52,916	25.31
St. Thomas and St. Dennis	2,082	69,420	33.34
Christ Church	2,076	48,574	23.40
St. Stephen's	1,988	78,919	39.70
St. James Goose Creek	1,492	51,006	34.19
All Saints'	1,489	71,880	48.27
St. David's	1,276	100,194	78.52
St. Mathew's	1,121	97,608	87.07
St. Peter's	1,082	40,757	37.67
St. Mark's	599	31,665	52.86
Back country	3,552	559,429	157.50
Total	81,728	3,269,871	—

Source: South Carolina Archives, Public Treasury of South Carolina, General Tax Receipts and Payments, 1761–1769 (1771), 64–65.

a. Total land and slave holdings of taxable inhabitants of each parish, not only in their home parish but in all others as well.

to hold office in the parishes in which their families had long been identified, rather than to serve on the vestries of either of the town parishes.[37] These families were involved in the social activities as well as the political life of the parish communities. In Prince William's Parish, for example, Stephen Bull of Sheldon usually entertained "the more respectable part" of the congregation at his plantation house every Sunday after divine service. The church was another social gathering place in this parish, with as many as seventy carriages likely to be drawn up before it every Sunday.[38] In addition, the more well-to-do families in each parish constantly engaged in social visiting.[39] Finally, the existence of parish-based commu-

TABLE 3.

Characteristics of Vestrymen and Churchwardens.

Parish	Years Vestry Minutes Extant (Before 1770)	Mean Value of Estates (£ Sterling)	Average Slaveholdings	Average Term Served on Vestry	Average Term Served as Churchwarden	Total Office-holders	Total Extant Inventories of Officeholders
St. John's Berkeley	1731–70	2,954	75	4.7	1.3	73	35
Christ Church	1708–59	3,176	42	3.7	1.6	64	26
St. John's Colleton	1738–70	3,162	63	4.4	2.5	50	30
St. Helena's	1726–70	3,061	49	5.9	1.3	91	37
Prince Frederick's	1734–63	1,042	20	4.0	1.5	70	28
St. Stephen's	1754–70	3,767	70	6.2	1.2	35	10
St. Mathew's[a]	1768–76	787	26	2.5	1.4	38	8
St. David's[a,b]	1768–76			1.7	1.4	43	2
St. Philip's	1732–70	8,934	87	3.8	1.4	84	23
St. Michael's	1759–70	8,000	80	2.3	1.6	40	14

a. Because St. Mathew's and St. David's were both founded in 1768 the membership of their vestries is included for all years up to 1776.
b. No average estate or slaveholdings included because inventories of only two officeholders are extant.

169

nities is reflected in the fact that many of the most prominent families resident in particular parishes were closely bound together by ties of marriage. In Christ Church, for example, Allens and Maybanks, Bartons and Cooks, Benisons and Capers, Bonds and Maybanks, Bullocks and Brewtons, Capers and Maybanks, Dorrills and Cooks, Gibbes and Benisons, Hexts and Boones, Holmes and Fowlers, Brewtons and Milners, and Brewtons and Pinckneys, all of whom were represented on the vestry, were related by marriage.[40]

The second group of parishes, including St. Helena's, St. Stephen's, and Prince Frederick's, shows certain similarities with the first group, especially in the areas of economic status and domination of vestry membership.[41] First, although the St. Helena's and St. Stephen's planters were collectively among the poorest in the province (see tables 1 and 2), the majority of those elected to church office were nevertheless men of high economic status. Those elected in Prince Frederick's, however, tended to be of lesser economic standing (see table 3).[42] Second, the tendency in St. John's Berkeley, St. John's Colleton, and Christ Church for the old settled families to dominate vestry membership was repeated in St. Stephen's, Prince Frederick's, and to a lesser extent in St. Helena's. A group of eight families that had arrived in South Carolina before 1700 served 97 of the total 118 terms of the vestry of St. Stephen's between 1754 and 1770.[43] In Prince Frederick's, 64.3 percent of those elected to church office were members of families that had settled in the province before 1700: 63.1 percent of all terms served as vestrymen and 66.7 percent of all terms as churchwardens.

In St. Helena's, however, the dominance of vestry membership by the old settled families was far less pronounced. The families that had settled in the colony before 1700 served only 115 out of the total 311 terms on the St. Helena's vestry (37 percent). The fact was that although the area encompassed by the parish was first settled during the early period of the colony's history, St. Helena's remained much less densely settled throughout the colonial period than some of the old tidewater parishes. The existence of uncultivated land in the parish continued to attract settlers throughout the colonial period. St. Helena's, therefore, had the characteristics of both an early and a late settled parish, and this is reflected in the membership of the parish vestry. In addition, repeating the example of those Charles Town residents who were elected to the vestries of

St. John's Berkeley, St. John's Colleton, and Christ Church, some officeholders in the St. Helena's and St. Stephen's vestries also lived in Charles Town and listed that town as their place of residence.[44]

Prince Frederick's, however, stands out in that no Charles Town residents, either planters or merchants, were elected to its vestry. The parish's distance from Charles Town was one factor in this phenomenon, since it meant that the Charles Town residents owning land in Prince Frederick's probably visited their plantations less frequently than those owning land closer to Charles Town, and hence would have been unable to attend vestry meetings. A perhaps more important explanation, however, was the relative newness of these families to Prince Frederick's. Here, the merchants had not inherited plantations held by their families for many years, but had acquired the land themselves with profits from trade.[45] As a result, these men had no particular identification with the parish itself or with the families settled there. On the other hand, those Charles Town residents who had inherited plantations in the early settled parishes that had formerly belonged to their fathers and grandfathers, maintained a strong sense of identification with those parishes and the families who lived there.

The third group consists of the two lower back country parishes, St. David's and St. Mathew's, both founded in 1768, and encompassing areas settled later than those of the parishes hitherto discussed.[46] Although the men elected as church officeholders here were considerably less wealthy than those elected in the parishes examined above, they were still probably among the wealthiest inhabitants of their parishes (see table 3). In contrast to the situation in the older tidewater parishes, no families in the lower back country parishes emerged to assume positions of political leadership. The thirty-eight men elected to church office in St. Mathew's between 1768 and 1776 represented thirty-three families, while the forty-three men who were elected in St. David's in the same period represented thirty-seven families.[47] This no doubt resulted from the fact that, as recent arrivals, the families who settled in these parishes had no particular identification either with the parishes or with the other families who lived there.

Like their counterparts who were elected to church office in the old tidewater parishes, those who served as vestrymen and churchwardens of the two Charles Town parishes, St. Philip's and St.

Michael's, were for the most part wealthy men. The mean values of the estates of the officeholders in St. Philip's and St. Michael's were £8,934 and £8,000, and their average slaveholdings eighty-seven and eighty, respectively.[48] In contrast to the practice of the tidewater parishes, however, in neither St. Philip's nor St. Michael's was there a tendency for the old settled families to dominate membership. For example, the forty men elected vestrymen and churchwardens of St. Michael's represented a total of thirty-six families. The rapid turnover in vestry membership in St. Philip's and St. Michael's reflected the fact that in Charles Town there existed a large pool of qualified men available to serve.

Moreover, whereas most of those elected vestrymen and churchwardens of the country parishes were planters, the overwhelming majority of those elected in St. Philip's and St. Michael's were merchants.[49] Indeed, the Charles Town merchants exerted a degree of political influence that extended beyond their predominance among the vestrymen and churchwardens of St. Michael's and St. Philip's, to include, as we shall see, dominance of the offices of Charles Town's town government. In the Assembly too, the merchants played a key role, for although the planters were elected to that body in greater numbers, it was nevertheless the merchants who, by controlling the most important committees, managed the business of the house and provided it with leadership.[50]

Few, if any South Carolinians were as committed as Landon Carter and other Virginians to the notion that public service was the hallmark of the man of virtue and the mark of a gentleman.[51] But the elite's dominance of vestry membership throughout South Carolina suggests that they were committed to the belief that they possessed the right to provide political leadership not only at the colony but also at the local level. Whereas 20.9 percent of all men who died in South Carolina between 1736 and 1775 and whose inventories are extant owned estates valued at £1,000 or more, 65.9 percent of those who served as vestrymen and churchwardens before 1770 in the parishes included in this discussion and whose inventories are extant were possessed of personalty valued at more than £1,000 sterling (see tables 4 and 5). The wealthier planters were strongly represented in the country vestries, and the merchants dominated the membership of St. Philip's and St. Michael's.

The duties of vestrymen and churchwardens in the country parishes

TABLE 4.
Value of Estates, 1736-75 (All Extant Inventories).

Value (£)	Number of Estates	Percentage of Total	Cumulative Percentage
1- 1,000	3516	79.08	79.08
1,001- 2,000	526	11.83	90.91
2,001- 3,000	170	3.82	94.73
3,001- 4,000	70	1.57	96.30
4,001- 5,000	47	1.05	97.35
5,001-10,000	79	1.77	99.12
10,001-60,000	35	0.78	99.90
Total	4443	—	—

TABLE 5.
Value of Estates of Vestrymen and Churchwardens,
1736-75.

Value (£)	Number of Estates	Percentage of Total	Cumulative Percentage
1- 1,000	73	34.06	34.06
1,001- 2,000	51	23.82	57.88
2,001- 3,000	24	11.2	69.08
3,001- 4,000	14	6.54	75.62
4,001- 5,000	8	3.73	79.35
5,001-10,000	25	11.68	91.03
10,001-60,000	19	8.86	99.89
Total	214	—	—

were relatively light. By law, the vestries were required to meet at least four times a year, but the business that had to be settled by the country vestries was often so little that they met less often. Between 1726 and 1770, for example, the St. Helena's vestry met on the average less than three times a year. Occasionally, as happened in St. Bartholomew's in 1726, the parishioners neglected to elect a vestry at all.[52] In contrast, so numerous were the Charles Town poor that the St. Philip's vestry, whose main responsibility was in caring for these people, met frequently.[53] Indeed, so much time and effort was required, especially by the churchwardens, in providing for the poor, that the office came to be regarded as particularly burdensome. "I have lately been Elected into an Office which is attended with some trouble," wrote the merchant Robert Pringle in 1740, "but there is no dispensing with it as it comes in Course that is being one of the Church Wardens."[54]

Those who refused to serve as churchwardens when elected were liable by an act of 1706 to a fine of £10 current money of South Carolina (less than £10s. sterling). This amount was raised to £10 proclamation money in 1758 (approximately £7 sterling).[55] However, despite the nominal size of the fine levied before 1758, few men declined to act as churchwardens. Including all parishes covered by this study, there were only twelve such instances before 1770, and all but two occurred in St. Philip's.[56] Beyond their commitment to the parish-based communities and their belief that they possessed the right to political leadership, at the local as well as the colony level, those members of South Carolina's elite who served as church officeholders, and in particular those who acted as vestrymen and churchwardens of St. Philip's, apparently did so from a concept of duty.

The government of Charles Town was directed not only by elected church officials, but by elected town officials as well. This puts it in contrast with New York and Philadelphia, which were incorporated cities, and also with Boston and the other major New England towns, which governed through the town meeting. The town officials included commissioners of the streets, commissioners of the workhouse and market, wood coal measurers, firemasters, and packers. At first, the Assembly had appointed these officers, but in later years they were elected annually at the same time and place as those chosen as vestrymen and churchwardens of St. Philip's.[57] The firemasters inspected buildings to ensure that their owners left ready the correct number of buckets and fire ladders; the commissioners of streets supervised the cleaning and resurfacing of roads; the packers ensured that all goods exported from Charles Town were properly packed and of sufficient quality; the wood and coal measurers made certain that wood and coal were sold at the prices prescribed by law; and the commissioners of the workhouse and market supervised the operation of those institutions.[58]

In the same way they dominated the membership of the vestries of the Charles Town parishes, the merchants also predominated among the elected town officials—many served at various times as both church and town officials. The only office to which a majority of those elected were not merchants was packer. The nature of the work involved here required that officeholders be qualified coopers and it was usually tradesmen of this class who were chosen.

After the merchants, it was the Charles Town mechanics and tradesmen who were elected in the largest numbers as town officials. Comparatively few of these men also served as elected church officeholders. In fact, in the period before 1770, only six mechanics in total were chosen to either of the town's vestries. However, this did not mean that tradesmen made up the majority of those town officials who did not also hold church office. In fact, 71 of the 173 men in this category were merchants, while, of the rest, only 31 can be identified as tradesmen.

The average value of the estates of the town officeholders, excluding those who also served as church officials, was considerably lower than that of the church officials; nevertheless, there were among the town officials many men of considerable economic standing. The mean value of their estates was £2,704 sterling, and, on the average, they owned sixty-four slaves.[59] Many Charles Town tradesmen were also plantation and slave owners, and these men frequently were elected as town officials. At the same, some Charles Town merchants, although chosen as town officials, were never elected to the vestry of either of the town parishes. Several of these men, especially those whose families had for some time owned plantations in the country parishes, may have been elected to the vestries of the parishes in which those plantations were located. Others, however, can be identified as dissenters who were legally unqualified and apparently personally unwilling to serve as elected officeholders in an episcopal church. Nonconformists had been settled in Charles Town from its very beginnings, and during the colonial period Presbyterians, Congregationalists, Baptists, Quakers, Arians, Lutherans, and Huguenots all built churches within the town.[60] A number of the merchants who were elected as town officers but never chosen as church officers were members of the nonconformists churches. On the other hand, a few dissenters, apparently untroubled by personal scruples and although in violation of the law were elected to the vestries of St. Philip's and St. Michael's.

An examination of the membership of the Fortifications Commission further reveals the merchants' dominance of Charles Town's institutions of government. This commission, the most prestigious in the colony, supervised the construction and maintenance especially of Charles Town's fortifications but also of those elsewhere in the colony.[61] The twelve members of this commission between 1755 and 1760 included eight merchants, a lawyer, a bricklayer, the colony's powder receiver, and one man of undetermined profession. Given the duties of those serving on a commission of this kind, the reason for membership of both a bricklayer and the powder receiver is obvious enough. The fact that no planters were members, and that apart from the necessary bricklayer and powder receiver, eight of the remaining ten members were merchants, indicates the degree to which the government of Charles Town was controlled by this group.

The concern of South Carolina's colonial elite to provide political leadership at the local level is reflected again in its dominance of the road commissions. In Virginia, the maintenance of roads and bridges was supervised by the county courts. In North Carolina, precinct courts administered the upkeep of roads and bridges, although after 1734 in the colony's southern precincts these duties were carried out by commissioners appointed by the Assembly.[62] In South Carolina until 1721, the Assembly appointed commissioners to supervise the construction and repair of particular roads, bridges, and ferries.[63] By an act of 1721, however, the Assembly established permanent road commissions in each parish. Additionally, some of the larger parishes were divided into precincts, each with its own road commission.

The authority of these commissioners extended to the building and maintenance of all ferries, roads, and bridges within the bounds of their parish or precinct. Each set of commissioners was assigned the power to levy assessments on the local inhabitants, as well as to summon all the residents of the parish or precinct and require that either they or their slaves work for a certain number of days each year at repairing the local roads, bridges, and ferries. The law further provided that each set of commissioners was to meet at least twice a year, with those who neglected to attend such meetings liable to a fine of £10 current money for each time absent. Finally, while naming the first sets of commissioners for each parish and precinct, the act also specified that in case commissioners died, left the province, or neglected their duty, the remaining commissioners were to choose replacements.[64]

At first there was probably not a close relationship between the membership of the permanent road commissions and that of the vestries. Only three of the nine men appointed by the act of 1721 as permanent road commissioners in St. Helena's, for example, served as parish officials in 1726 or afterward.[65] However, a very close relationship emerged later. For example, the twenty road commissioners of St. John's Berkeley between 1760 and 1770 included seventeen who were also either vestrymen or churchwardens,[66] and all seven road commissioners of St. Stephen's when that parish was established in 1754 were at one time or another elected as church officials in that parish.[67]

In each parish or precinct the remaining road commissioners named replacements for those who died or neglected their duty, but because none of the journals of the road commissions are extant, with the exception of that for St. John's Berkeley 1760–70, no comprehensive list of those who were members of the permanent road commissions can be compiled. Yet evidence is available that indicates that these commissioners tended to be men of high economic status. The mean value of the estates of the men appointed as the original commissioners by the act of 1721 was £2,141 sterling, and, on the average, they owned sixty-eight slaves.[68] The overlapping membership of the road commissions and the vestries further suggests that the road commissioners were men of high economic standing. However, these road commissioners in the area beyond the tidewater were usually of more modest means. Thus, the average estate value and slaveholdings of those appointed by an act of 1747 for the lower back country were £595 sterling and thirteen, respectively.[69]

Despite the existence of permanent road commissions within each parish, the Assembly continued to appoint commissioners to undertake the construction and repair of particular roads and bridges. These commissioners served less frequently as church officials than did the members of the permanent road commissions. Thus, only three of the thirteen men named to supervise the construction of particular roads and ferries in St. Helena's Parish between 1733 and 1755 were ever elected to church office in that parish,[70] while none of those appointed in St. John's Colleton by acts of 1751 and 1758 were ever elected to church office in that parish.[71] Yet despite the fact that many of the commissioners named to supervise particular projects never served as elected church officeholders, the members of these commissions were mostly drawn from the ranks of the wealthier planters (see table 6).

At various times the Assembly also appointed commissioners to cut and clear particular creeks and rivers. Again there does not appear to have been much overlap between these commissioners and elected church officeholders. Only three of the ten men nominated by acts of 1738 and 1753 to clear a section of the Black River where it passed through Prince Frederick's Parish were also elected to church office in that parish.[72] Included in the eight men appointed by acts of 1717 and 1733 to clear creeks in Christ Church were only two who also served as vestrymen and churchwardens in the parish.[73] Nevertheless, as table 7 indicates, the majority of those who were nominated as commissioners to clear creeks and rivers were wealthy men with more than 60 percent of them owning estates valued at more than £1,000 sterling.

It is clear that apart from those who served as vestrymen, churchwardens, and permanent road commissioners, there existed in each parish a pool of planters, a large number of whom belonged to the wealthiest 20 percent of the population. These men made up the majority of those appointed as commissioners of particular public works at the local level. In this manner the colony's economic elite extended its supervision to all levels of local government.

Neither the permanent road commissioners nor those appointed for particular projects were always thorough in the performance of their duties. In the period before 1770 the permanent road commissioners of Christ Church, St. James Santee, St. James Goose Creek, St. Thomas and St. Dennis, and John's Island, as well as the commissioners of six particular projects, were presented for neglect by the province's grand jury.[74] Generally, however, the commissions functioned effectively. The Dutch engineer John William Gerard De Brahm had only praise for the manner in which South Carolina's roads and bridges had been constructed; and John Bartram, a Philadelphia naturalist who visited South Carolina in 1765, claimed that "no province in America generally has finer roads."[75] The fact that those appointed as permanent road commissioners, together with those nominated to oversee particular projects, were drawn from the ranks of the colony's wealthier inhabitants, combined with the fact

TABLE 6.

Value of Estates of Commissioners of Particular Roads,
Bridges and Ferries, 1736–75.

Value (£)	Number of Estates	Percentage of Total	Cumulative Percentage
1- 1,000	57	43.80	43.80
1,001- 2,000	35	26.92	70.72
2,001- 3,000	15	11.53	82.25
3,001- 4,000	4	3.06	85.31
4,001- 5,000	7	5.37	90.68
5,001-10,000	6	4.61	95.29
10,001-20,000	6	4.61	99.90
Total	130	—	—

TABLE 7.

Value of Estates of Commissioners for Clearing and
Cutting Rivers and Creeks, 1736–75.

Value (£)	Number of Estates	Percentage of Total	Cumulative Percentage
1- 1,000	26	36.04	36.04
1,001- 2,000	23	31.97	68.01
2,001- 3,000	9	12.49	80.50
3,001- 4,000	5	6.93	87.43
4,001- 5,000	2	2.76	90.19
5,001-10,000	6	8.33	98.52
10,000-20,000	1	1.38	99.90
Total	72	—	—

that those appointed usually performed their duties conscientiously
and efficiently, further indicates that the South Carolina elite believed that it was their duty to provide effective leadership at the
local level.

The fact that such strong institutions of local government as existed in Virginia and Massachusetts failed to develop in South
Carolina resulted neither from indifference on the part of the merchant and planter elite nor from the phenomenon of a jealous Commons House of Assembly's declining to share its right and privileges
with local institutions.[76] Rather, this failure was the consequence of
settlement patterns, which in turn resulted from geographic circumstances. Carolina society was much smaller and more compact than,

for example, Virginia's, and as long as the population remained confined to the low country, the relative proximity of most colonists to Charles Town, combined with the excellent road and river system, made for ease of access to the legislative, administrative, and judicial institutions in Charles Town.

Both in the hinterland and in Charles Town itself the functions of local government were adequately and efficiently performed by the vestrymen and churchwardens, the elected town officials, the road and creek commissioners, and to a lesser extent the justices of the peace. Occasionally demands were made that the institutions of local government be strengthened, but the proposals made to this end were modest in content and unaccompanied by pressure from the hinterland communities.[77] It is worth noting that when during the course of the 1750s and 1760s the emigration of large numbers of people into the back country was accompanied by a demand there for strong institutions of local government—a demand stimulated by the sheer distance of the new areas of settlement from Charles Town—the Assembly responded with understanding and indeed alacrity. This response culminated in 1769 with the passing of the Circuit Court Act which established in the back country four circuit courts with highest jurisdiction in both criminal and civil matters.[78]

The institutions and offices of local government in colonial South Carolina were dominated by the wealthy planters and merchants, a dominance that grew from their sense of responsibility especially to their local communities and their belief that it was their particular duty to provide political leadership. Some men of modest means, including small planters and tradesmen, participated in government at the local level, but the majority of those holding local office were drawn from the colony's elite.[79] The most powerful and hardworking local government officials in the colony were the vestrymen, churchwardens, and town officials of St. Philip's. The domination of these offices by the merchants reflected their powerful political position. In the Assembly, too, although outnumbered by the planters, the merchants dominated political leadership through their control of the key committees. Finally, it might be suggested that in South Carolina, as elsewhere, there existed a close relationship not only between the rise of the Commons House of Assembly to a position of increased power and prestige and the emergence of an economic and social elite,[80] but also between the establishment of institutions of local government in the early years of the eighteenth century and the emergence in the same period of an elite struggling to establish its political identity and authority.

NOTES

1. Carl Bridenbaugh, *Myths and Realities: Societies of the Colonial South* (New York, 1968), 59–60; M. Eugene Sirmans, *Colonial South Carolina: A Political History, 1663–1763* (Chapel Hill, N.C., 1966), 254–55.

2. Bridenbaugh, *Myths and Realities,* 54–118; Lewis E. Frisch, "The Fraternal and Charitable Societies of Colonial South Carolina," B.A. thesis (Johns Hopkins University, 1969); Mark A. DeWolfe, ed., *Journal of Josiah Quincy, Junior, 1773, Proceedings of the Massachusetts Historical Society,* XLIX (1916), 424–81.

3. Bridenbaugh, *Myths and Realities,* 75, 116; Sirmans, *Colonial South Carolina,* 245, 250–51.

4. J. H. Plumb, *Sir Robert Walpole: The Making of a Statesman* (London, 1956), 42–54; Michael Zuckerman, *Peaceable Kingdoms: New England Towns in the Eighteenth Century* (New York, 1970), 10–45; Charles S. Sydnor, *American Revolutionaries in the Making: Political Practices in Washington's Virginia* (New York, 1965), 74–85.

5. For the best analysis of these attitudes, see Robert Weir, " 'The Harmony We Were Famous For': An Interpretation of Pre-Revolution South Carolina Politics," *William and Mary Quarterly,* 3rd ser., XXVI (October 1969), 473–501.

6. David J. McCord and Thomas Cooper, eds., *The Statutes at Large of South Carolina,* 10 vols. (Columbia, S.C., 1836–41), III, 268–69. This act superseded a 1721 law which limited the jurisdiction of justices to cases involving less than £10 current money (ibid., II, 131–32).

7. South Carolina Archives (hereafter, SCA), Transcripts of Records in the British Public Record Office Relating to South Carolina (hereafter, BPRO), XXIII, 184–85.

8. William Simpson, *The Practical Justice of the Peace and Parish Officer, of His Majesty's Province of South Carolina* (Charles Town, S.C., 1761), 49.

9. Ibid., 67.

10. McCord and Cooper, *Statutes,* IV, 51–52, 158–62; George C. Rogers, Jr., *The History of Georgetown County, South Carolina* (Columbia, 1970), 67.

11. McCord and Cooper, *Statutes,* VII, 343–47, 352–65, 371–84, 385–97, 397–417.

12. Ibid., 166–76, 178–83.

13. Sirmans, *Colonial South Carolina,* 166.

14. I. Ferguson, "County Courts in Virginia, 1700–1830," *North Carolina Historical Review* (hereafter, *NCHR*), VIII (January 1931), 14–40.

15. Simpson, *The Practical Justice of the Peace,* 1. For lists of those named to this office before 1770, see A. S. Salley, ed., *Journal of His Majesty's Council for South Carolina,* May 29, 1721–June 10, 1721 (Atlanta, 1930), 12–13; *South Carolina Gazette,* June 15, 1734; April 12, 1737; November 4, 1756; March 28, 1761; April 3, 1762; May 9, 1768; February 2 and October 18, 1769; October 18, 1770.

16. *South Carolina Gazette,* November 15, 1737.

17. SCA, BPRO, XXIII, 356–57: James Glen, "A Description of South Carolina," in *Historical Collections of South Carolina,* ed. Bartholomew Rivers Carroll, 2 vols. (New York, 1836), II, 221.

18. SCA, BPRO, XXII, 22; XXIII, 85.

19. *South Carolina Gazette,* November 5, 1737.

20. Ibid., February 10, 1733.

21. McCord and Cooper, *Statutes,* II, 242–43. For different election procedures in Virginia, see W. H. Seiler, "The Anglican Parish in Virginia," in *Seventeenth Century America: Essays in Colonial History,* ed. James Morton Smith (Chapel Hill, N.C. 1959), 126.

22. McCord and Cooper, *Statutes,* II, 78, 135–36, 593–98, 606–7.

23. Ibid., II, 395.

24. A. S. Salley, ed., *Minutes of the Vestry of St. Helena's Parish, South Carolina, 1726–1812* (Columbia, S.C., 1919), 8.

25. E. C. Hannum, "The Parish in South Carolina, 1706–1868," M.A. thesis (University of South Carolina, 1970), 49–50; E. J. Boucher, "Vestrymen and Churchwardens in South Carolina, 1706–1778," M.A. thesis (University of South Carolina, 1948), 22.

26. Boucher, "Vestrymen and Churchwardens."

27. McCord and Cooper, *Statutes,* II, 396–99, 683–91; III, 50–53, 135–40; Hannum, "The Parish in South Carolina," 48.

28. SCA, BPRO, IX, 22–23.

29. Vestry Minutes of St. John's Berkeley, 1731–1911, Dalcho Historical Society, Charleston, S.C. (hereafter, DHS); Vestry Minutes of Christ Church, 1708–1759, DHS.

30. Vestry Minutes of St. John's Colleton, 1738–1874, DHS.

31. Transcripts, A21, 82–83, Reverend Bryan Hunt to the Secretary, May 6, 1728; B5, 416 Reverend Levi Durand to the Secretary, November 18, 1763; B5, 418, Reverend Levi Durand to the Secretary, October 1, 1760, Library of Congress, Society for the Propagation of the Gospel (hereafter, SPG).

32. Ibid., B10, 354, Reverend Levi Durand to the Secretary, December 29, 1741.

33. For examples of men of modest means elected to the vestries of St. John's Berkeley and Christ Church, see Richard Waterhouse, "South Carolina's Colonial Elite: A Study in the Social Structure and Political Culture of a Southern Colony, 1670–1760," Ph.D. diss. (Johns Hopkins University, 1973), 216, 221.

34. These families were Arnold, Boone, Cole, Davis, Gibbes, Hext, Ladson, Mathews, Middleton, Raven, Sams, Stanyarne, Turguit, Underwood, and Waight.

35. For example, John Colleton, who came to South Carolina in the 1720s, was twelve times a vestryman of St. John's Berkeley, and both his sons, Peter and John, were elected to office in that parish.

36. Thus, of the 64 men who served as vestrymen or churchwardens of Christ Church, 1703–59, only twenty-eight were from families that had arrived in the colony before 1700. Further, men in this category were elected to only 34 percent of all terms served on the vestry and twenty-nine percent of all terms served as churchwardens.

37. Those elected to church office in St. John's Berkeley who owned houses in Charles Town included Elias Ball, Sr., Elias Ball, Jr., Nathaniel Broughton, Thomas Broughton, Daniel Huger, and Isaac Mazyck. The Charles Town–based merchants and lawyers who were elected to the Christ Church vestry included John Atkins, William Boone, George Logan, Jacob Motte, and Andrew Rutledge. Of those elected to church office in St. John's Colleton, William Boone, James Carson, John Gibbs, Alexander, Hugh, and Thomas Hext, and Alexander McGilvrey, all owned houses in Charles Town. Boone, Carson, and two of the Hexts listed Charles Town as their place of residence.

38. Frederick Dalcho, *An Historical Account of the Protestant Episcopal Church in South Carolina* (Charleston, S.C., 1820), 383.

39. Elise Pinckney, ed., *The Letterbook of Eliza Lucas Pinckney* (Chapel Hill, N.C., 1972), 34–35.

40. *South Carolina Historical Magazine* (hereafter, *SCHM*), II (April 1901, 141, 242; XX) (January 1919), 66, 69; XXI (April 1920), 73; XI (April 1910), 116. The parish register for St. Helena's indicates that many of those who held church office in this parish too were bound together by ties of marriage. For the register, see Joseph W. Barnwell and

Mabel L. Webber, "St. Helena's Parish Register," *SCHM*, XXIII (January, April, July, October 1922), 8–25, 46–71, 102–51, 171–204.

41. Salley, ed., *Minutes of the Vestry of St. Helena's Parish;* Minutes of Prince Frederick Winyah, 1734–1763, DHS; Vestry Minutes of St. Stephen's, 1754–1935, DHS.

42. By 1769 the Prince Frederick's planters, who prospered increasingly through the 1750s and 1760s from the indigo which they grew along the Black River, were listed among the wealthiest in the province. Three factors explain why those elected to church office in the period before 1763 tended to be men of relatively modest means. First, the planters who prospered from indigo were presumably elected to the vestry in the late 1760s and 1770s, whereas those elected before 1763 were men who had not yet profited from indigo. Second, the dissenters who lived in the parish—the Huguenots, Presbyterians, and Baptists—outnumbered those who adhered to the Church of England by two to one. Many of the parish's richer planters may well have been dissenters who were ineligible for vestry membership. Third, that no residents of Charles Town who owned plantations in the parish were elected to the vestry may also explain why the average estate and slaveholdings of Prince Frederick's officeholders were lower than those of church officeholders in other parishes.

43. These families included the Cordes, Gaillards, Porchers, Peyres, Sincklers, Canteys, Coopers, and Palmers.

44. Those elected to the St. Helena's vestry who owned houses in Charles Town included the merchants John Chapman and Thomas Middleton and the planters William Elliott, Sr., and Richard Wigg, Sr. (SCA, Will Book, 1726–1727, 618; Will Book, 1767–1771, 384; Will Book, 1760–1767, 651; Will Book, 1774–1779, 595; SCA, Inventories, vol. Y, 215–16; SCA, Judgment Rolls, 1755; 88A; SCA, Ship Registers, I, 45–46, 134, 138–39, 155, 163). The St. Stephen's planters who owned houses in Charles Town included Samuel Bonneau, Samuel Cordes, and Philip Porcher (SCA, Will Book, 1771–1774, 215; Will Book, 1783–1786, 75; Will Book, 1786–1793, 234; Will Book, 1793–1800, 340).

45. Rogers, *Georgetown*, 20.

46. McCord and Cooper, *Statutes*, IV, 230–32, 300–302. On the settlement of the back country, see R. L. Meriwether, *The Expansion of South Carolina, 1729–1765* (Kingsport, Tenn., 1940).

47. Minutes of St. Mathew's, 1768–1838, DHS; Minutes of St. David's, 1768–1832, St. David's Protestant Episcopal Church, Cheraw, S.C.

48. Vestry Minutes of St. Philip's, 1732–1910, St. Philip's Episcopal Church, Charleston, S.C. Minutes of the Vestry of St. Michael's, 1759–1824, 1824–1869, St. Michael's Protestant Episcopal Church, Charleston, S.C.

49. Of 124 men elected as vestrymen and churchwardens of St. Michael's and St. Philip's, 82 were merchants. In compiling this information on professions I have referred to the following: SCA, Judgment Rolls, 1703–1784; SCA, Will Books, 16 vols., 1671–1785; *South Carolina Gazette*, 1732–76; Richard Walsh, *Charleston's Sons of Liberty: A Study of the Artisans, 1763–1789* (Columbia, S.C., 1959).

50. Waterhouse, "South Carolina's Colonial Elite," 291–92.

51. Jack P. Greene, *Landon Carter: An Inquiry Into the Personal Values and Social Imperatives of the Eighteenth Century Gentry* (Charlottesville, S.C., 1965), 33–35; Sydnor, *American Revolutionaries in the Making*, 60–106.

52. SCA, Church Commissioners Book, 1717–1742, 45.

53. In 1767 it was calculated that 130 adults and 31 boys and girls were maintained by the parish; these did not include many transient poor who were also so maintained. In 1759 the St. Philip's vestry levied a poor tax of £6,000 current money, whereas in the same year the St. John's Colleton vestry levied a poor tax of only £348 4s. current money. (J. H. Easterby, ed., "Public Poor Relief in Colonial Charleston: A Report to the Com-

mons House of Assembly about the Year 1767," *SCHM.*, XLII [April 1941], 84; St. Philip's Vestry Minutes, April 30, 1759, June 25, 1759; St. John's Colleton Vestry Minutes, October 1, 1759.)

54. Walter B. Edgar, ed., *The Letterbook of Robert Pringle,* 2 vol. (Columbia, S.C., 1972), I, 211. See also the resolution of the St. Philip's vestry, October 3, 1756: "That the trouble of the Churchwardens is so greatly increased and likely more to increase, that it can't be expected any person in future will serve the Office."

To partially relieve itself of the burden of caring for the poor, the St. Philip's vestry in 1761 demanded that the St. Michael's vestry accept responsibility for the poor who lived south of Broad Street. But by the terms of the act establishing the parish of St. Michael's, its vestry was specifically exempted from the duty of caring for the poor, including those who lived within its boundaries. The vestry of St. Michael's therefore declined to accede to the demand. (McCord and Cooper, *Statutes,* VII, 79–84; Vestry Minutes of St. Michael's, May 11, 1761.)

55. McCord and Cooper, *Statutes,* II, 292; IV, 49–50.

56. Vestry Minutes of St. Philip's, April 18, 1757; April 11, 1760. The fact that in each parish studied the average number of terms served as vestryman exceeded that served as churchwarden may reflect an unwillingness on the part of colonial South Carolinians to accept the responsibilities of the more burdensome office. Yet it is also worth noting that in each parish seven vestrymen and only two churchwardens were elected annually. For statistical reasons, therefore, it was likely that the average term served on the vestry would exceed that served as churchwarden.

57. SCA, Archdale's Laws, 1696, 36–40; McCord and Cooper, *Statutes,* II, 77, 96, 216–19, 264–65, 615–17; III, 497–501, 690; VII, 7–12, 17–22, 41, 58–60. Most of the relevant acts are no longer extant. Although the names of those elected to these offices were not recorded in the vestry minutes before 1742, annual elections for these offices first took place several years earlier (*South Carolina Gazette,* April 2, 1737; McCord and Cooper, *Statutes,* III, 497–501, 516).

58. *South Carolina Gazette,* December 14, 1738; May 3, 1740; August 7, 1755; November 4, 1756; McCord and Cooper, *Statutes,* III, 497–501; George C. Rogers, Jr., *Charleston in the Age of the Pinckneys* (Norman, Okla., 1969), 20–21.

59. These figures are based on the 57 extant inventories of the 173 men who were elected as town but not as church office holders.

60. Fulham Palace Transcripts, Nos. 298, 299, and 300, Charles Woodmason's Account of South Carolina, Georgia & co. (1766), Library of Congress; George N. Edwards, *A History of the Independent or Congregational Church of Charleston, South Carolina* (Boston, 1947), 1–20; Leah Townsend, *South Carolina Baptists, 1670–1805* (Florence, S.C., 1935), 5–23; George Howe, *History of the Presbyterian Church in South Carolina,* 2 vols. (Columbia, S.C., 1870, 1883), I, 122–28, 201–2.

61. Journal of the Commissioners of Fortifications, 1755–1769, South Carolina Historical Society (hereafter, SCHS); Jack P. Greene, *The Quest for Power: The Lower Houses of Assembly in the Southern Royal Colonies, 1689–1763* (New York, 1972), 254–55.

62. I. Ferguson, "County Courts in Virginia," 22–25; Paul M. McCain, *The County Court in North Carolina Before 1750* (Durham, N.C., 1954), 12, 124; Alan D. Watson, "Regulation and Administration of Roads and Bridges in Colonial Eastern North Carolina," *NCHR,* XLV (Autumn 1968), 400–401.

63. McCord and Cooper, *Statutes,* IX, 2–3, 3–6, 6–8, 8–11, 11–12, 14–17, 17–21, 21–22, 24–25, 26–28, 29–31, 32–35, 36, 38–39, 39–41, 41–43; SCA, MS Law No. 249.

64. McCord and Cooper, *Statutes,* IX, 49–57.

65. Ibid., IX, 53.

66. Records of the Commissioners of the High Roads of St. John's Parish, Berkeley County, 1760–1798, SCHS.

67. McCord and Cooper, *Statutes,* IV, 8–10.

68. These figures are based on the twenty-eight extant inventories of the eighty-seven men named as commissioners by the act of 1721.

69. Ibid., IX, 144–47. These figures are based on the sixteen extant inventories of the thirty-four men named as road commissioners by this act.

70. Ibid., IX, 80–82, 93–95, 133–34, 178–79.

71. Ibid., IX, 161–63, 193–94.

72. Ibid., VII, 489–91, 503–4.

73. Ibid., VII, 477–78; IX, 76–78.

74. *South Carolina Gazette,* March 30, 1734; November 5, 1737; March 27, 1742; March 28, 1743; November 5, 1744; April 15, 1745; May 1, 1756; January 25, 1770; SCA, BPRO, XXII, 73–83.

75. J. W. G. De Brahm, "Philosophico-Historico-Hydrogeography of South Carolina, Georgia, and East Florida," in *Documents Connected with the History of South Carolina,* ed. P. G. J. Weston (London, 1856), 178; John Bartram, *Diary of a Journey Through the Carolinas, Georgia and Florida, from July 1, 1765 to April 10, 1766, Transactions of the American Philosophical Society,* XXXIII, part I (1944), 22; Klaus G. Loewald, ed., "Johann Martin Bolzius Answers a Questionnaire on Carolina and Georgia," *William and Mary Quarterly,* 3rd ser., XV (April 1958), 232. For an example of a zealous road commissioner insisting that even Charles Pinckney, perhaps at that time the most prestigious figure in the colony, contribute his share to the upkeep of the roads, see Pinckney Family Papers, William Murray to Colonel [Charles] Pinckney, August 23, 1748, Library of Congress.

76. This is the contention of Sirmans, *Colonial South Carolina,* 252.

77. SCA, Commons House Journals, January 28, December 3, 1741; April 10, 1753; Sirmans, *Colonial South Carolina,* 252.

78. Richard Maxwell Brown, *The South Carolina Regulators* (Cambridge, Mass., 1963), 64–82, 96–111, 138–39.

79. At the Assembly level the dominance of the wealthy planters and merchants was even more complete. Few small planters and no tradesmen were elected to the Assembly after 1720. (See Waterhouse, "South Carolina's Colonial Elite," 285, 288–90.)

80. For the suggestion of the correlation between the appearance of economic and social elites and the lower houses' demand for increased authority, see Greene, *The Quest for Power,* 11.

The Development and Structure
of Local Government
in Colonial New York

NICHOLAS VARGA

The existence of local government in colonial New York was, in the main, the result of popular pressure. Had it been left entirely to the provincial authorities—whether Dutch or English—the people would have been governed by centralized, appointed, and primarily executive governmental institutions. The province-level officers would not yield control to any local units even of their own creation until the demand became too threatening to ignore. Local government, thus, is not merely a minor facet of colonial history, but indeed part of the continuing struggle for popular participation in government.

The Dutch did establish a modicum of local government in the "patroonships." These grants, first authorized in 1629, were a quasi-feudal device to attract immigrants and to control them once they settled in New Netherlands. For any enterprising man who transported fifty adults to the province, a vast tract of land and plenary

186

authority were patented. The proprietors of such manors (to give them their English name) enjoyed definite judicial powers. These were, in particular, the high and low jurisdictions so familiar to historians of the medieval period. Such broad authority was granted because the proprietors were responsible, like their medieval analogues, for good order among these new immigrants and for their loyalty.

These earlier Dutch grants proved rather inconsequential as governmental agencies, and did not survive for long. Although five patroonships were established, only Rensselaerswyck lasted into the English period. Curiously, even after the British conquest, New York's governors were attracted to this form of grant. Between 1680 and 1696 a number of manors were established. These proved somewhat more durable than the older Dutch grants and differed in a few details from these earlier establishments.[1]

On parchment, at least, the proprietors were not only landlords but also the agents of local government. Their tenants were subject to manorial courts. One, the court leet, served a dual function as an agency to make local ordinances and also as a court to punish violators of these same regulations. The other (the court baron) was restricted to a judicial function. It dealt with disputes arising from tenancy and also heard small civil disagreements between the tenants. Neither of these were courts of records; thus, how they functioned or indeed whether they existed can not be fully determined. Even if the proprietors did not regularly convene and use these particular agencies, they had been given the authority and might well have acted informally.

Gradually, however, the local government functions of these manors were absorbed into the developing county government. What previously had been done by the manorial proprietor and his bailiffs could still be done by the same men under commissions as colonels of the militia and justices of the peace. In time, the surviving manors would come to be treated during the eighteenth century as the functional equivalents of either townships or precincts—local units that developed much later. By then too, there was evidence that the proprietors no longer enjoyed "control" over the local officers who served the manor.[2]

While the patroonships and manors were moving along their brief arc into governmental oblivion, another more vital development was taking place. Compact settlements that persisted in their demands were reluctantly being chartered as towns. This clamor arose first among the English settlements on Long Island. These were peopled by New Englanders who had crossed Long Island Sound but who would not permanently yield the privileges of local government to which their ancestry and experience had accustomed them. In old England, they had enjoyed a limited right to make local ordinances and to be regulated by local officers—albeit mainly appointed. They had brought this system with them to Massachusetts and Connecticut. Here in the New World, the government of the township, now thoroughly responsive to local needs, became their primary unit of local government. Though they lived within a territory ruled by Dutch law, customs, and officials, they wanted their villages chartered.

The provincial officials (the director and Council, appointed by the West India Company) were initially unwilling to grant this demand. They recognized the local government advantages in the patroonships but the proprietors of these units were mortal individuals. A grant to one man could be limited or resumed at relatively short but inevitable intervals. Towns, however, are ruled not by one mortal person but by a group, and groups are by their nature more formidable, resourceful adversaries. The director and Council wanted to maintain a unitary structure in which their decisions became the law for all inhabitants and their own appointees alone enforced their will.

Nevertheless, the persistence of the Long Island Englishmen finally secured limited concessions from the New Netherland authorities. In 1644, Hempstead was chartered—to be followed the next year by Flushing and Gravesend. The success of these English-bred petitioners proved infectious. Their Dutch neighbors also demanded incorporation. In 1646, the settlements of Gowanus, Red Hook, the Wallabout, and the Ferry were aggregated under the charter given to Breucklen. Six years later, Fort Orange (Albany) was organized under a local government. This process continued to the end of the Dutch era in 1664, by which time Newtown, Flatlands, Westchester, Jamaica, Harlem, and Kingston had also been established.

All these localities operated under governments formed according to a common model. The public affairs of each town were directed by a court made up of magistrates (called *schepens*) and a prosecutor-sheriff known as the *schout*. Together, the schepens and schout administered the common lands. The town court enacted local regulations affecting lands, fences, highways, schools, and churches. However, neither these regulations nor any other action of the town court was effective until it had been approved by the provincial authorities. Thus, the concessions made by the director and Council were carefully circumscribed.

Furthermore, all the local officials were appointed by the director and Council. The Dutch practice, however, made this a less autocratic prcedure than it might at first seem. The freemen of the town nominated their fellows for appointment as magistrates. The schepens and schout were chosen from this list. On the other hand, Dutch custom also dictated that there be twice as many nominees as positions to be filled. Thus, the choice of the provincial officials was a real one—if also subject to popular influence.[3] With so many checks, one wonders why the Dutch governors were so reluctant to establish local units. Their yielding so little, so late, and to such pressure should indicate how deeply embedded was the preference for a unitary administration.

In the midst of the process establishing town governments on Long Island, another proposal, even less welcome to the provincial authorities, was made. The mixed Dutch-English population living on the tip of Manhattan petitioned the home authorities in the early 1650s for a municipal charter. They were asking for an elected government similar to the one then operative in old Amsterdam. Prudently, the West India Company granted the request, but its provincial director, Peter Stuyvesant, delayed implementing the order during the rest of the decade. The denizens of New Amsterdam persisted in their demands so that, if only with a glacial slowness, Stuyvesant was gradually forced to yield point after point.

The details of the struggle are less significant than the characteristic attitudes that it exposed. The provincial authorities worked stubbornly to avoid establishing local, elective government jurisdictions, while these were exactly what the people were demanding and by persistence forcing on their officials.

In view of this tension, it is not surprising that in 1664 when a small English fleet appeared in the harbor few, if any, could be found to defend the incumbent Dutch regime. The English commander, acting for James, the duke of York, offered such generous terms that even old Stuyvesant's own appointees urged capitulation. Thus, Dutch authority was quickly replaced by that of England and the process of converting the local governmental institutions was begun.[4]

Since Englishmen in their native land enjoyed a well-established and varied structure of local government, one might have assumed that the displacement of the Dutch would mean a rapid development of a similar structure in New York. While some concessions were made and English forms came more and more to be observed, there was no greater willingness on the part of the early English authorities to share government with local officers and corporations than had been the case under the Dutch. The ill-fated Stuart dynasty, of which James (New York's lord proprietor and later King of England) would prove a tragic exemplar, was already noted for disregarding constitutional precedent. In general, the Stuarts preferred a unitary, unencumbered structure of government that was responsive to their inspired will. By this time, however, they had also come to accept the necessity of restraining some of their more arbitrary tendencies temporarily, and thus in the glow of the Restoration there was a gradual development of New York's governmental institutions according to the native English model.

Several months after the conquest, the agents of the duke of York convened an assembly of deputies from the Long Island towns and Westchester for the promulgation of a code of laws. While Dutch law and practice would be continued in Albany and in much of the Hudson River Valley, a new code, derived from the laws of Massachusetts and Connecticut (sans their peculiar religious restrictions), was to be effective in the southernmost (and most English) part of the province. The Duke's Laws, as they were called, dealt with many things but were especially significant in how they provided for local government.

Long Island, Westchester, and Staten Island were formed into a county (that most fundamental of English local government units) named Yorkshire. Like its counterpart in the mother country, New York's Yorkshire was divided into "ridings." The East Riding was the far, bleak end of Long Island which later became known as Suffolk County. The West Riding joined Staten Island with the western end of Long Island. Westchester and part of the northern shore of Long Island were conglomerated into the North Riding. For the whole county one high sheriff was appointed while each riding was to be served by an undersheriff and a board of justices. These latter officers were to meet three times each year to hear and decide civil

and criminal matters and to review the administration of local affairs. Such meetings, it should be recalled, also offered an occasion
to gossip, influence, and discuss matters of general concern informally.
It would be surprising to find these officers and their later counterparts talking only about the things on the official docket.

The work of the riding courts was subject to direct provincial influence in two ways: the governor or any member of his Council
who happened to be present when one of these courts was meeting
had the right to preside. There is little evidence that this right was
often exercised. The other control was through appeals: the judicial
decisions of these Yorkshire bodies could be reviewed by the province Court of Assizes, that is, the governor, Council, and assembled
justices of the peace. This higher body was thus made up of either
the appointees of New York's lord proprietor or those named by his
governor and Council.[5] The principle of election or popular representation was not operative in the upper levels of the provincial
government.

There was, however, an elective element introduced into the town
governments under the Duke's Laws. The freemen of each patented
locality were initially to elect eight overseers and one constable.
These replaced the Dutch schepens and schout and were given a
number of new responsibilities more in keeping with the English
practice. In the following year, half the board of overseers were to
retire and new members elected. One of the retiring overseers was to
be named constable whose office was symbolized by a six-foot staff
emblazoned with the duke's, and later the King's, arms. Either the
constable or his staff (preferably both) had to be present at meetings
of the town court. Furthermore, no ordinance could become effective without the constable's approval. Together, the overseers and
constable for each town appointed fenceviewers, surveyors of highways, and poundmasters—whose titles adequately describe their
civic duties.

Among the additional responsibilities of these town courts was
the collection of taxes modeled on the customary English levies,
the poll and property taxes. All males sixteen years and older who
were liable for military service were also required to pay a poll tax.
Specified varieties of real and personal property were made subject
to a tax of one penny for each pound of valuation. The taxes themselves and the rates were established by the provincial authorities,

but the town overseers and constables were required to administer the law. The high sheriff of Yorkshire ensured the overall enforcement.

This sytem was particularly obnoxious to the English, who insisted that at the Dutch surrender they had been promised their full rights. Among these, they argued, was the right to be governed by laws that had their consent—especially laws that taxed them. In good Stuart fashion, the governor replied that "nothing . . . was required but obedience and submission to the laws as they appeared in the duke's commission." This was then no more palatable a doctrine than it would later appear to the descendants of these same New Yorkers, but the circumstances restricted their response to various persistent obstructions and harassments of the provincial authorities. Some governors with more patience, others with less, continued to enforce the Duke's Laws.

Under that code, a new function was assigned to the towns. Now every able-bodied male aged sixteen to sixty was liable for militia service. This meant maintaining proper arms, training regularly, and mustering on call of the governor. Such duties had not been previously required because the Dutch relied, in the main, on regular troops, for their defense. This new militia force was organized by towns with the captains, lieutenants, and ensigns appointed by the governor from lists submitted by the militia companied through the town court. The higher officers—who commanded the whole force of a riding—were commissioned by the governor without prior local nomination. The captains and lieutenants were required to inspect the arms of their men quarterly; if any were defective, the owners were fined. The companies were mustered on four days during the year for training. Once a year, the companies of a riding would be gathered for joint maneuvers. Every other year, Yorkshire's whole militia was drawn up in a grand show.[6] However limited as a military force, this system provided a sense of civic solidarity that had been lacking during the Dutch period.

The duke of York also instructed his provincial agents to reform the municipal government of the capital. The existing Dutch city corporation was summarily replaced in June 1665 by one formed according to an English model. In place of the schout, burgomasters, and schepens, the governor named a sheriff, mayor, and aldermen for the ensuing year. This change was considered a violation of the surrender terms which provided for the continuation of the incumbent magistrates. The Dutch and English inhabitants protested a number of other violations as well but nothing roused them so much as the summary disappearance of their so recently won right to nominate candidates for municipal office. The Stuart governor merely asserted the propriety of his actions and accommodated popular sentiment by dividing the offices among the English and Dutch; the former got the mayoralty and two aldermanic seats while the latter had to be satisfied with the sheriff and three aldermen. Their commission was ambiguously worded to permit the gradual substitution of English laws and usages for the Dutch. The change was not fully accomplished until 1674 when the Duke's Laws were officially put into force.[7]

The occasion for this action was the resumption of English control after the brief 1673–74 Dutch interlude. The results of the second Anglo-Dutch War and the terms of peace made clear that English control of the now-again "New York" could not be challenged by a distant and weakened Dutch Republic. James, New York's proprietor, had less need to accommodate the Dutch in his province and acted accordingly.

The gradual change in New York City's municipal government was matched by a similar emergence of Albany as an English-form county. As in New York, the Duke's Laws were applied in 1674 to the Hudson Valley, although Dutch titles remained in use for a number of years. Even after 1680, the magistrates were called by their equivalent English title of "justice" but they still retained the powers of their Dutch predecessors. About this same time, the governor sought to relieve the problem of appeals to the provincial authorities at the capital by establishing a subordinate court sitting at Albany. This was to be made up of five or more magistrates from Albany and three or more from Schenectady.[8] The process would not be carried further until a province-wide representative assembly was established.

This specific development was promoted by a mercantile protest and the arrival of a wise governor. In 1681 some of the merchants of New York City refused to pay customs on an incoming cargo because the tax had been imposed by proprietary authority rather than being freely granted by a representative body. Surprisingly, the action of these protesters was supported by the Province Council whose members had been appointed by the lord proprietor. To resolve the resulting impasse, James dispatched Colonel Thomas Dongan to New York with instructions to convene an assembly made up of deputies from the various towns. This Dongan did within a few months after his arrival in 1683.[9]

The representatives of the people of New York seized the opportunity to summarize the kind of government and laws to which they thought themselves entitled. In the Charter of Liberties, the New York Assembly sought to secure the rights guaranteed in the Magna Carta and the Petition of Right (1628). These were: regular representative assemblies, trial by jury, no taxation except by consent of an assembly, no quartering of troops in private homes, and the like. Most significant for the development of local government was the nearly simultaneous passage of a law dividing New York into ten counties—Suffolk, Queens, Kings, Richmond, New York, Westchester, Orange, Ulster, Dutchess, and Albany. (There were two dependencies that were also named counties but these soon disappeared from the governmental structure of the province and so need not be mentioned.)

Insisting on the establishment of counties was particularly striking when it is recalled that these deputies had been elected from townships. In 1683 New Yorkers were obviously demanding not only the rights of Englishmen but also the same basic territorial structure that was traditional in the mother country. They did not want a gradual dispersion of governmental powers by means of town charters since such grants could, by bargaining, be used to bolster the influence of the central administration. What these New Yorkers wanted was the immediate establishment of large units located below the province level. It was a characteristic and indicative demand.

The response of Governor Dongan and even his master was favorable. Dongan provisionally agreed to the charter and the statutes enacted by this first Assembly. James, too, approved these actions but before his decision could be reconveyed back to New York, his brother died and he ascended the throne as King James II. This made New York a royal province and the actions of the Assembly were reviewed by the Committee on Trade and Plantations, which recommended disallowing the New York Charter because it derogated from both the crown's and Parliament's authority. On receiving this news, Governor Dongan obeyed the formal requirements of the crown while acting, as best he could, in accord with the expressed will of the people.

There were several instances to indicate how well Dongan dealt with the demand for county government. He did establish a regular set of county courts as well as appoint an appropriate number of justices of the peace. The vestiges of Dutch governmental institutions were erased from Albany and Ulster. When people complained about the difficulty and cost of appealing from local courts to the provincial court of assizes, he abolished the latter body and substituted instead a court of oyer and terminer that was convened twice a year in each county. This court could act on all indictments for treason, felonies, and misdemeanors.[10] In England it acted normally on action of the grand jury, and thus the establishment of this court in New York presumes the appearance of the other necessary institution. Though little understood or valued today, the grand jury then had a larger function. It was not merely a check on the police and prosecutors, but was also considered by colonial New Yorkers as the political "voice" of the county.[11]

There were also some minor changes in the town governments. The overseers and constables were replaced by three annually elected commissioners. They in turn appointed a supervisor who was responsible for administering the town's affairs and its expenditures. These modifications remained in force until they were in turn supplanted by the system established in the aftermath of the "Glorious Revolution."[12]

After the conversion of New York into a royal province, Governor Dongan completed the reform of its municipal governments. In 1686 he issued a new charter for New York City according to the pattern described in a petition submitted three years earlier. Dongan in the meanwhile had acted according to the terms of the petition while awaiting formal approval from London. In the Dongan charter, the island of Manhattan was divided into six wards named for the major points of the compass plus the Dock Ward and the Out Ward. The former was located along the shore of the East River while the latter included Harlem and the northern part of the island. Annually, each ward elected an alderman, assistant, and constable; these elections were customarily conducted by the incumbent aldermen. The governor retained the right to appoint the mayor and sheriff each year. In addition, the city was now given an officer (the recorder) who was responsible for its legal business and who, if need be, could preside in the mayor's court. This was made up of the aldermen who individually also served as "JPs." The mayor and common council could enact local ordinances but these remained in force only for three months unless they were confirmed by the provincial authorities. On the other hand, the municipal finances now became the responsibility of a chamberlain or treasurer who was appointed not by the governor but by the mayor and common council. The mayor alone licensed taverns and inns at no more than 30s. per license. These funds were subject to the order of the corporation, but no account of these expenditures could be required by the governor.[13] Dongan's charter, while not fully applying the elective principle, made the municipal corporation more representative than it had previously been. Also, its powers had been augmented and its structure further elaborated. A similar structure was established in Albany at the same time.

The Dongan era ended in 1688 when the province momentarily lost its identity in the Dominion of New England. James II had finally decided to consolidate the administration of his American colonies into a larger unit devoid of representative institutions. His experiment with executive rule proved short-lived when his reign ended in the "Glorious Revolution." There was a good deal of confusion at this turn of events and it would take until 1691 to channel the contrary political and governmental currents effectively.

In New York this confusion took the form of the turbulence known as Leisler's Rebellion. Except for one provocative suggestion, this brief interlude had no significant effect on the development of New York's local government. The ill-fated Leisler attempted to rally support by denouncing Dongan's charters for New York City and Albany and by opening all major offices to election. While this may have appeared to be the general direction in which popular sentiment had been heading, Leisler's proposal gained no eager acceptance, nor would it come back to haunt New York politics after its author had been executed.[14] New Yorkers preferred a municipal structure that combined appointive and elective elements even well after independence.

In 1691 a new governor with authority from William and Mary put an end to this brief unsettled period. He also established an elective Assembly and this body, convened in April 1691, would finally lay the basis for the varied structure of local government that served New York from that time until the American Revolution.

The attachment New Yorkers felt for the county unit was evident in their first General Assembly. One of the earliest laws passed organized the province into ten counties—the same as under Governor Dongan. The boundaries were defined mainly in terms of the townships included in each county rather than geographic reference points. Little change was made in these arrangements down to the time of the Revolution, except that in 1717 Livingston Manor was shifted from Dutchess to Albany County. On the eve of the Revolution, the number of counties was increased by two but these had little effect on the government or politics of New York.[15]

With the establishment of the county unit, it became possible to rationalize this level of government by the appointment of familiar officers and the erection of traditional courts. These, such as the sheriff, judges, and justices of the peace, were appointed by the governor nominally with the advice and consent of the Provincial Council. The terms of these county officials were indefinite and they served at the "good will and pleasure" of the governor. Eventually, the most potent voice in these appointments was that of favored members of the Assembly. These were given, it was said, the "administration" of the county.[16]

The representatives must certainly have used this power to their own advantage but this probability cannot be stretched to mean the development of a tightly constructed political "machine." The correspondence of Henry Beekman with his political agent in Dutchess County makes clear that such influence with the governor was exercised, in the main, according to customary rules of courtesy and deference rather than merely as political patronage. Beekman would willingly and gracefully submit a name proposed by his local opponents for a militia commission or other post, if propriety and community harmony required it.[17]

There being no lords-lieutenant in the Province of New York, the most formidable officer in the county was the sheriff. He was a recognizable derivative of the English practice and law; nevertheless, the New York sheriff was shorn of certain judicial and ceremonial functions that are assigned this officer in Blackstone's *Commentaries*. The American sheriff published all proclamations, supervised elections, executed the administrative and judicial decisions of the county courts, upheld law and order in the community, and collected royal revenues.[18] This last function might, however, be left

in desuetude if someone else obtained a commission as "ranger."
In that case the latter became responsible for collecting quitrents
and protecting the royal rights in whales, mines, treasure trove, and
forfeitures.

The sheriffs were also responsible for the incarceration of prisoners.
In colonial New York, these would include not only criminals but
debtors as well. Initially, the prisoners were lodged in a fortified
room in the sheriff's home and he was reimbursed for this encroachment on his privacy. As the county prospered, a court house would
be built and a strong room included in the plans. A high mark of
local pride was reached with the building of a separate jail. In any
case, the sheriff was held personally responsible for his prisoners,
and if any escaped he was obliged to cover their liabilities. The
sheriff of Albany County, Abraham Yates, had to pay £59 sterling
one year for prisoners who had slipped out of his custody.[19]

To be appointed sheriff, one's origins might be relatively common
but good connections were essential. Abraham Yates, for instance,
had been a shoemaker, then turned attorney, and would eventually
have letters addressed to him as "Merchant." In 1754, he got the
proprietor of Livingston Manor to support his bid for the shrievalty.
Successful, he soon opined to his patron that he worked so diligently in his new office that he was "a Slave to the County."

In 1761 Yates would attempt to rise still higher by offering himself as a candidate for one of Albany's seats in the Assembly. Again,
he had Livingston support—even an offer of £50 to finance his
canvass for votes. Unfortunately, the other Albany "grandees" had
decided on a full slate which effectively closed out Yates' bid. His
failure was no reflection on the office of sheriff since Theodorus
Snediker of Orange County successfully made the transition, although a number of years intervened between his service as sheriff
and his winning a seat in the Assembly. Yates would eventually become an alderman of the city of Albany and finally a leader in the
movement for American independence.[20] Other sheriffs enjoyed a
less spectacular career—few would serve in posts of greater prestige
or pelf.

One significant power of the sheriff related to Assembly elections. Each county sheriff could, within limits specified in the
gubernatorial writ, determine the day on which the election would
be held. This made it possible for the sheriff to surprise or other-

wise disadvantage one group or another. It is known that this power was used to influence elections. To whatever advantage, the sheriff would eventually have to give notice of the date and place of the election. He would, at the appointed time, read the writ and ask the voters to divide according to which of the candidates they favored. Surveying each group, the sheriff would then declare who had the larger body of voters and thus had won. Such a "vote" might prove inadequate, so the sheriff would then conduct a "poll." In this procedure, each voter presented himself to a clerk named by the sheriff and, under the scrutiny of "inspectors" appointed by the candidates, would record his choice. Oral and recorded voting may be abhorrent to us today, but it was considered the "manly" way to do things in pre-Revolutionary New York.[21] Furthermore, it was the only possible procedure until all voters were subjected to prior registration. At the end of the poll, the sheriff would write the results on the writ, seal it, and send it back to the governor.

Periodically, though not at regular intervals, a New York governor would issue a "commission of peace" and name the judges of the county court and the justices of the peace. These last were not the grand conservators of the peace as were their English namesakes. The latter were appointed from among men who enjoyed an annual income of £100; consequently, they were entrusted with broad supervisory powers. The New York JPs were for the most part prosperous but not wealthy—brewers, shoemakers—hardly men of the weight of their English counterparts. Nevertheless their basic jurisdiction was similar; it extended "not only [to] Assaults and Batteries, but Libels, Barratry, and common Night-walking, haunting Bawdy-Houses, and the like Offences."[22]

As the Province of New York grew in numbers and complexity, the general increase in judicial business made it necessary to enhance the powers of the JPs. In 1737 all disputes of debt, trespass, and the like not exceeding 40s. became subject to decision by a justice of the peace. The threshold for adjudication was later raised to £5 sterling—much to the annoyance of William Smith, Jr., who denounced the justices of the peace as illiterate "genii." However much this arrangement bothered lawyers like Smith, it was favored by the immediate beneficiaries and probably the public as well since the entrance level was raised in 1769 to £10 sterling. The parties to the suit always had the right to be heard before a jury of six men.

Furthermore, three or more JPs could decide criminal matters that fell short of punishments endangering life or limb.[23] The main qualification for this office, at least as described by a critic, was "a Weight and Influence with the Vulgar."[24] Since few New Yorkers could have been professionally prepared for the post, this jaundiced definition can be given some credence.

There were, however, men in each county who had enough understanding of the law and procedure to be named judges. These two or three constituted the court of common pleas, whose jurisdiction and practice were similar to the Common Bench at Westminster. The county court held two sessions each year. After the ordinary business was completed, the justices of the peace joined the judges for a meeting of the court of general sessions of the peace. Previously, the general sessions were an occasion for considering local regulations, but this practice ceased after county government was fully established in New York. Thereafter, this quasi-legislative function was performed by an elected board of supervisors.

A number of county judges bore other responsibilities as well. Some of them simultaneously served as members of the General Assembly. Examples of this combination can be cited from almost every county, but possibly the more familiar were Isaac Hicks and David Jones of Queens County, John and Abraham Lott of Kings, and William Willett and John Thomas of Westchester County. Some, like Richard Merril of Richmond and Cornelius Van Brunt of Kings, donned the judicial dignity only after they had finished their service as elected representatives. A few, such as Philip Ver Planck of Cortlandt Manor and Henry Beekman, served in the lesser capacity of JP.[29] Having judicial and legislative authority thus exercised by the same people does not seem to have bothered colonial New Yorkers; separation of powers was a later concern.

The capstone of the county judicial system was a "hybrid" court which combined a few of the county judges with the justices of the Supreme Court. Together, they became the bench for the court of oyer and terminer and general jail delivery. The jurisdiction of this body under the title "oyer and terminer" had been introduced earlier by Governor Dongan. General jail delivery permitted the combined judges and justices to try all persons incarcerated at the time the court was convened in a particular county. It was in this circuit service that Chief Justice James De Lancey became such a familiar personage. He used his annual swing around the province to make politically advantageous connections.[26]

The county as a whole was also served by a number of miscellaneous officers who were appointed by the governor in his civil capacity. Among these were the clerks to keep necessary records and to conduct correspondence for all the administrative and judicial agencies in the county. County clerks tended to remain in office for long periods of time. Henry Livingston, for instance, served Dutchess County from 1742 until the Revolution. In this post, he was also the political agent of Henry Beekman, the county's almost-as-durable assemblyman. The governor also named coroners whose functions are too familiar to need description, while others to deal with testamentary matters were commissioned as "surrogates."

There was another class of appointments made by the governor under his title "captain general." In this capacity, he had the authority to name all militia officers and do this without the concurrence of the Provincial Council. The specific number of militia companies varied with the county but each one had its military force organized as a regiment with a colonel, lieutenant colonel, major, and adjutant. The companies were commanded by captains with assorted lieutenants and ensigns. At least one of the companies in each county was likely to be a cavalry unit, while New York City alone boasted a Blue Artillery Company. There were few occasions for the militiamen to demonstrate their martial skills, although they did some garrison duty around Albany during King George's War (1744–48).

Just as several civilian commissions might be held by the same person, so militia officers served in other capacities. During the eighteenth General Assembly in the mid-1720s, fourteen of the twenty-seven representatives sported military titles: six were colonels, one a major, and seven were captains.[27] Like the civil commissions, these too were distributed according to customary protocol rather than merely as patronage.[28]

County government was not all appointive; there was another — an elective — element. The most prestigious of these county offices was that of assemblyman. Each of the ten counties had two seats with two added for the capital, so that New York had four representatives while certain privileged subdivisions like Rensselaerswyck, Livingston Manor, and Cortlandt Manor, as well as the town of Schenectady and the borough of Westchester each enjoyed the distinction of one assemblyman apiece. The apportionment of these seats was not finally fixed until the mid-1720s and thereafter remained essentially unchanged until the Revolution. The Long Island counties (Suffolk, Queens, and Kings) were slightly underrepresented, while the apportionment for the metropolitan counties (New York, Richmond, and Westchester) was balanced and Orange, Ulster, Dutchess, and Albany together were slightly overrepresented. The disparity, however, was not striking and favored an area of rising population.[29]

As already noted, assemblymen also tended to serve as county judges, JPs, or militia officers. Much of their time was taken by local legislation on which the applicable rule was "courtesy," that is, all other delegations deferred to the wishes of the group of representatives seeking the enactment to raise funds for a new courthouse, or to name a new set of highway commissioners, or the like. Finally they should be identified as county officers because they were paid from the county treasury rather than the provincial coffers. They might, like Henry Beekman, seek to oblige the county board of supervisers by periodically donating their pay vouchers. In New York City, however, candidates for the Assembly would commit themselves in advance of their election not to accept the wages to which they were entitled by law. Some guardians of the public morals reprehended this practice as tantamount to bribing the voters. Nevertheless, it was continued and even expanded to include substantial donations for the poor of the city.[30]

The highest elective office within the county was a seat on the board of supervisers. These were chosen annually—one from each township or, in the sparsely settled regions, from each precinct. These officers had first appeared in the laws prepared under Governor Dongan in 1682. When the county government was fully and formally established in 1691, the judges and JPs were supposed to assume the administration of local affairs, but by 1703 elected boards of supervisers were reestablished. The judicial responsibilities were left to the appointed "commission of peace," while the remaining functions were exercised by annually elected officers. The men chosen as supervisers, like most other local officials, tended to come from the "middling sort" and like the others were prepared to perform their civic duties diligently and regularly.[31]

The number of precincts within a county depended on the distribution of people and thus was changed as the counties grew. Dutchess county, for instance, was originally divided into three precincts; then in 1737 was reorganized into seven; a quarter-century later it got two more and two more in 1769. Dutchess was also one of the few New York counties that had no local subdivisions other than precincts. As a result of this process of development, the number of supervisors varied from county to county and also over time within a particular county.[32] There was no English equivalent for this elective institution.

The board of supervisors took over the ordinance-making and administrative functions which had been exercised by the pre-1691 riding court. In the main, the supervisors insured that the other officers of the precinct, particularly the tax assessors and collectors, did their duty. Added to these precinct officers were others, generally including a precinct clerk, constables, overseers of the poor, and overseers of the highways. Possibly the most complete listing of precinct officers may be found in Franklin Delano Roosevelt's edition of the records of the Crum Elbow precinct in Dutchess County. While the functions of some officers are not immediately evident from their titles, most were responsible for such things as keeping the pound, making sure fences were in good repair, and being prepared to inventory the estates of any who died without having made a will.[33]

The variety and multiplicity of these offices should indicate how pervasive the control of government was in colonial New York. On the other hand, much of this authority was exercised by annually elected officers, thus spreading the burden and insuring that authority would not be viewed as some distant, god-like power but a familiar tool to achieve the necessary level of order in the community. Furthermore, the system, so different from that of the mother country, offered colonial New Yorkers schooling in how to manage their own local affairs.

The county body politic had another significant type of officer, who were distributed throughout the counties but owed their position to specific provincial statutes. They were the liquor excisemen, highway commissioners, and the loan officers.

An excise on liquor had been collected as far back as the Stuyvesant regime. After a hazy interval, a new excise law was passed in 1699 requiring retailers to pay one-eighth ounce of Mexican silver per gallon of distilled liquor and three-quarters ounce of silver for every barrel of beer or cider. The justices of the peace were responsible for enforcing the law in the counties, while the mayors of New York, Albany, and Westchester were the enforcement agents in their respective municipalities. In 1714 commissioners were appointed to collect the excise in each county. Their names were from among the noteworthy families of the province, such as Curger, Schuyler, Livingston, Hicks, and Rutsen. One, Leendert Lewis, was at the same time serving as an assemblyman from Westchester. A quota was assigned each county and the commissioner retained 10 percent of the total amount he collected.[34]

Three years later this arrangement was superseded when Gilbert Livingston offered to collect the excise for five years and agreed to pay the provincial treasury over four thousand ounces of silver per year. Unfortunately, the war with Spain had, by 1721, depressed the consumption of liquor to such a level that Livingston was £3,000 in arrears and had no hope of full payment. He and his sureties therefore petitioned the General Assembly for relief.[35] Clearly, another system for collecting the liquor excise had to be established.

Even before Gilbert Livingston was freed of his obligations, a new liquor excise law had been enacted. This statute, annually renewed, would remain in operation until the early 1750s. By this act, the collection of the excise was "farmed" to the highest bidder.[36] Whoever succeeded in this auction had himself inserted into the statute. The names of these "farmers" lacked the luster of the earlier commissioners but they remained on the roll for long periods of time. There was a fair sprinkling of men who simultaneously held other offices. Among these were Adam Lawrence (a sheriff), Valentine Hulet Peters and Ryck Suydam (both county judges), Henry Vandenbergh (a county clerk), and Paul Michaux who was also an assemblyman.

Complaints against the excisemen were slow to accumulate, but by the early 1750s familiar charges were heard. The "farmers" of the excise had a monopoly of licensing the sale of alcoholic beverages and thus could extort additional sums from the tavern keepers. In the *Independent Reflector,* a critic noted how in one county (probably Kings) the "farmer" was only required to pay £41 per year even though there were nearly as many outlets as in New York City. This meant that the fortunate "farmer" collected as much in licensing fees as his city colleague but was not required to collect even one-twentieth as much in excises. The remedy proposed was to abolish the practice of farming, then to require the delivery of all excises and licensing fees to the treasury except 5 percent to be kept by the commissioners.[37] The *Reflector's* proposal was in fact adopted and remained the basic law until the end of the colonial era.[38] Nevertheless, complaints soon arose against the new commissioners. By 1755 the excisemen were charging 6s. per bond from each tavern keeper when the going rate for such a transaction was 13d.[39]

The regulation of highways was subject to similar abuse. By various acts, highway commissioners were appointed for each county. Periodic amendments ensured that each county's commission was kept up to full strength and active. The number varied but a 1721 law may be taken as setting the basic pattern. Therein, each major subdivision of Queens, Kings, Westchester, Dutchess, Orange, and Albany were assigned three commissioners. The names included a number of assemblymen as well as scions of the more important families. Their specific function was to lay out the roadways. If the route passed through private property, the commissioners could purchase the necessary land at the value set by two JPs and twelve freeholders. The commissioners were paid for their fatigues at the rate of 6s. per diem.[40] Their work was rather routine and apparently the subject of little controversy.

It was otherwise with the overseers of highways—at least those who held their position by appointment. In New York City, for instance, the surveyors of highways were, like their English equivalents, named by justices of the peace. Since in New York the latter were not the weighty personages their counterparts in England were, it is understandable that their appointees also suffered by comparison. In 1752, a letter bearing the initials M.K. (presumably from a poor widow) was published in the *Independent Reflector*. "Widow K" complained about being summoned to work on the roads. Although she was a householder and thus subject to this service, she could hardly do the actual work but had to pay the half crown per day penalty instead. The editor of the *Reflector* amplified her complaint by noting how common it was for people to pay the penalty while no accounting of these sums was ever required of the surveyors.[41] The English officers, on the other hand, must have been more strictly regulated and in any case their income was limited to nine pence of every pound they collected. There must have been less of this particular abuse in the towns and county precincts where overseers of the highways were elected annually since no complaints were ever recorded and too extortionate an official could easily have been replaced.

There was another group of statutory officers in the counties, at least after 1737. In that year a public banking structure became operative in New York. It was established as a means both of supporting an emission of paper money and also of providing for an expansion of credit. Over £40,000 in paper currency was authorized. The sum was then apportioned to all the counties along a scale between New York City which got £10,000 and Richmond which received only £1,600. These monies were to be loaned out for a period of twelve years at an annual interest of 5 percent. The loans were to be made on lands and houses, with the limits for each type of mortgage specified in the act. Each county had two officers who were responsible for administering these funds. These loan officers were chosen by a majority of the board of supervisors with the concurrence of three judges. If the supervisors were unable to decide, the choice passed entirely to the judges.[42] The legislation was so carefully drawn and so efficiently administered that no notice was ever taken of the operations of these loan offices. Nor was any complaint registered by imperial authorities who would a few years later demolish a similar arrangement in Massachusetts. Although the author of the New York measure cannot be determined with certainty, a likely candidate for the honor is James Alexander since he is recorded in the *Assembly Journal* as explaining the bill to his colleagues.[43]

For at least four of the counties, there was still another governmental agency that had a claim on their purses. The freeholders of New York, Richmond, Westchester, and Queens met annually in their respective counties on the second Tuesday of January under the supervision of two JPs to elect a brace of churchwardens and ten vestrymen. Upon election, these "worthies" were required to collect a tax totaling almost £400 sterling for the support of six Protestant ministers. Whether the act required that these clergymen be in communion with the Church of England was a matter of dispute, but since it was the governor of New York who had the authority to name the ministers, it regularly worked out that way. Furthermore, whether or not this act "established" the Anglican Church was equally a subject for fruitless, bitter contention.[44]

The last significant level of local government in colonial New York was that of the towns and municipalities. Almost half the population lived within such local jurisdictions. The reorganization of these after the English conquest, especially of the towns, set the basic pattern for the few later developments. Towns, in fact, operated under the system established by the Duke's Laws for the remainder of the English era. City governments, established by Governor Dongan in 1686, also continued along the general guidelines he set.

Nevertheless, there was some growth in the structure and operations of New York City after 1731. In that year, the corporation successfully petitioned Governor John Montgomerie for a revision of the city's charter. While generally satisfied with the Dongan grant, there were several desirable amendments, the corporation thought, including one providing for the election of the mayor and other officers. To its petition, the corporation affixed a "sweetener" of £1,000. Montgomerie cheerfully accepted the bribe as well as most of the amendments but not, unfortunately, the popular election of the mayor. Not even the American Revolution could dislodge this prerogative from the higher levels of government.

The Montgomerie charter marked a major change in the character of the city corporation. Until then, it had been "closed" as city corporations were in England but thereafter became, according to Carl Bridenbaugh, "more responsive to public opinion in respect to services offered and . . . judicial activities."[45] The growth and spread of population was accommodated by the insertion of a new ward (named for Governor Montgomerie) in the northeastern section. Gubernatorial control of the ordinance-making power was loosened so that a regulation was effective not merely for three months but for a full year when it lapsed unless it had been approved by the governor. The mayor now could appoint his own deputy and his authority was expanded as clerk of markets. The common council, however, disputed the mayor's new prerogatives and eventually succeeded in wresting the power to rent market stalls from the mayor.[46]

Possibly the most important function of the mayor and aldermen of New York was as a judicial body. The cases that came before the mayor's court were much the same as those tried in a county court.

Here, however, the judges (except for the mayor or recorder) were elected by the people and were subject to annual review by the electorate. A full bench was the mayor or recorder with four aldermen. The court sat once a week on civil matters such as the 1736 judgment it rendered for William Bradford who needed a decree to recover £28 he had lent to John Peter Zenger—both publishers of newspapers but only the latter has achieved historical fame. More interestingly, however, the court also dealt with smuggled goods. Its records are replete with cases curiously entitled. Archibald Kennedy *qui tam* versus Twenty-Eight Casks of Rum or Richard Nicolls *qui tam* versus Thirty-Seven Casks of Gunpowder.[47] Since no owner appeared to claim these "waifs," the court's work was quickly done. As a result, the royal treasury was richer by one-third the value of the contraband, the governor too got his third, and the complainant was rewarded with the remainder.

The New York Corporation performed a number of other functions as well. It could, as in 1731, borrow £1,000 from James De Lancey at an annual interest of 8 percent by mortgaging certain lands. Or it might grant lots extending 200 feet into the East River. Such property might, at first glance, seem unattractive but it was coveted for dockage and ferry sites. The mayor, aldermen, et al. had to be vigilant against encroachment of the common lands. In peacetime they provided a storehouse for gunpowder, while in wartime they bought arms to protect the province. At all times they had to be ready with a silver box and a diploma granting the freedom of the city to some visiting dignitary.[48]

Both the appointed and elected officers of the city corporation held other posts as well. Some mayors and recorders (like Stephen Bayard, Edward Holland, Francis Harrison, and Daniel Horsmanden) were also members of the Provincial Council. In that body, they were gubernatorial advisers, members of the upper legislative house, and also judges in the highest court of appeals in the province. Several aldermen, especially during the mid–eighteenth century, simultaneously sat in the New York General Assembly. They thus doubly breached the wall of separation between legislature and judiciary since they were both elected representatives at the city and provincial levels and judges and justices of the peace. Though not so common as to be the rule, a number of these aldermen had started as collectors or assessors in their wards, then rose to assistant, later securing their election as aldermen, and finally a seat in the Assembly.

Not all citizens were equally willing to serve the municipality. Stephen De Lancey, for instance, excused himself from accepting the honor of alderman for the West Ward because he already served the public as an assemblyman. Later, William Smith, Sr., was equally loath to serve as constable of the same ward. Each was fined substantially for refusing these offices.[49]

Elections to city posts were held annually in each ward with the incumbent aldermen supervising the process. A particular election might be close but rare was it for a city-wide effort to be mounted. During a couple of the years in the mid-1730s the municipal elections were contested by factions named "Who Ares" and "Who are Nots."[50] This cryptic division seems to have disappeared shortly after Governor Cosby's death, whereafter the elections subsided to their more customary level of fragmentation and mild concern. The absence of something to oppose made cohesive party organization difficult, especially since New Yorkers objected to any influences from outside their own ward.

The participants in these municipal elections were a clearly defined but numerically imprecise group. The ordinary title to the elective franchise was acquired by men when they reached adulthood and also owned a freehold worth at least £40. They had the right to vote wherever they held the requisite amount of property or else (so New Yorkers argued) they would be taxed without granting their consent. In New York City and Albany, however, the franchise was also extended to freemen of the respective corporations. These were mechanics who had completed their apprenticeships within the municipality or who upon immigration had paid the stipulated fees. If a newcomer to New York considered himself a "merchant" and wanted to participate in civic life, he paid about £3 sterling while an "artisan" was charged only 20s. In the first decade of the eighteenth century, the city fathers were anxious to attract industrious citizens and so briefly cut the fees to £1 sterling and 6s. respectively, and even these fees could be waived for a particularly desirable tradesmen.[51] What proportion of the city's population was enfranchised as a result of these laws and practices cannot be established with precision, although the tendency of recent scholarship has been to raise the ratio of poten-

tial voters to total adult population to something approximating
"democracy."

The only other jurisdiction comparable to New York City was
Albany, whose government also had received its fundamental structure under Governor Thomas Dongan. In its charter, Albany was
divided into three wards with two aldermen, two assistants, and one
constable elected annually from each. The governor appointed the
mayor but quite often merely accepted the candidate preferred by
the merchant clique. Together, the mayor and common council appointed the treasurer and various other officers. So staunchly com-
pacted was the Albany Corporation that it could, on occasion,
even defy a royal commission for an alien town clerk.[52]

There were other somewhat less imposing municipalities. Westchester and Schenectady were unique in that each also had the
right to elect a member to the General Assembly. Their structure
differed, however, in that the mayor of Schenectady was appointed
by the governor and "his honor" of Westchester was locally elected
from among the aldermen. The latter were chosen from the assistants and these in turn were elected by the freemen of the corporation.[53] This arrangement insured stability as is evident from the
fact that Isaac Willett held the mayoralty for the decade of the
1740s, while Nathaniel Underhill served for most of the following
decade. Both Willett and Underhill also held other local authority.

Another contrast may also be found in the tendency of the Westchester and Long Island towns to follow the example of New England, from which many of their original inhabitants had migrated.
To a greater extent than their counterparts in the Hudson Valley,
these tended to rely on regular and frequent town meetings to determine local affairs. Although annual town meetings were held
along the Hudson River, they were mainly to elect officers and to
review affairs of the past year; in the interim between such gatherings, more reliance was given to the municipal officers.

Of the still smaller towns, the most recent detailed study has
been made of Kingston, originally a Dutch fur trading post on the
west bank of the Hudson. From 1711 to 1776, over a hundred and
thirty men served on its board of trustees—a dozen at a time. Some
of the Kingston officers had a long tenure and significantly, they
tended to be young at the time of their initial election, being on
an average between thirty and forty years old. Furthermore, only

four of the Kingston trustees could be considered "gentlemen" with many yeomen farmers but most being artisans: shoemakers, carpenters, blacksmiths, brewers, and the like. From a 1728 list of freeholders it is evident that at one time or another nearly half of them served as trustees. There are other indices to demonstrate that local government in Kingston was broadly participatory as well as vigorous. Although no equivalent study has been made for any other township, there is evidence to justify the conclusion that local government experience provided the critically needed base for the American idea and practice of popular sovereignty.[54]

Viewed in the light of the above data, local government should be considered an important part of the life of colonial New Yorkers. Like us today, their contact was more often with the town, municipality, precinct, or county officers than with those of the province or higher. There were, of course, a number of differences between their governmental operations and ours; education, for one thing, was not a matter of public concern during the English period of New York's history. Their lives, however, like ours, were intimately regulated by the rules, customs, or officers of their localities. Most significantly, this level of government was subject to notable popular influences.

If on the eve of the American Revolution some keen observer looked at the structure of New York's local government, he would be surveying familiar terrain. The general form still carried the character of English county and municipal government but there were also significant adaptations to American conditions. Our observer, however hard he tried, would discern no significant changes in that structure after the mid–eighteenth century. There had been minor adjustments to accommodate the settlement of new territories but this did not significantly affect the basic framework. Nor could he discern even with the sharpest vision any remnants of specifically Dutch institutions. The Dutch were an important socio-political factor, but they like all New Yorkers operated within a local model of English character.

Neither was there any evident trend toward centralization. What the county sheriffs, judges, and supervisors were doing early in the eighteenth century, they were still doing later. There were some political developments that may be judged as having a centralizing tendency. The emergence, after 1765, of the General Assembly as a more cohesive political institution and the appearance of organized factions pointed in that direction. The Assembly, as noted above, was an extension of local governance and political factions also had local roots.

If our observer moved a decade or two forward in time, he would find that the structure of New York's local government had provided a comfortable framework for revolutionary organization and governmental operations. Committees of observation, correspondence, and safety might be formed, but these in the main tended to utilize the familiar mechanisms and offices. The general acceptance of the earlier structure is symbolically evident in the continuation of the practice of appointing New York City's mayors even after independence, as before. What had worked before the Revolution was not discarded summarily.

With such "reluctant" revolutionaries, how can a historian explain the difference between the structure of local government in England and colonial New York? Speculation suggests the source was the pragmatic, adaptive character of the English which initially spawned the variations in New York. There may also have been another element. The English had a less thoroughly rationalized authoritarian tradition than either France or Spain. Instead of professionals and bureaucrats, the English government relied, in some measure, on "amateurs"—a landlord, for instance, who also served as justice of the peace.

In the northern colonies, there was not time enough nor willing subjects to conglomerate the "cake of custom," which was so important to the government of Old England. With "republican" New England as the magnet, the home authorities were drawn to establish a local level of government in New York with a strong elective (and thus necessarily, "amateur") element. Instead of paying taxes or fees to support one of the "better sort" in public service, rather ordinary New Yorkers gave their time and talents directly or elected some neighbor. At some future election, it would come their turn to collect taxes or protect the tranquillity of the town. These might be men of some position in the province but they lacked the imposing character and multiple connections of their English counterparts.

The effect of this development was greater than was intended or could have been foreseen. Englishmen recognized popular participation in government as a source of social cohesion and strength. Edmund Burke, in his October 3, 1777, letter to the Bell Club of Bristol, argued:

> In a free country every man thinks he has a concern in all public matters. . . . They sift, examine, and discuss them. . . . And this it is that fills free countries with men of ability in all stations. . . . [I]n other countries none but men whose office calls them to it having much care or thought about public affairs, and not daring to try the force of their opinions with one another, ability of this sort is extremely rare in any station of life. In free countries, there is often found more real public wisdom and sagacity in shops and manufactories than in the cabinets of princes where none dares have an opinion until he [the prince] comes into them.

Burke obviously saw England as the paradigm of a "free country" where the discussion of public affairs was more widespread. New York, which Burke had served for a time as colonial agent, had pushed the process beyond debate to actual administration by multiplying offices and by electing many of its public servants. This process of simplification and extension arose out of practical necessity because New York's society lacked the bracing influence of the solid social structure and "worthies" which existed in England. The pragmatic adaptation and reliance on "amateurs" (both thoroughly English) produced in New York a people who would eventually seek a future separate from that of the mother country.

NOTES

1. Patricia Bonomi, *A Factious People* (New York, 1971), 20, 31–32.

2. Irving Mark, *Agrarian Conflicts in Colonial New York, 1711–1775* (reprint, Port Washington, N.Y., 1965), 56–68; Patricia Bonomi, "Local Government in Colonial New York: A Base for Republicanism," in *Aspects of Early New York Society and Politics,* ed. Jacob Judd and Irwin H. Polishook (Tarrytown, N.Y., 1974), 46.

3. Herbert L. Osgood, *The American Colonies in the Seventeenth Century* (reprint, Gloucester, Mass., 1957), II, 47–50, 107–8.

4. Henry H. Kessler and Eugene Rachlis, *Peter Stuyvesant and his New York* (New York, 1959), 127–29, 250–68; Osgood, *Colonies in the 17th Century,* II, 108, 388; Carl Bridenbaugh, *Cities in the Wilderness,* paperback ed. (New York, 1971), 64–65. For details of the municipal administration during the later years of the Dutch period, see Berthold Fernow, ed., *Minutes of the Executive Board of Burgonmasters of New Amsterdam* (reprint, New York, 1970).

5. Osgood, *Colonies in the Seventeenth Century,* II, 119-23.

6. Osgood, *Colonies in the Seventeenth Century,* II, 122, 128, 134-38, 352-53, 392; Historical Records Survey, WPA, *Transcript of Early Town Records of New York, Town Minutes of Newtown, 1638-1688* (New York, 1940), I, ix (hereafter, HRS. WPA).

7. Osgood, *Colonies in the Seventeenth Century,* II, 123-24.

8. Osgood, *Colonies in the Seventeenth Century,* II, 282-83.

9. Osgood, *Colonies in the Seventeenth Century,* II, 162-65.

10. Marcus Benjamin, "Thomas Dongan and the Granting of the New York Charter, 1682-1688," in *The Memorial History of the City of New York* ed. James Grant Wilson (New York, 1892), I, 406, 408; Osgood, *Colonies in the Seventeenth Century,* II, 166-68.

11. *New York Weekly Journal* (NYC), April 8, 1734.

12. HRS, WPA, *Newtown Minutes, 1638-1688,* I, ix.

13. Bejamin, "Dongan," 411-13, 425-26.

14. Jerome R. Reich, *Leisler's Rebellion* (Chicago, 1953), 64, 66, 72, 76, 81; Osgood, *Colonies in the Seventeenth Century,* II, 450, 460-64.

15. Charles Z. Lincoln et al., eds., *The Colonial Laws of New York from the Year 1664 to the Revolution* (Albany, 1894-96), I, 268, 915; IV, 903-5, 931, 944.

16. William Smith, Jr., *The History of the Province of New York,* ed. Michael G. Kammen (Cambridge, Mass., 1972), I, 260.

17. Henry Beekman to Henry Livingston, January 7, 1745, Henry Beekman Letters, New York Historical Society (hereafter, NYHS).

18. Cyrus Harreld Karraker, *The Seventeenth Century Sheriff* (Chapel Hill, N.C., 1930), 150-56.

19. Abraham Yates Junior, Journal, October 31, 1757 Autograph Letter Series, VI, New York Public Library.

20. Alice P. Kenney, *The Gansevoorts of Albany* (Syracuse, 1969), 84-88.

21. Cadwallader Colden to John Catherwood, January 3, 1748, George Clinton Papers, William L. Clements Library, Ann Arbor, Mich., VII; Colden to George Clinton, January 24, 1748, ibid.; *New York Weekly Journal* (NYC), November 5, 1733.

22. William Livingston et al., *The Independent Reflector,* ed. Milton M. Klein (Cambridge, Mass., 1963), 352; Bonomi, "Local Government," 37.

23. Smith, *History,* I, 261.

24. Livingston, *Independent Reflector, 353.*

25. Smith, *History,* I, 261; see also Edmund B. O'Callaghan, ed., *Calendar of New York Colonial Commissions, 1680-1770* (New York, 1929), 18, 44, 56, 73, 74; and Nicholas Varga, "New York Government and Politics during the Mid-Eighteenth Century," Ph.D. diss. (Fordham University, 1960), 419-73 passim. These are lists compiled from county histories, the calendar of commissions, etc.

26. Smith, *History,* I, 265-66; Edward Floyd De Lancey, "Memoir of the Honorable James De Lancey Lieutenant Governor of the Province of New York," in *Documentary History of the State of New York,* ed. Edmund B. O'Callaghan (Albany, 1851), IV, 634, 639.

27. Bonomi, *Factious People,* 303; Varga, "New York Government," 419-73 passim.

28. Beekman to Livingston, January 21, 1747, Beekman Letters. There might however be an occasional dismissal from office to prove the governor's power and displeasure. See Lewis Morris to Colden, January 17, 1734, *The Letters and Papers of Cadwallader Colden,* NYHS, *Collections,* LI (New York, 1919), II, 101.

29. Charles Worthen Spencer, "Sectional Aspects of New York Provincial Politics," *Political Science Quarterly,* XXX (September 1915), 416.

30. Beekman to Livingston, January 5, 1741; January 7, 1747, Beekman Letters; *New York Weekly Post-Boy* (NYC), October 10, 1743; *New York Mercury* (NYC), November 13, 1752; Livingston, *Independent Reflector,* 278-84; Smith, *History,* I, 259.

31. Bonomi, "Local Government," 33.

32. Lincoln, *Colonial Laws*, I, 1034; II, 956; IV, 615, 1104; Bonomi, "Local Government," 46.

33. Franklin Delano Roosevelt, ed., *Records of Crum Elbow Precinct, 1738-1761*, Collections of the Dutchess County Historical Society, VII (1940).

34. Lincoln, *Colonial Laws*, I, 248, 423, 835-36.

35. Ibid., I, 931; II, 51, 80, 119.

36. Ibid., II, 2.

37. Livingston, *Independent Reflector*, 61-68, 228-34.

38. Lincoln, *Colonial Laws*, III, 951-52.

39. *New York Gazette and Weekly Post-Boy* (NYC), February 15, 1755.

40. Lincoln, *Colonial Laws*, II, 68-72.

41. Livingston, *Independent Reflector*, 69-75.

42. Lincoln, *Colonial Laws*, II, 1015-38; IV, 156-58, 708; V, 149; see also Theodore Thayer, "The Land Bank System in the American Colonies," *Journal of Economic History*, XIII (Spring 1953), 145-59.

43. I, 729, December 5, 1737.

44. Lincoln, *Colonial Laws*, I, 329, 544, 577, 579; Livingston, *Independent Reflector*, 267-77; *John Englishman* (NYC) April 9, 1755; Smith, *History*, I, 233-45; R. Townshend Henshaw, "The New York Ministry Act of 1693," *Historical Magazine of the Protestant Episcopal Church*, II (1933), 199-204.

45. Bonomi, "Local Government," 47, quoted in Carl Bridenbaugh, *Cities in Revolt*, paperback ed. (New York, 1971), 8; Bridenbaugh, *Cities in the Wilderness*, 304; Sidney I. Pomerantz, *New York: An American City, 1783-1803* (New York, 1938), 125, 143.

46. Smith, *History*, I, 210; *Minutes of the Common Council of the City of New York* (New York, 1905), V 40, 67, 163, 188, 207; VI, 85, 209, 262.

47. Richard B. Morris, ed., *Select Cases of the Mayor's Court of New York City, 1674-1784* (Washington, D.C., 1935), 491-94, 593, 620.

48. *Minutes of Common Council*, IV, 44, 45, 227, 328, 421.

49. *Minutes of Common Council*, III, 50; V, 156.

50. *New York Weekly Journal* (NYC), October 7, 1734; October 6, 13, 1735.

51. Mark, *Agrarian Conflicts*, 94-95; Robert Francis Seybolt, *The Colonial Citizen of New York City* (Madison, Wisc., 1918), 4, 6, 14, 16, 18.

52. Kenney, *Gansevoorts*, 58-61.

53. Robert Bolton, *History of the County of Westchester* (New York, 1881), II, part I, 308; Jonathan Pearson, *A History of the Schenectady Patent* (Albany, 1883), 130.

54. Bonomi, "Local Government," 45, 33-36, 48-50, 138.

Local Government in Colonial Pennsylvania

WAYNE L. BOCKELMAN

Four units of local government existed in Pennsylvania during the colonial period: the county, the township, the borough, and the city. Of these the county was the main unit, to which the others were related in varying degrees. The township was the most closely related, for it was a subdivision of the county. The borough, a form rarely found in colonial Pennsylvania, was more of an independent entity than the township but still within the jurisdiction of the county. Only three boroughs existed at the end of the colonial period: Chester, erected in 1701; Bristol, in 1720; and Lancaster, in 1742. The city, of course, was Philadelphia, organized as a corporation since at least 1701; even it, however, was not completely separate from the county in which it was located.[1]

During the years from 1682 to 1776, eleven counties were created in Pennsylvania. Three were erected in 1682 when the colony was established under the proprietorship of William Penn: Bucks, Chester,

216

and Philadelphia Counties. All three were situated in the south-eastern corner of Pennsylvania along the Delaware River. The next county created was Lancaster, in 1729. It was formed from the western part of Chester County, and its creation indicated the west-ward expansion of Pennsylvania's population. As this expansion con-tinued, more counties resulted. In 1749 and 1750, respectively, York and Cumberland Counties were taken from Lancaster County, and in 1752 parts of Lancaster, Chester, and Philadelphia Counties were de-tached to form Berks. Also in 1752 the northern part of Bucks County became Northampton County. Berks and Northampton lay to the north and northwest of the original counties, indicating the movement of settlers in that direction as well as to the west. The creation of Bedford, Northumberland, and Westmoreland in the early 1770s completed the process of county formation during the colonial period. Bedford was detached in 1771 from the western part of Cum-berland County, Northumberland was formed in 1772 in the north-central part of Pennsylvania from its five contiguous counties, and Westmoreland was erected in 1773 out of the southwestern corner of Bedford.[2]

The structure of county government as it existed at the end of the colonial period was based upon the Charter of Privileges of 1701, which set the framework of Pennsylvania's government until 1776, and upon various statutes adopted during the eighteenth century. By using the mode of selection as a basis, the various officials can be divided into three categories: elective, elective-appointive, and appointive. The first are those officials who were chosen directly by the electorate. The second are those whom the voters nominated but whose final selection and appointment were made by the gov-ernor of Pennsylvania. The third category includes those appointed by provincial and by county authorities.

The solely elective officials were the county commissioners and the county assessors. The commissioners appeared first in 1711 as of-ficials appointed by the Assembly. Several times during the follow-ing decade the Assembly changed the number of commissioners in each county and the appointees who held those positions. Finally, in 1722, the office was made elective, and the number of com-missioners was set at three. The shift to an elective body was gradual, however, and was not completed until 1725. In that year an act was passed which combined previous acts and specifically stipulated that there were to be three commissioners, with one being chosen yearly. The 1725 act also implied, as had the 1722 act, that there was a limit of three years' service at one time. This was not complied with, however, and in 1732 such a limit was placed on a commissioner by forbidding his reelection at the end of his term.[3] As for the assessors, an act of 1696 provided for the yearly election of six assessors, with no limit on their length of service; this practice continued throughout the colonial period.[4] The election of a commissioner and the assessors occurred on October 1 of each year.

The primary responsibility and function of the commissioners and assessors was handling the financial business of the county. This involved calculating county expenses and levying and collecting county taxes to cover those expenses. It also involved levying and collecting some provincial taxes. Originally, the assessment, collection, and disbursement of the county taxes were the responsibility of the justices of the peace, in conjunction with the grand jury and, after 1696, the newly created assessors. In 1718 the commissioners were given this task, along with the assessors. Limits were placed, however, on the amount of tax that they could impose on county residents.[5] The provincial taxes—specific property and capitation taxes —had been handled in the late seventeenth century by two or more of the assemblymen from each county, with assistance from the justices or "other substantial freeholders." In 1699 the justices replaced the assemblymen and held the primary responsibility for the taxation process until 1711. In that year the commissioners were created to levy and collect these provincial taxes, along with the county assessors, and they continued to do so whenever the Assembly legislated such taxes.[6]

Whatever taxes were being raised, provincial or county, the same procedure was followed. The commissioners issued an order that a list be made of the residents in each township and their property. The kinds of property that formed the basis of assessment were defined by the Assembly, and by the end of the colonial period included land, livestock, "bound servants and negroes," various types of mills, "forges, furnaces, mines, house rents, ground rents, trades or occupations, and all offices and posts of profit." Prior to 1758 the constable in each township gathered this information; after 1758, a township assessor was elected to do this work. Once gathered, the information was given to the county assessors, who proceeded to rate those liable for taxation, including single freemen over twenty-one. (From 1758 to 1774 the township assessors joined them, but in 1774 the task reverted solely to the county assessors.) The county assessors divided the county into districts and appointed a tax collector for each district to inform the taxables of their rates. After the taxables had had an opportunity to appeal to the commissioners if they felt an injustice in their rates, the collectors collected the tax and paid it to the county treasurer, an official appointed by the commissioners and assessors to handle the funds.[7]

The revenue from the provincial taxes went to the provincial treasurer for provincial expenses. The revenue from the county taxes was under the control of the commissioners and assessors and was used for county expenses: "to defray the charges of building and re-pairing of court houses, prisons, workhouses, bridges and causeways at the ends of bridges or for destroying wolves, foxes and crows, with such other uses as may redound to the public service and benefit of the said counties."[8] Remuneration for most local officials and, until 1732, a county's assemblymen also came from the county treasury.[9]

The elective-appointive officials were the sheriff and the coroner. Both these offices began with the first Frame of Government in 1682 and were continued in the succeeding frames (1683 and 1696) and the Charter of Privileges in 1701. The electorate voted for two candidates for each office, and the governor appointed one of the two highest vote-getters in each case. If the governor did not make an appointment, the nominee with the highest number of votes received the office. Yearly election was stipulated in the early Frames of Government, but under the Charter of Privileges, the term of office was lengthened to three years. In 1706, however, the term was restored to one year for both the sheriff and the coroner, and this remained so for the rest of the colonial period. In 1730 a limit of three years of service at one time was imposed on the sheriff, with no reelection until another three years had lapsed. Usually, a sheriff was reelected twice for a total of three years. The coroner was under no such restriction regarding reelection, and consequently, some served for many years.[10] Both officials were chosen at the October 1 election.

The sheriff had important administrative functions in judicial and electoral matters. His responsibilities in the judicial area included

selecting jurors, making arrests, serving summonses, and executing
the decisions of the justices of the county courts. In the matter of
elections, his responsibilities were appointing clerks to help with the
elections, checking electors to make certain they were qualified to
vote, taking charge of the ballot boxes after the election, and certifying the names of those elected—the assemblymen to the Assembly, the county commissioners and assessors to the justices of
the court of quarter sessions, and the sheriff and coroner to the governor. In the absence of the sheriff, the coroner was to perform these
duties, but the latter's main functions were to view dead bodies if
occasion required, to summon inquests to investigate unnatural or
suspicious deaths, and to summon or arrest the sheriff if necessary.[11]

The third category was the appointive officials. Of those appointed
by provincial authorities, perhaps the most important was the justice
of the peace, chosen by the governor. Under the First and Second
Frames of Government (1682 and 1683), this official was actually
an elective-appointive one, like the sheriff and coroner, and had a
term of one year. But in 1701, if not earlier, the justice became a
solely appointive official, with no specified term of office. Although
single appointments were sometimes made, usually all of the justices
for a county were appointed at the same time. The occasions for
such appointments were the arrival of a new governor, the existence
of several vacancies on the county court, or the need for additional
justices. A justice's most important responsibilities were connected
with his service on the county courts, but on an individual basis,
he could settle suits for debts under 40s.[12]

Collectively, the justices constituted three courts: the court of
quarter sessions, the court of common pleas, and the orphans' court.
Before 1707, there had been only one court, which had jurisdiction
over both civil and criminal cases and sat twice a year as an orphans'
court. In 1707, however, by an ordinance of the governor, the
separate courts of quarter sessions and common pleas were established. Because of a long struggle over judicial powers between the
Assembly on the one hand, and the governor, the proprietor, and
the crown on the other, it was not until 1722 that the Assembly
passed a judiciary act that was accepted in England. That act, which
formed the basis of Pennsylvania's judicial system for the rest of the
colonial period, continued the existence of the two separate courts.
However, the same justices served both courts, for the custom was

to issue joint commissions. An attempt in 1759 to split the composition of the two courts was disallowed by the King in 1760.[13] As for the orphans' court, an act passed in 1713 required the justices of the quarter sessions court to act as justices of the orphans' court. This practice prevailed, although an effort was made, unsuccessfully, in 1759 to transfer jurisdiction over orphans to the common pleas court.[14]

The court of common pleas handled "all manner of pleas, actions, suits and causes, civil, personal, real and mixed." The court of quarter sessions tried such criminal cases as assault and battery, breach of the peace, and drunkenness, but, unless a special commission of oyer and terminer was granted, the Supreme Court of Pennsylvania tried such major crimes as treason, murder, burglary, rape, and arson. The orphans' court had jurisdiction over the estates of orphans in the county, with the power to summon the guardians or trustees for an accounting of those estates.[15]

The quarter sessions court had additional functions of an administrative and appointive nature. Among the most important of these were caring for the poor, authorizing the building of county roads and the maintaining of both county and provincial roads, and recommending to the governor those who should receive tavern licenses.[16] The fulfillment of the first two of these responsibilities involved the yearly appointment, since at least 1706, of one or more overseers of the poor for each township and borough, and, until 1762, of overseers of the highways for the county. Another appointive function of this court was selecting the constable for each township from the two top candidates nominated by the electorate.[17]

The clerks who were responsible for keeping the records of the three county courts were also appointed by the governor. The office of clerk existed from the beginning of the colony, at first serving, of course, the then sole court. Even after the split into two courts in 1707, there seems to have been only a single clerk, for not until 1715 are there references to the separate offices. Following the procedure defined in the Charter of Privileges in 1701 for selecting the clerk of the peace, the clerk of quarter sessions was appointed by the governor from three candidates nominated by the justices of the quarter sessions court.[18] No evidence was found, however, that the appointment of the prothonotary of the common pleas court resulted from a similar procedure. In fact, since the same person usually held both offices, as well as clerk of the orphans' court, and since commissions were usually issued simultaneously, it would seem that the appointment of the prothonotary followed pro forma that of the quarter sessions clerk. In at least two instances, however, a person's appointment as prothonotary preceded his appointment as clerk of quarter sessions, and in another instance, the justices made nominations for the clerkship two months *after* the governor had appointed the prothonotary. Moreover, in the last case, the prothonotary's name headed the list of the three submitted. This suggests that the nomination process was not a particularly meaningful or influential one and that the governor essentially retained the prerogative of appointing whomever he wished.[19]

A local office of great significance for the daily and continuing life of the county was the recorder of deeds. Beginning in 1682 the governor had appointed a master of the rolls for the colony, who, after 1706, was to serve an enrollment office in each county either by himself or through a deputy. In 1715 the office of recorder of deeds was clearly established in each county and the manner of appointment defined. The Assembly stipulated that, initially, the prothonotary or county clerk should act as recorder in each of the counties except Philadelphia, where a specifically named person was appointed by the Assembly. Replacements were to be named by the justices of the quarter sessions court. From the minutes of the Provincial Council, however, it would seem that succeeding appointments were made by the governor without any role being played by the justices.[20]

Another office of similar importance was the register of wills, actually the deputy register. A registry office for the colony was created in 1682, and by 1700 an official with the title of register-general existed who evidently could appoint deputies in the counties. In 1706 the Assembly stated definitely that there "shall be an officer called register-general, to be commissionated by the governor from time to time . . . , which register-general shall keep his office at Philadelphia, and shall from time to time constitute a sufficient deputy to officiate for him in each of the other counties."[21] Usually, the register-general appointed the same person serving as recorder, who, in turn, was usually the clerk of the various county courts. Like his superior, the deputy register was "empowered to take probates of wills and grant letters of administration."[22]

One local official, the collector of excise, was appointed by the Assembly. The office dated from the early days of the colony when a duty was imposed on the importation of wine, rum, brandy, and other alcoholic beverages to raise revenue for the provincial treasury. Later the duty was changed to an excise on alcoholic beverages retailed and sold in Pennsylvania.[23] At first, the governor appointed a collector or collectors for the colony. In 1711 the Assembly assumed the appointive power, naming a collector who could appoint others under him. Beginning in 1730 a collector was named for each county, and he served, until 1756, for the duration of the excise. In 1756 provision was made for yearly appointments, but not until 1769 did the Assembly make appointments on such a basis; in the interim, collectors were allowed to continue automatically for the period of the excise. Before making an appointment, the Assembly usually received petitions from individuals within a county who wanted the office, probably because it paid a certain percentage of the revenue collected.[24]

Two other county officials were appointed by provincial authorities: the county surveyor by the surveyor-general of the colony, and the sealer of weights and measures by the governor.[25] How regularly such appointments were made is unclear.

Finally, two officials, the county treasurer and the clerk of the commissioners, were appointed at the county level. The county treasurer's office began, it seems, with tne creation of the assessors in 1696. They made the appointment until 1718, when the county commissioners joined them in naming this official. (From 1711 to 1718 both the commissioners and the assessors appointed a subtreasurer in the county for handling the provincial taxes, but after 1718 the county treasurer assumed this task.[26]) The clerk of the commissioners dated from at least 1722, when there is a reference to "their clerks"; prior to that time, the clerk of the peace was supposed to perform such tasks as issuing precepts from the commissioners. The commissioners alone were authorized to appoint the clerk, but in at least one county, the assessors also participated.[27]

The officials of the townships into which the counties were subdivided helped to administer the affairs of the county. Perhaps the most important official was the constable, whose functions in many ways paralleled those of the sheriff at the county level. Among his

TABLE 1.
County Offices

Official	Selected By
Elective:	
Commissioners	Electors
Assessors	
Elective-Appointive:	
Sheriff	Two candidates for each office
Coroner	nominated by the electors; one
	appointed by the Governor
Appointive (Provincial):	
Prothonotary	
Clerk, quarter sessions	
Clerk, orphans' court	Governor
Justices of the peace	
Recorder of deeds	
Sealer of weights and measures	
Deputy register of wills	Register-General
County surveyor	Surveyor-General
Collector of excise	Assembly
Appointive (Local):	
County treasurer	Commissioners, or commission-
Clerk, county commissioners	ers and assessors

varied duties, he served warrants issued by the justices of the peace, assisted the county's collector of excise in collecting duties, enforced the law that forbade drinking in public houses on Sundays, apprehended rioters, and presided over township elections. For most of the colonial period he also played a role in the taxation process by gathering information for the county assessors on the real and personal property of inhabitants within his township.[28] The constable was an elective-appointive official, nominated yearly in April by the electors in each township, who voted for two candidates, and appointed by the county's court of quarter sessions from the two top candidates.[29]

One elected official in the township participated in the county's taxation procedure and another in its election procedure. The township assessor was created in 1758 to join the constable in gathering the data upon which tax assessments were made and to assist the county assessors in levying the rates on the taxables in his township. The former task became solely the township assessor's in 1759, but the latter joint responsibility continued until 1774, when it reverted to the county assessors alone.[30] Aiding the sheriff in conducting the county's elections was the inspector of the election, an official existing since at least 1706 but only on the township level since 1752. Each year in late September, at the same time that the township assessor was elected, electors in the township chose one person to receive their votes at the regular election held on October 1 for the county's assemblymen, commissioner, assessors, sheriff, and coroner. The inspector was also charged with administering an oath to electors whose qualifications for voting might be challenged at the polls.[31]

The holders of two offices served the court of quarters sessions in carrying out its duties of caring for the poor and of maintaining the roads in the county. From at least 1706 to 1771 the justices of the quarter sessions court appointed yearly one, two, or more overseers of the poor in each township (after 1771 the number was set at two) from names suggested by the outgoing overseers. These officials could, with the approval of three (later two) justices, lay a tax on inhabitants "to be employed for the relief of the poor, indigent and impotent persons inhabiting within the said townships."[32] For the "opening, clearing, amending and repairing" of roads, each township elected one or two supervisors of the highways in March of each year beginning in 1765. The office actually dated from the 1680s but on a countywide and then a precinctwide basis and as an appointive office until 1762 (the justices of the quarter sessions court made the appointment). With the approval of at least two justices, the supervisors could levy a tax to raise money for hiring laborers and buying the materials necessary for road maintenance.[33]

To complete the list of formal township officials is the poundkeeper. Established at the township level in 1729, this official was elected in May of every year and was to care for stray horses, cattle, or sheep. If the animals were not claimed within three months, he was authorized to sell them, after first getting a warrant from a justice of the peace within the county. To pay for the construction and maintenance of pounds in the township, the overseers of the poor could assess inhabitants "in the same manner as they are directed by the act for the relief of the poor."[34]

Like the townships, the three boroughs had a local assessor, overseer of the poor, a constable (actually high constable), and (at least

TABLE 2.
Township Officials

Official	Selected By
Elective:	
Township assessor	Electors
Inspector of the election	
Supervisor of the highways	
Poundkeeper	
Elective-Appointive:	
Constable	Two candidates nominated by the electors; one appointed by the justices of the quarter sessions court
Appointive:	
Overseers of the poor	Justices of the quarter sessions court

in Lancaster) an inspector of the election, for, like the townships, they were subordinate units of the county in matters of county and provincial taxes, care of the poor, the administration of justice, and county elections. The main difference from the township was that a borough's high constable was an elective rather than an elective-appointive official.[35]

There were other officials in the boroughs, however, that were peculiarly theirs. Four burgesses were elected in Chester and two each in Bristol and Lancaster, with the burgess who received the highest number of votes holding the position of chief burgess. Five councilmen in Bristol and six assistants in Lancaster assisted the burgesses and were chosen yearly, like the burgesses, by the boroughs' "freeholders and housekeepers."[36] All three boroughs had a town clerk, who was elected in Lancaster but appointed in Bristol and probably in Chester, and a clerk of the market, a position held by the high constable in Bristol and Chester and by an appointee removable by the burgesses and assistants in Lancaster.[37]

These officials had powers, and the boroughs' inhabitants had rights, that indicate a sizeable degree of self-government. Indeed, in many respects these powers and rights made the borough more nearly equal to rather than subordinate to the county. The burgesses and the constable (and in Lancaster the assistants) could call town meetings at which inhabitants could "make such Ordinances and

Rules . . . as to the greatest part of the Town-meeting shall seem necessary and convenient for the good Government of the said Town."[38] In Bristol and Chester this power included the creation of "such other Officers as by the Burgesses and Freemen shall be judged needful for assisting and serving the Burgesses in managing the Affairs of the said Borough, and keeping of the Peace therein."[39] Furthermore, the burgesses were granted judicial authority within the borough similar to that of the justices in the county for they were "impowered and authorized to be Conservators of the Peace . . . and shall have Power by themselves and upon their own view . . . to remove all Nuisances and Incroachments out of the said Streets as they shall see Occasion: With Power also to arrest, imprison and punish Rioters and Breakers of the Peace, and to bind them and all other Offenders and Persons of evil Fame to the Peace or good Behaviour, as fully and effectually as any of the Justices of the Peace in the said County can do."[40]

In theory there were limits to the borough's self-government, but in fact the restrictions were not too severe. Although the charters granted no power to tax, Bristol and Lancaster did acquire such power during the eighteenth century. While the burgesses were seemingly required to receive approval from the court of quarter sessions for their judicial actions, they did not do so in practice. Even though only the chief burgess of Chester was automatically a justice of the peace in the county, in fact a burgess in each borough was usually included in the list of justices for the county.[41] Moreover, with the subsequent legislation which granted taxation power to Bristol and Lancaster, additional borough officials were created, which further enhanced the self-rule of those boroughs. In 1746 Bristol was authorized to elect yearly two or more assessors to levy assessments for maintaining a house of correction or workhouse, "and also for building a market house, public stalls and bridges, repairing town wharves, regulating the streets and highways, and to and for such other public uses as they the said Burgesses or either of them . . . shall judge necessary for the year ensuing." The high constable was designated the collector of the borough tax, and the burgesses and councilmen were given power to appoint a treasurer for the borough as well as the officials of the workhouse. Almost thirty years later, in 1774, the Lancaster burgesses and assistants received power to appoint three surveyors or regulators of streets, lanes, and alleys "as often as there shall be occasion," and the qualified inhabitants in the borough were allowed to elect yearly two supervisors of the highways and two assessors who were to lay a rate on the inhabitants "to be employed for the amending, repairing and keeping clean and in good order the streets, lanes, alleys, and highways" of Lancaster.[42]

The increased authority and power given to the boroughs, and the similar grant to the townships with the creation of the poundkeeper in 1729 and the township assessor in 1758 and the shifting of the inspector of the election in 1752 and the supervisors of the highways in 1765 to the township level, suggest a trend toward decentralization and greater self-government for these units during the eighteenth century. In part, of course, this is true, for certainly the addition of more elective officials in the boroughs and townships gave eighteenth-century Pennsylvania a greater voice in their own government at that level. Yet, in spite of this, the county was still clearly the dominant unit of local government: county officials retained the ultimate responsibility and authority, especially in relation to the township, and the county remained the unit of representation in the Assembly. Indeed, the changes that occurred might be seen as providing a better way for dispatching the county's affairs rather than depriving the county of its power and role.[43]

As important as the county offices were because of their necessary and invaluable functions in the life of the county, they were also important because of the role of some of them in the larger context of provincial politics. In varying degrees during most of the colonial period, two main political parties or, more properly, factions contested for power in Pennsylvania. The Quaker party, whose composition and leadership included non-Quakers, especially after 1756, usually controlled the Assembly and used it to challenge the proprietor and his policies. The Proprietary party, as its name suggests, defended and supported the proprietor's interest and government. At first, it also consisted of Quakers but later became a party mainly of Anglicans and Presbyterians. It was generally unpopular among the voters and less organized than the Quaker party; therefore it rarely won elections. In the latter half of the 1760s these two parties seemingly joined forces, at least at the provincial level, to preserve their control of Pennsylvania against the possible rise to power of such ethnic-religious groups as the Scotch-Irish Presbyterians and the German Lutherans and Reformed. This truce, perhaps even collu-

TABLE 3.
Borough Officials

Official	Selected By
Elective:	
Assessor (for county and provincial taxes)	Electors
Inspector of the election (Lancaster)	
High Constable	
Burgesses	
Councilmen (Bristol)	
Assistants (Lancaster)	
Assessors (for borough taxes — Bristol and Lancaster)	
Supervisors of the highways (Lancaster)	
Town clerk (Lancaster)	
Appointive:	
Overseers of the poor	Justices of the quarter sessions court
Borough treasurer (Bristol)	Burgesses and councilmen
Workhouse officials (Bristol)	
Town clerk (Bristol and probably Chester)	
Surveyors or regulators of streets, lanes, and alleys (Lancaster)	Burgesses and assistants
Clerk of the market (Lancaster)	

sion, between the two parties stemmed from the organization of a third party, the Presbyterian party, which subsequently played a leading role in the oncoming of the American Revolution in Pennsylvania.[44] As these political groups in Pennsylvania contended for power, county offices and officials were often drawn into the struggle.

Because of his control over the election process, the sheriff was one of the most important officials politically. The Quaker party was usually successful in winning and controlling this office and in using it for the party's benefit.[45] The Proprietary party, while not without interest in the office of sheriff, often floundered in its attempts at organizing an opposition because of an inability to achieve unity among Proprietary supporters. This is what happened, it seems, in 1764 when an effort was made to contest the Quaker party ticket in Lancaster County. A Proprietary leader in Philadelphia, Samuel Purviance, Jr., wrote to a Proprietary leader in Lancaster, James Burd: "I wish the unhappy Contests abt Sheriff could be reduced to two Competitors, on our side (suppose Coll Worke & Jamy Anderson) [.] it would unite our Friends to act with more Spirit & prevent their hurting the public Cause." A week later, however, Burd reported: "We Judg'd it most propper to leave the Shirriffs Blank."[46]

Even if unsuccessful in electing Proprietary partisans, the Proprietary authorities could influence the selection of the holder of the sheriff's office because of the power of the governor to appoint one of the two top candidates for the office. It would appear that this power was sometimes used, for an examination of the election returns in newspapers in the 1760s and early 1770s reveals that the person whose name appears second was in several instances appointed to the office rather than the first person listed. Since the newspaper listings seem to have been in the order of voters' preferences, the governor evidently could and did exercise his prerogative. Even so, of course, his selectivity was limited to the two top choices of the electorate, and if the electorate's inclination was anti-Proprietary, the governor could do little about circumventing that inclination, except to appoint an individual whom he might regard as the lesser of two evils.

In addition to withholding appointment, a subtle pressure that could be applied by the Proprietary group was the withholding of bond for performance as sheriff. In 1774 an important Proprietary leader threatened the sheriff of Northumberland County over the latter's tolerance of and involvement in illegal gambling: "I told Nagle it was well for him that this was the last year of his office. Otherwise it would be impossible that he could either get Security for his performance of it or that the Governor could intrust any Men with the Office of Sheriff who played for half Joes."[47] As with the power of appointment, this also was probably a limited coercive power, since there were wealthy Quaker supporters who must have provided security for the Quaker party candidates. Nevertheless, it was another means by which the Proprietary group could exert influence.

As the body which administered county affairs and as the only county offices over which the electorate had the complete power of selection, the offices of the three county commissioners and the six county assessors also became involved in provincial politics. In the late 1760s either the Proprietary group in Lancaster or a group aligned with the new Presbyterian party began a determined effort to gain control of those offices. The group started in 1767 (at the latest) and evidently met with some success. In 1768 a ticket for commissioner and assessors was drawn up which, if successful, would give the party "the command at the board." "The Plan begun & now pursued is to gain the Majority at the Board[.] we last Year got a good footing there & if our present Ticket carries we have it & may then do something more, indeed I think if that point is carried something more will be done next Year." The "something more" was to reelect Isaac Saunders, a strong Proprietary supporter who had been defeated in 1765, to the Assembly. The short-range hope for moving toward that goal, however, was not fully realized in the 1768, for the group's candidate for commissioner, Adam Orth, was defeated.[48] (Absence of information on the assessors elected that year prevents any statement on whether the one particular candidate it pushed, James Keimer, was successful.) The following year, another attempt was made, with Adam Orth again as the candidate for commissioner on the "new Ticket" and with six candidates for assessor. A strenuous campaign ensued, a campaign in which, a Lancaster lawyer noted, "the Struggle seems to be chiefly about the Board."[49] This time, all the party's candidates won.

The appointive offices under the control of the executive branch of the provincial government were drawn into provincial politics because they provided an obvious opportunity for the Proprietary party to establish a power base within a county. The most numerous of the appointive officials were the justices of the peace, who, on the eve of independence, numbered more than two hundred in Pennsylvania's eleven counties. Because their appointment came from the governor, thus identifying them with the Proprietary party, some men were reluctant to accept such appointments for fear of alienating voters and possibly threatening their aspiration for elective office, especially the Assembly. In 1751 Governor James Hamilton wrote: "It is inconceivable what an inveteracy there is in those people against the Magistracy, to which they so much prefer a seat in the Assembly, that tho there are several in the House, whom I put into commission of the peace, yet they will not qualify for fear of losing their popularity."[50] In spite of the identification of these offices with the Proprietary party, however, county courts were not, it seems, Proprietary strongholds. Quakers were often appointed to the justiceships, so many, in fact, that William Peters complained to Proprietor Thomas Penn in 1764: "By your having always given the Preference to the Quakers in the Commissions of Peace and every Favour you could bestow on them they have obtain'd great Influence in the Country which they have always and now especially so ungratefully make use of against you."[51]

The offices that seem to have been more suitable for the building of a Proprietary power base, and to have been used for such, were the clerks of the three courts, the recorder of deeds, and the register of wills. Those offices were "Lucrative Posts," as Edward Shippen, the holder of those positions in Lancaster County, characterized them, and thus they were highly desirable.[52] Also attractive was the tenure that came with the offices. A well-placed friend of Shippen assured him that "The Office of Prothonotary is in its own nature an office during good behaviour and until a person is legally convict of ill behaviour he in my opinion cannot be divested of the office."[53] Because of these advantages, appointment to the offices provided a way for the proprietor and his governor to reward Proprietary supporters—and also to incur an obligation on their part to the Proprietary family and interest.

Edward Shippen offers an example of how the holder of those offices served as a conduit from Philadelphia to the county and from the county to Philadelphia. In his capacity as a link between the Proprietary leaders in Philadelphia and the residents and party supporters in Lancaster, Shippen carried out the pursuit of Proprietary politics in the county. In 1756 he attended a meeting for the selection of candidates to run for the Assembly and proposed the names of two men who were "agreeable to Cous. Allen [William Allen, the Chief Justice of Pennsylvania from 1751 to 1774 and the dominant Proprietary leader in the period from the 1740's to the 1770's] & ye other Gentlemen in Philada."[54] In 1761 Shippen made plans to campaign for the reelection of the Proprietary party's candidate for the Assembly, as he revealed in a letter to Allen: "As soon [as] I have sealed up this Letter I shall mount my horse & go down to Mr. Work & others & endeavour [to] engage their Votes & Interest & on my Return shall proceed to Dennegal & talk with Mr. Tate ye Minister & Some of ye leading Men there and shall write to Mr. Elder ye

Minister at Paxton and to Jno Harris to do all they can in ye Affair and these whom I have An Opportunity to see & can confide in I Shall mention Your Name but shall leave it out in my Letters."[55]

In his capacity as a link between Lancaster and the Proprietary authorities in Philadelphia, Shippen served as an avenue to those who possessed the powers of appointment and patronage, and thus his support was sought for and by aspiring officeholders. In 1767 a promoter of James Bickham for an appointment as justice of the peace solicited Shippen's aid because the person "imagined if I would have written to the Governor in favour of their Man, the point would have been gained." In 1773, after emerging as the top vote-getter in the contest for sheriff, John Ferree asked Shippen to recommend him to the governor for appointment.[56] Shippen's promotion of a candidate, however, did not mean automatic appointment, nor did his disapproval mean rejection. His suggestions for the magistracy in 1767 of Michael Hubley and in 1773 of Peter Grubb, who had recently married one of his granddaughters, were not translated into appointments, and his lack of support for James Bickham in 1767 did not prevent Bickham's receiving a justiceship. In fact, others within the county besides Shippen suggested names and politicked for their particular candidates, which caused Shippen, at one point, to complain: "as this business has been managed of late Years, everything is to be carried Over the heads of the old Magistrates."[57] Nevertheless, whatever the competition for influence and whatever the limitations upon his own influence in Philadelphia, the fact that aspirants sought Shippen's backing implies that it was thought to be of value.

Because important political power rested in the county in Pennsylvania, and because political parties in Pennsylvania sought to use that power to obtain and maintain political control of the province, county government was more than simply a part of a governmental structure. The interaction that occurred between the local and provincial levels in colonial Pennsylvania and the important relationship that existed between local and provincial politics drew the county into the larger context of provincial affairs. County officials functioned as transmitters of local wishes to provincial authorities and as translators of provincial policy into local reality. With the increased number of locally selected officials during the eighteenth century and the frequency with which elections occurred (voters

went to the polls at least four or five times each year by the end of
the colonial period), a county's residents were actively and constantly involved in the political process and, as a result, gained familiarity with and valuable experience in the process of self-government.

NOTES

1. Elgin R. L. Gould, *Local Self-Government in Pennsylvania*, Johns Hopkins University Studies in Historical and Political Science, ed. Herbert B. Adams, 1st. ser. (Baltimore,
1883), I, no. 3, 27; William P. Holcomb, *Pennsylvania Boroughs*, Johns Hopkins University
Studies in Historical and Political Science, ed. Herbert B. Adams, 4th ser. (Baltimore, 1886,
IV, no. 4, 7, 33; Edward P. Allison and Bois Penrose, *Philadelphia, 1681-1887* (Philadelphia, 1887), 8 (extra volume in Johns Hopkins University Studies in Historical and Political Science).

2. A list of the counties and the dates of their creation can be found in the *Pennsylvania
Archives* (hereafter, PA), end ser. (Harrisburg, 1874-1890), III, 716-17; 3rd ser. (Harrisburg, 1894-1899, XXIV, iv-vi.

3. Sylvester K. Stevens and Donald H. Kent, eds., *County Government and Archives in
Pennsylvania* (Harrisburg, 1947), 97; James T. Mitchell and Henry Flanders, comps., *The
Statutes at Large of Pennsylvania from 1682 to 1809* (Harrisburg, 1896-1915; hereafter,
SL), ch. 179, II, 370, ch. 180, II, 374; ch. 182, II, 389, ch. 195, III, 6; ch. 215, III, 84;
ch. 221, III, 129; ch. 231, III, 178; ch. 254, III, 296; ch. 284, IV, 11; ch. 330, IV, 235. For
a more detailed discussion of the development of the county commissioners, see Clair W.
Keller, "The Pennsylvania County Commission System, 1712 to 1740," *Pennsylvania
Magazine of History and Biography* (hereafter, *PMBH*), XCIII (July 1969, 372-82; and
Clair W. Keller, "Pennsylvania Government, 1701-1740," Ph.D. diss. (University of Washington, 1967), ch. 6. On p. 218 Keller notes that some commissioners in the 1720s served
longer than three years.

4. Gould, *Local Government* 27; Stevens and Kent, *County Government*, 96-97;
Staughton George, Benjamin Nead, and Thomas McCamant, *Charter to William Penn, and
Laws of the Province of Pennsylvania, Passed between the Years 1682 and 1700* . . . (Har-
risburg, 1879), 257.

5. George, Nead, and McCamant, *Charter and Laws*, 146-47, 233, 256-57; *SL*, ch. 32,
II, 35; ch. 231, III 175; ch. 284, IV, 146.

6. George, Nead, and McCamant, *Charter and Laws*, 222, 254, 280; *SL*, ch. 86, II,
111; ch. 170, II, 370-71; ch. 180, II, 374-75; ch. 182, II, 389-90.

7. The general procedure was laid down in several acts, with the act of March 20, 1724/
25 (*SL*, ch. 284, IV, 10f.) being the operative one for the rest of the colonial period.

8. *SL*, ch. 284, IV, 13.

9. Ibid., 13, 23; ch. 329, IV, 233-34; Keller, "Pennsylvania Government," 252. Remuneration to the commissioners and assessors for collecting the provincial taxes came
from the provincial treasury (see *PA*, 8th ser. [1931-1935], VIII, 6690-91 for an example).

10. Stevens and Kent, *County Government*, 289, 306; Francis Thorpe, comp. and ed.,
*The Federal and State Constitutions, Colonial Charters, and Other Organic Laws of the
States, Territories and Colonies Now or Heretofore Forming the United States of America*
(Washington, D.C., 1909), V, 3058, 3067, 3078; *SL*, ch. 161, II, 273; ch. 315, IV, 183;
ch. 321, IV, 214.

11. Stevens and Kent, *County Government*, 295-96; 307-8; *SL*, ch. 98, II, 132; ch. 398,
V, 165-66; ch. 539, VII, 32; ch. 683, VIII, 334. The sheriff and the coroner were paid on
the basis of fees established by the Assembly.

12. Thorpe, *Constitutions,* V, 3058, 3067; *SL,* ch. 106, II, 148; Keller, "Pennsylvania Government," 162; *Colonial Records* (Harrisburg, 1838-1853), IV, 152; William Henry Lloyd, *The Early Courts of Pennsylvania* (Boston, 1910), 105; George, Nead, and McCamant, *Charter and Laws,* 219. Like the sheriff and the coroner, the justice's fees were set by the Assembly.

13. George, Nead, and McCamant, *Charter and Laws,* 131, 205, 321; Keller, "Pennsylvania Government," 158-62; Lloyd, *Early Courts,* 57, 80, 93-94, 98, 102; *SL,* ch. 106, II, 148, 156; ch. 255, III, 298; ch. 450, V 464; Thorpe, *Constitutions,* V, 3058, 3067.

14. Lloyd, *Early Courts,* 230-31; *SL,* ch. 197, III, 14; ch. 450, V, 463-64.

15. *SL,* ch. 255 III, 306; Lloyd, *Early Courts,* 52, 94-96, 230; *SL,* ch. 197, III, 15. A special court for the trial of Negroes was established in 1705 consisting of two justices commissioned by the governor and six freeholders. (Lloyd, *Early Courts,* 105; *SL,* ch. 143, II, 234).

16. George, Nead, and McCamant, *Charter and Laws,* 115, 233, 258; Gould, *Local Self-Government,* 29-30; Lloyd, *Early Courts,* 18, 254-56; Sylvester and Kent, *County Government,* 409, 469; Thorpe, *Constitutions,* V, 3079. The King's highways and public roads were laid out by the governor and Council. Until 1718, when the commissioners were given the responsibility, the justices also had charge of bridges in the county; after 1732 the concurrence of the justices was theoretically necessary for the building and repairing of bridges. For a discussion of this, see Keller, "Pennsylvania Government," 241-42.

17. To examine sites for roads, the justices were authorized, since at least 1699, to appoint six viewers "as often as they find needful" (*SL,* ch. 55, II, 69; see also George, Nead, and McCamant, *Charter and Laws,* 285-86). In addition to all these appointments, the justices of the quarter sessions court in at least four counties filled vacancies among the officials of the houses of correction and workhouses in those counties (*SL,* ch. 229, III, 169; ch. 498, VI, 282).

18. Stevens and Kent, *County Government,* 184, 231; George, Nead, and McCamant, *Charter and Laws,* 131, 321; Thorpe, *Constitutions,* V, 3079; *SL,* ch. 169, II, 339; ch. 216, III, 103, 104; *Colonial Records,* X, 47.

19. *Colonial Records,* IX, 663; X, 43, 47; *PA,* 3rd ser., IX, 16-18, 19; Quarter Sessions Docket, 1754-1782 (Bucks County Court House), June 12, 1770.

20. Stevens and Kent, *County Government,* 166-68; Thorpe, *Constitutions,* V, 3050, 3058, 3067; *SL,* ch. 136, II, 211; ch. 208, III, 56.

21. *SL,* ch. 133, II, 196-97; Stevens and Kent, *County Government,* 258; George, Nead, and McCamant, *Charter and Laws,* 119; *SL,* ch. 103, II, 139; ch. 106, II, 156.

22. *SL,* ch. 133, II, 197.

23. George, Nead, and McCamant, *Charter and Laws,* 138; *SL,* ch. 164, II, 289; ch. 276, III, 408.

24. *SL,* ch. 85, II, 107-8; ch. 181, II, 385; ch. 313, IV, 159; ch. 412, V, 260; *PA,* 8th ser., VII, 5887, 5895, 5949, 5956, 5961.

25. Stevens and Kent, *County Government,* 464, 490, 491; *SL,* ch. 73, II, 89.

26. Stevens and Kent, *County Government,* 360; George, Nead, and McCamant, *Charter and Laws,* 257-58; *SL,* ch. 180, II, 375; ch. 231, III, 189.

27. *SL,* ch. 284, IV, 17, 23; ch. 215, III, 84; Keller, "Pennsylvania Government," 221; Stevens and Kent, *County Government,* 120.

28. *SL,* ch. 331, IV, 241; ch. 119, II, 177; ch. 618, VIII, 7; ch. 539, VII, 32; ch. 431, V, 337; ch. 284, IV, 10; George, Nead, and McCamant, *Charter and Laws,* 222, 257, 280-81. Legislation regarding the township assessor redefined the role of the constable (see note 30).

29. George, Nead, and McCamant, *Charter and Laws,* 22, 69, 455-56; Lancaster County Miscellaneous Papers, 1772-1816, 147 (Historical Society of Pennsylvania, hereafter, HSP); Quarter Sessions Docket of Philadelphia County.

30. *SL,* ch. 431, V, 340; ch. 437, V, 382; ch. 692, VIII, 379. From 1762 to 1772 the

township assessors assisted the supervisors of the highways in levying the tax for the maintenance of roads (see relevant sources listed in note 33 and *SL*, ch. 653, VIII, 185).

31. *SL*, ch. 137, II, 212; ch. 396, V, 153; see also ch. 296, IV, 78; ch. 350, IV, 333;
ch. 539, VII, 32.

32. *SL*, ch. 154, II, 252; ch. 635, VIII, 75.

33. George, Nead, and McCamant, *Charter and Laws*, 136, 233; *SL*, ch. 57, II, 73; ch.
479, VI, 186; ch. 526, VI, 424. The power to levy assessments dated from 1762; prior to
that, the overseers could only summon the inhabitants to work on the highways.

34. *SL*, ch. 301, IV, 116, 119.

35. Information on the assessor and the overseers of the poor can be found in the laws
referred to in notes 30 and 32. Reference to the high constable is found in the charters of
Chester, Bristol, and Lancaster, which are available in Samuel Hazard, ed., *The Register of
Pennsylvania*, (Philadelphia, 1829), III, 264-65, 312-14; and J. I. Mombert, *An Authentic
History of Lancaster County in the State of Pennsylvania* (Lancaster, 1869), appendix,
141-46. Reference to an election inspector in Lancaster Borough is found in a January 22,
1774 act (*SL*, ch. 689, VIII, 356-57). No evidence was found in the statutes regarding an
election inspector in Bristol and Chester, but it does not seem unlikely that such an official
existed.

36. Hazard, *Register*, 264, 313; Mombert, *Lancaster*, appendix, 142. The Lancaster
charter adds the stipulations of at least one year's residence and a house and ground "of the
yearly value of five pounds or upwards" (142). Reference to Bristol's councilmen is found
not in the charter but in the Minutes of the Bristol Council (Keller, "Pennsylvania Government," 313). It is not known whether councilmen existed in Chester; Keller speculates
that "It is probably [sic] since Chester had four burgesses, additional councilmen were
not thought necessary" (ibid.)

37. Information on the town clerk in Bristol is taken from Keller, "Pennsylvania Government," 313, and is assumed to be true for Chester as well; the office is specifically mentioned in Lancaster's charter. Reference to the clerk of the market is found in the respective
charters. A discussion of the government of Chester and Bristol can be found in Keller,
"Pennsylvania Government," 305-19, and of Lancaster in Jerome H. Wood, "Conestoga
Crossroads: The Rise of Lancaster, Pennsylvania, 1730-1789," Ph.D. diss. (Brown University, 1969), 36-48.

38. Hazard, *Register*, 165, 314; Mombert, *Lancaster*, appendix, 145.

39. Hazard, *Register*, 264, 313. This was probably the basis for the councilmen in
Bristol and the town clerks in Bristol and Chester. Although no such authority was granted
in the Lancaster charter, some borough officials were appointed by the Burgesses (see
Wood, "Conestoga Crossroads," 60).

40. Hazard, *Register*, 264. Similar language is found in the Bristol charter (313) and the
Lancaster charter (Mombert, *Lancaster*, 143).

41. Keller, "Pennsylvania Government," 314-15, 317.

42. *SL*, ch. 367, V, 33-36; ch. 689, VIII, 348-51.

43. Keller notes that "There is some evidence that, in 1740, the township was evolving
into a unit of self-government" ("Pennsylvania Government," 209). His evidence includes
town meetings in one township of Chester County at which business beyond that authorized
by the Assembly was transacted and the existence in the township of an official not specifically authorized by the Assembly.

44. James H. Hutson, *Pennsylvania Politics, 1746-1770* (Princeton, 1972), 209-15,
237-43; see also William Hanna, *Benjamin Franklin and Pennsylvania Politics* (Stanford,
1964), 188-91.

45. Hanna, *Franklin*, 103, 165-66.

46. Purviance to Burd, September 10, 1764, Shippen Papers, VI, 107, HSP; Burd to Pur-

viance, September 17, 1764, ibid., 109. The discussion in this section of the political role of county offices is drawn from Wayne L. Bockelman, "Local Politics in Pre-Revolutionary Lancaster County," *PMHB*, XCVII (January 1973), 45-74.

47. Edward Shippen, Jr., to Edward Burd, May 28, 1774, Papers of Edward Burd, HSP, quoted in David Hawke, *In the Midst of a Revolution* (Philadelphia, 1961), 81.

48. William Atlee to James Burd, September 20 and September 26, 1768, Shippen Papers, VI, 213, 215, HSP. After the election, the name of John Carpenter appears in the Minute Book of the county commissioners, Lancaster County Court House.

49. Jasper Yeates to James Burd, September 17 and September 19, 1769, Shippen Papers, VII, 17, 19, HSP.

50. Hamilton to Thomas Penn, February 22, 1750/51, Penn Papers, Official Correspondence, HSP, quoted in Hanna, *Franklin*, 45.

51. Peters to Penn, June 4, 1764, Penn Papers, Official Correspondence, IX, quoted in Hanna, *Franklin*, 166. Beginning in the mid-1760s, however, appointments to justice-ships may have been used more frequently than previously for patronage purposes. See James Hutson, "Benjamin Franklin and Pennsylvania Politics, 1751-1755: A Reappraisal," *PMHB*, XCIII (July 1969), 307n.

52. An Account of the Estate Possessed by Edward Shippen at Lancaster—1764, Shippen Papers, VI, 137, HSP.

53. William Allen to Edward Shippen, July 25, 1753, Shippen-Balch Papers, I, 34, HSP.

54. Edward Shippen to Joseph Shippen, September 13, 1756, Shippen Papers, II, 71, HSP.

55. Shippen to Allen, September 15, 1761, Edward Shippen Letter Books, American Philosophical Society.

56. Edward Shippen to James Burd, November 24, 1779, Shippen Papers, VIII, 65, HSP.

57. Shippen to Joseph Shippen, February 7, 1769, Shippen Papers, X, 91, HSP.

The Government
of Eighteenth-Century Philadelphia

JUDITH M. DIAMONDSTONE

The history of governing Philadelphia in the eighteenth century can be comprehended by tracing through the fabric of its early social and political life two distinct but related threads of experience. The first of these stretches back across space and time to English practices evolved over nearly a thousand years. The English experience of town, not to say urban, development was certainly present in the minds of early Philadelphians, who had roots in London, Dublin, Bristol, and other provincial towns of Great Britain. They may have imperfectly understood the political reasoning behind ancient practices, but they were familiar with the pattern of English town government at the end of the seventeenth century. The pattern varied considerably in detail but hardly at all in basic arrangements. Thus, early Philadelphians, looking about for suitable governmental arrangements for their town, had an adequate model ready at hand in their own early experience and that of their forebears.[1]

The other experience that shaped local government in Philadelphia was the developing relationship between many early "adventurers" to Pennsylvania and their landlord and governor, William Penn. The settlers felt uneasy when all political power and total control over land sales and titles lay with one man, even a good man. The concern to protect property and privileges was both great and real.[2] Early Pennsylvanians were most interested in knowing what sort of administrator Penn was, how accessible he would be, what sort of practical and durable limits on his power he was willing to agree to. For the later town government, the experience of working with William Penn from 1682 to 1701 was decisive.

The significance of these two factors warrants a brief but careful examination of their meaning for the Philadelphians who established early in the eighteenth century the forms of local government that would persist to the Revolution and beyond. Let us look first at the long-range past of the Philadelphian-Englishman and then at the short-range past of the Philadelphian vis-à-vis the proprietor.

When small commercial towns began to develop in feudal England, classes of men emerged who had no place in the existing society of mutual obligation and service. The town dweller and the man of business were unprotected against the power of the local lord. The search for some legal form that would define their social and political obligations as well as limit the power of others to command them led to the evolution of two forms: the gild, both craft and commercial, and the town corporation. It is the latter that Philadelphians transformed into a New World town government. The town or municipal corporation was a device to bind some or all of the town's residents into a legal body, with specified rights and obligations and with provision for internal change and self-perpetuation. Over time the corporation in most places came to be managed by the more substantial citizens for the benefit of all the inhabitants; it took care of both the administrative and commercial business of the town and its dealings with the emerging centralized power of the crown.[3]

Town corporations were originally rather simple in form, because town life was simple and the scale and frequency of problems was small. As towns grew larger and more complex, so did their corporations. Their spokesman, the mayor, came to have others associated with him, a council or aldermen; meetings for deliberation, once open to all the townsmen, grew unwieldy and were restricted to chosen representatives; the tedious business of commercial regulation and inspection was consolidated in the hands of paid officials. No two English corporations are identical in particulars, but all followed the same broad pattern. Where towns remained small, with a slow rate of growth, and hence were more medieval in character, the corporations functioned better. They were able to manage the problems they had, and in some cases though not all, the smaller the town remained, the more likely it was that the interests of the substantial burgers who ran things and the interests of the ordinary householder might coincide.[4]

Where towns grew rapidly, in size or commerce or both, the corporation was less successful. Townsfolk became less interested in close regulation of trade and more interested in having the town provide clean streets, good drinking water, and perhaps a public school. Town government was changing over from a medieval patron of local autonomy to the more modern supplier of public services.[5] This transformation showed signs, in England, of raising very substantial problems, which were to be faced by colonial corporations when conditions were equivalent.

First, there was the problem of administrative efficiency, however modestly one defines the term. As the scale and frequency of problems enlarged, the occasional volunteer efforts of otherwise busy citizens were less adequate than before. Salaried officials required salary expenditures, increasing the need for corporation income. In addition, the question of administrative efficiency led naturally to the question of executive supervision, which few corporations could readily provide.

Second, there was the problem of money. If the primary task of a municipal corporation altered from providing a framework for community regulation to providing a constantly escalating level of community services, clearly some adequate and expanding sources of income were needed. This raised additional hard questions about the power to tax, about who and what was taxable, about representation of those taxed, and about accountability for the receipt and expenditure of the money. All these questions bore on the structure of the town community and the nature and power of the corporation.

Third, there arose the problem of common interests in a community that was rapidly enlarging and diversifying. As long as the interests of all the townsmen were roughly identical, it did not matter much that the corporation was governed by men of one class or of a few families; nor did it matter that not all residents were "members" of the town corporation. What met the needs of some, met the needs of all. But with divergent interests and the loss of a homogeneous community feeling, it became important to know for whom the corporation governed, whose interests predominated, and whose were freely ignored.

These problem areas were emerging in many of the town corporations familiar to the emigrant Pennsylvanian, as were some of the immediate solutions tried out. Why would early Philadelphians feel the need for such a medieval form of government in a New World setting that lacked the medieval inheritance, that invited if not commanded rapid growth and expansion, and that was an ocean away from the power of the King? There are two parts to the answer, one general and one specific to Philadelphia. In general, men struggling to subsist and prosper on the shore of a wild land, their backs to the sea and their lives filled with uncertainty, took comfort in much that was familiar from their past life, simply because it *was* familiar; it helped them orient themselves to the needs and tasks they must and might meet in order to survive. But Philadelphians faced an additional concern in the person of their proprietor, a powerful local lord whose prerogative was limited only in vague and general ways; their situation was fluid, and hence uncertain, and their own rights and obligations were not clearly defined. Their experience with William Penn convinced them by 1701 that it was wise to ask him to create the Corporation of Philadelphia.

Penn did a lot of advance planning for Pennsylvania, knowing that plans made in England might well be changed by firsthand experience; but he seems to have made little allowance for the wishes or needs of the settlers, only for the demands of the environment. Altering the plan did not seem to Penn to call for a collaborative effort; he thought to make the needed changes himself, consulting whomever he thought best, but obligated to no one.[6]

But the most generous arrangements were valueless if they could be changed at will or on a pretext by the proprietor. Like any man, Penn looked to his own interests first and, like most upper-class Englishmen, was readily exasperated by opposition. Furthermore, consensus, not controversy, was the Quaker value. In disagreement with the townsfolk Penn proved stubborn and uncompromising; as a public administrator he was careless and often arbitrary.[7] It was not surprising that the settlers attempted common action. People grown uneasy thought some permanent community agent was necessary. A town corporation functioned briefly in 1691, dealing successfully with proprietary power.[8]

Penn spent little time in Pennsylvania, and in his absence (1684–99) men developed ways of governing themselves. They were frustrated, however, by Penn's efforts to keep nearly all Pennsylvania's business in his own hands, despite the distance. Protection for the community against Penn's power, legal authority for some independent town government, and a way of institutionalizing the common interests and identity of the townsfolk were real concerns of politically active Philadelphians when in 1701 Penn announced his departure for England and asked them to "think, therefore, since all men are mortal, of some suitable expedient and Provision for your safety, as well in your Privileges as Property, and you will find me ready to Comply with whatsoever may render us happy, by a nearer Union of our interest."[9]

Pennsylvanians responded to Penn's broad offer with proposals for legislation and drafts of three important charters, as well as lesser ones. The Frame of Government became the provincial constitution, Penn rejected the Charter of Property, and the city charter established a municipal corporation for Philadelphia that endured to 1776.[10] The history of governing Philadelphia in the eighteenth century is the story of how the Corporation that gave Philadelphians what they wanted in an old familiar struggle with lordly power and prerogative failed to be what they needed to deal with the rapidly expanding problems of a thriving commercial town. Here is that story.

The town corporation of Philadelphia chartered by William Penn in 1701 had to meet two basic needs in governing the trading town on the Delaware: first, it had to provide needed services to the inhabitants, including the maintenance of public order; and second, it had to guard and foster local autonomy as against the political authority of both province and proprietor. But the city of Philadelphia was not, under the charter, a collection of inhabitants nor even an area of settlement marked out by the building of streets and houses. It was defined by a plan on paper—the plan drawn by William Penn even before he saw Pennsylvania. The plan provided for a city one mile wide and about two deep, running east and west across a neck of land between the Delaware and the Schuylkill Rivers. Streets and public squares were laid out symmetrically on paper, but settlement did not always adhere to the plan. In 1701 the little cluster of houses stretched back only about three squares from the river, but it ran along the Delaware bank for more than the mile that Penn had allotted. The town government had jurisdiction over the uninhabited woods and meadows running west to the Schuylkill, but none over the inhabitants north and south of the town lines.[11] People living outside the "city limits" either accepted the government of the county or organized into small, unincorporated towns.[12] In this sense the city of Philadelphia came to resemble in the late eighteenth century the historic city of London, a small, legal-geographical enclave within a vaster area of human settlement and activity.

The charter created "the mayor and commonalty of Philadelphia." The "commonalty" did not include all inhabitants within the legal bounds; rather it was limited to those who became freemen of the city.[13] From that limited body of citizens the Common Council chose new members; aldermen, when any were needed, were chosen from among the councilmen; the mayor was chosen from among the aldermen, and he returned to their ranks when his mayoralty year was completed. The original officers and councilmen were selected by Penn, and the occasional vacancy was filled by the choice of the remaining members. This government had originally no genuine citizenry that might play a part in the Corporation; it had only a limited and inactive body of freemen, on whose behalf theoretically the corporation did its business.[14] The result was a governing body not elected but self-selected. The Common Council was the Corporation.

Penn initially chose a mixture of political friends and foes for the Corporation, filling the key offices—mayor, recorder, sheriff, and clerk—with his own supporters. Changes in the Common Council— a body of only twenty-two men in 1701—depended on the wishes of whatever faction held a majority of votes there; the dominant party decided whom to choose to membership and whether new members should be chosen at all. Corporation government was thus

"closed", like most of its English contemporaries and in striking contrast to the New England town, to full or even meaningful citizen
participation.[15]

This arrangement did not, so far as we know, alarm or distress
either the substantial merchants and craftsmen who made up the
Corporation nor the less prosperous, less powerful residents of
Philadelphia, at least not until well into the eighteenth century.
Although Quakerism fostered a powerful sense of equality in religion, the social distinctions and class attitudes of English society
were perfectly comfortable on the Delaware. The able and the
wealthy, and they amounted to the same people, felt it their obligation to rule and to discharge the burden of government, just as the
"weighty Friends" carried much of the burden of business of the
Quaker meetings.[16] The bulk of the inhabitants expected the duties
of office to fall on the able and affluent, who had time and funds to
devote to them as well as proven competence in business affairs. So
long as there was no substantial division of interests among classes
of Philadelphians, the middling and lower classes did not feel un-
represented. The closed nature of corporation government in a New
World environment would be a problem only if and when "the
mayor and commonalty" lost their identity with the rest of Philadelphia and were unresponsive to the needs of the townsfolk. For the
time, in the early eighteenth century, the corporation structure did
not prevent the town government from doing either of its two jobs.[17]

Corporation obligations for the "better ordering" of Philadelphia
make an impressive list for a small group of men to accomplish, and
the list expanded as the town did. The Corporation was responsible
for that forerunner of the police department, the night watch. Its
responsibility for "better regulation of trade" meant organizing and
supervising a public market and public fairs; building and repairing
the market place and stalls; setting the price of staples by ordinance; inspecting the bakeries; maintaining standard weights and measures, and
inspecting tradesmens' weights for conformity to the standard;
regulating the admission of applicants for the freedom of the town;
regulating the number of public carters as well as their rates, the size
and construction of their wagons, and the speed at which they might
haul goods through the streets; and constructing and maintaining
wharves, bridges, and ferries.[18]

Corporation members inspected the streets and supervised the water courses (a sort of gutter down the middle) and later the pitching (which slanted the streets downward from center to curb for runoff) of the streets. They supervised the paving of the streets from the time when that advance seemed desirable until the responsibility was taken over by the streets commissioners. They inspected the public water supply (private pumps) and also the public slaughterhouses, dealing with "nuisances" or other offenses against public health or quiet. They inspected chimneys to guard against fire hazard and could be called on to deal with other sorts of hazards or nuisances, such as timber, straw, or firewood left piled on a public wharf. They inspected both bread and flour being packed for export. They surveyed the streets when new ones were required. They provided and maintained a public burying ground, as well as a jail and a fire engine. They maintained order and suppressed riots, which could mean anything from collecting stray dogs to preventing violence on election day. If they did not perform these tasks personally, they arranged for workmen or officials to do them and handled the details of materials and payment.[19]

Beyond these responsibilities, all of which in much expanded form are still part of city government, the Common Council met and deliberated, drew up and passed city ordinances, gathered money (chiefly as fees, in small amounts), audited accounts, received petitions, chose committees, made representations to the provincial legislature, heard reports, hired and removed officials, and authorized payments. It kept a city court four times a year, in which the aldermen supplied the bench of judges; the council itself often heard appeals from its own court. It also undertook a variety of ceremonial functions: addressing a new governor, reading publicity the King's declaration of war (or peace), or giving itself an annual banquet.[20]

All in all, this was a great deal of rather tedious work (even allowing that much of it was let slide) for a body of usually fewer than thirty men, most of them occupied in fostering their own fortunes; hence, they gave the business of the town a morning here or there or occasionally a few hours out of their working day. There were no full-time officials, and none was salaried but the recorder, the Corporation's legal officer. The various clerks, the wharfinger, and so on, were paid in fees, which they had to collect themselves. Though Philadelphia was small, its growth was rapid; hence, every job was expanding.[21] All supervision was carried on by committees, with

all the attendant problems of getting members together and agreeing on which workmen to hire, and so on. All decisions required
a full council meeting; there was no delegation of authority that
would permit some official, or even some committee, to go ahead
and just do what needed doing, say, with regard to the streets.[22]

These administrative problems seem obvious to us, but they
were not so apparent in the eighteenth century; so the system continued in the traditional fashion, never quite so incompetent as to
drive men to change it but never so capable that men felt all their
municipal needs were well met. If the Corporation had been able to
provide itself with adequate executive and administrative officials,
it might well have managed as a deliberative body—investigating,
enacting ordinances, and devoting its remaining energy to representing city interests before the Pennsylvania Assembly. Its failure
to do so can be explained at least as much by the lack of money as
by the lack of imagination.

The Corporation, like many a modern municipality, was handi-
capped early and late by inadequate funding. Its income came from
fees and fines, which had to be collected laboriously in small amounts
—two shillings and sixpence here, three pounds there, and so on.[23]
The Corporation had no power to tax. The charter empowered the
corporation "to make . . . such and so many good and reasonable
laws, ordinances and constitutions (not repugnant to the laws of England and [Pennsylvania]) as to the greatest part of them at such
common council assembled . . . shall seem necessary and convenient
for the government of the city.[24] But in practice such a loose grant
of authority was a handicap in the eighteenth century. Public men of
that day accepted the notion of "specifically delegated powers,"
which required special acts of the legislature to authorize specific
powers. English corporations of this period frequently appealed to
Parliament for similar acts and for reasons similar to those that affected the Philadelphia Corporation: appeals failed in England when
the local and national political contexts were not complementary.
The same may be said for Philadelphia, where an appeal to the Assembly for an act empowering the Corporation to tax the town was
heard and considered in the context of bitter factional politics,
where legislature and Corporation were often dominated by opposing parties.[25] The notion of implied powers and loose construction
was either unknown or unconvincing until the nineteenth century.

Men *were* convinced, however, that the power to tax all the inhabitants could not lie with a group of men so little subject to the townsmen's influence as was the Philadelphia Common Council.

In any case, the lack of taxing power was most damaging to the Corporation's ambitions to govern the town. In 1706 the Corporation asked the provincial Assembly and the proprietor for a new charter. The text is lost, but the proposed new charter probably did include the power to tax: neither Penn nor the Pennsylvania Assembly responded favorably. In 1709 and in 1711 the Corporation tried again to get an act conferring the taxing power. The legislature was unwilling to invest the Corporation, a closed and self-perpetuating body, with the power to tax nonmembers (the great majority of Philadelphians); in addition, it was in no mood to gratify the Proprietary party, which then had a stronghold in the Corporation. Still, the need for money for public purposes in the city was obvious. The need was met in 1712 by an act requiring the popular election of six tax assessors for the city. The assessors and the Common Council were to agree together on the financial needs of the city; then the assessors set the tax rate required to raise the needed money. Thus was the principle of "no taxation without representation" adhered to in early Philadelphia.[26]

The Act of 1712 was significant for the future of the town government of Philadelphia. The political and administrative failure to make the municipal corporation an effective form of government led, as it did in England, to the creation of "statutory authorities." These were independent and usually uncoordinated administrative agencies that each had responsibility for some limited aspect of the actual government of the town. This development was ultimately fatal to the closed corporation. Making positive use of its status as symbol and spokesman for the community's common interest, the Corporation might have become the coordinating agency and merged into a competent and responsive government. But through incapacity and perhaps lack of energy, the Corporation gradually lost all touch with the responsibilities that it could not handle. These passed to the statutory authorities, which had only the smallest administrative link to the Corporation and which often displayed political antagonism. These authorities, having a limited responsibility to deal with, such as assessing taxes or keeping the streets in good repair, often managed very satisfactorily. The Corporation, with less and less to do, became more and more segregated from the real interests of the growing citizenry of Philadelphia.[27]

Let us note here that, in following the English model of fragmenting municipal authority by establishing new public bodies by statute, the Pennsylvania Assembly, and the citizens who influenced it, missed an opportunity to adapt the corporation to the times and make it politically responsive to the citizens. The tax assessors after 1712 might have been made ex officio members of the Common Council; the privilege of voting for councilmen might have been expanded from the closed arrangements of the charter to a more modern structure—anyone eligible to vote for tax assessors would also be eligible to vote for councilmen. In this way the Corporation might have been made more representative and a more directly responsible body than it ever could become with the semifeudal assumptions that under lay its charter and with the social traditionalism that animated many of its members.[28]

Alas, the charter that was so secure against the efforts of a powerful proprietor was also impervious to desired change from within. Like a suit of armor, it protected but it also confined. One might say the same of the social traditionalism: it produced the sense of security that enabled men to deal with their differences and work together without a destructive distrust of basic assumptions; but it also insulated them against an imaginative rethinking of the end and aim of self-government in a town community. In fact, political responsiveness to the general community does not appear to have been an important goal of the Corporation; response to the interests of the Philadelphia upper class, or at least of those well-to-do families from which most Corporation members were drawn, was far more important. Private self-interest animated the Philadelphia Corporation far ahead of service to the community.[29]

As a focus for the sense of local autonomy, the Corporation gradually lost its force in that direction. With the growing social differentiation of Philadelphia over the span of the eighteenth century, the increasingly upper-class merchant elite that made up the Corporation lost its sense of common interest with the remaining inhabitants. What had William Allen—merchant prince, land speculator, and public benefactor—in common with a Philadelphia tradesman, a laborer, or a sailor? Or Edward Shippen, fur merchant and landowner—what had he in common with a baker or a seamstress?[30]

The sense of local autonomy that was appropriate was also changing over the century. In 1701 there had loomed a monumental contest with the proprietor; it never materialized. Penn went away, was distracted by business in England, suffered a stroke—simply never became the formidable opponent that had once seemed likely. His successors, caring little for his "holy experiment," were content if their province was a profitable investment. No clear powerful structure existed against which the sense of local autonomy could be organized. The Assembly was perhaps the logical antagonist. Yet as the political life of Pennsylvania developed, the ferocity of the factions meant that party alliances across the province were more important than town unity against the rest of Pennsylvania.[31]

Town government soon found itself at an impasse. Without money, it could not meet town needs; money could only be obtained at the cost of the Corporation's own independence, authority, or identity with the community; declining authority and declining sense of identity with the town meant reduced likelihood that the Corporation would make an energetic effort to govern, represent, and symbolize the town. Decade by decade it lived through a metamorphosis into a kind of chamber of commerce for the great merchants of Philadelphia.[32]

Before 1730 the essential problem of town government in Philadelphia was exposed, if not obvious, to contemporaries, and a traditional kind of solution had been tacitly agreed to, although no evidence suggests there was any profound, wide-ranging, or free speculation about other possible alternatives. Indeed, the situation in eighteenth-century Philadelphia seems in its general shape not very different from the situation in twentieth-century Philadelphia, as well as many other modern cities. The failure of the governing structure seems obvious, but the means to change and the desired new direction are not so clear. Often it seems to lie in solutions that are familiar but inadequate. The structure usually has sprung from a community that no longer exists, but it has inertia as well as vested interests; so it persists. The questions that would elicit the nature of the new community are seldom asked, and the structure of a government that would reflect it is seldom pursued. Traditional-mindedness is not limited to the eighteenth century.

The unconscious and inarticulate strategy of Philadelphians two centuries ago was to keep the comfortable Corporation with its ties to the ancient past and its upper-class traditionalism, but to add to it in some fashion that would aid in meeting urban needs. The establishment of the popularly elected tax assessors in 1712 was a portent of future developments; for if the solution was a statutory authority when the Corporation did not have legal power to act (as with taxation), then why not a similar solution when the Corporation did not have the capacity to act? And if politics interfered, if it was impossible to get the necessary act passed, there were still other ways to work within the concept of adding new agencies separate from the Corporation. Over the course of the eighteenth century, three parallel developments affected local government: first, the rapid rate of growth that made Philadelphia larger than most English provincial towns by the middle of the century and expanding more rapidly as well; second, the inability of the Corporation, given its rigid constitution, its traditionally minded members, and its place in the provincial political struggle, to meet the demands of the town; and third, the appearance of other bodies or agencies that could and did provide the needed services.[33] These emerging public service agencies of colonial Philadelphia fell into two categories: statutory authorities and voluntary associations.

The number of statutory authorities actually created and the years in which they began their work would not give a complete picture of this process. Many appeals to the Assembly went unheeded, and in some cases legislative efforts were successfully opposed by the Common Council, leaving a problem area in limbo for a time longer. The town watch, for example, was an inadequate service and a persistent headache from the 1720s onward. The town had early been divided into wards, each of which elected a constable as its chief law enforcement officer. Each night the town watch was headed by a constable, who supervised a force of householders drawn from all wards. Various arrangements were tried, altering the length of duty, the time, the work; as an experiment, men were allowed to pay money instead of giving their time, and the money was used to hire watchmen. No arrangements worked well, and private citizens complained both of the annoyance of watch duty and of the inadequacy of the watch. Frequently they forgot to pay their watch money, thus complicating the hiring of substitutes; or they refused to pay on the grounds that they would serve their watch duty but then they never appeared. At times the constables must have spent more time preparing the lists of who was eligible to watch, notifying them, arranging substitutes, collecting money, making lists of those who did not pay or those who failed to show up for watch duty than they spent actually watching out for the nighttime safety of the town. The popularity of a job such as the constable's (the night watch was not his only responsibility) may well be imagined, and it was necessary to levy fines against those who refused the job when elected to it. A fine of £10 Pennsylvania currency was a cheap price to pay to avoid the nuisance of being constable, and many paid it.[34]

This unsatisfactory state of affairs attracted the notice of the grand jury on several occasions, and the Common Council made a surprisingly energetic effort to deal with the problem (despite the fact, or perhaps because of it, that Corporation members were among the delinquent citizens who had not met their obligation to watch or pay). In 1743 the council resolved that a regular paid watch was the answer, and they applied to the legislature for authority to establish one (really for the power to tax to pay for it); but no action was taken. The same sequence of complaint, debate, resolution, and petition was gone through again in 1749, after some intervening efforts at reform of the existing system; again, the reform failed in the legislature. In the following year, the Assembly acted to establish independent "Wardens of the Watch", a statutory body that was popularly elected and raised money by taxing the inhabitants with the cooperation of the tax assessors. The wardens were also given responsibility for lighting the streets (but not for cleaning or paving them) and in 1756 for control of the public pumps that provided the town's water supply. In this case the willingness of the Corporation to perform the task was frustrated by the lack of taxing power and by the political situation.[35]

Other services passed out of Corporation hands, some early and some late. Appointing overseers of the poor in Philadelphia was a power granted to the Corporation in 1705, when its identity with the community was still strong; but the overseers could tax only at a fixed rate—one penny per pound on all real and personal property. As the century wore on, this sum of money was increasingly inadequate; Corporation members joined the overseers in soliciting private contributions in addition to the tax. But in 1749 the overseers of the poor were incorporated by the Assembly, made subject to popular election, and authorized to hold property. This last meant not only the power to receive bequests and endowments but also the authority to open an almshouse and institutionalize the care of the poor. In 1766 Philadelphia and several outlying townships were consolidated for the purpose only of caring for the poor, and voting for overseers was limited at this time to those who had contributed at least £10. The Common Council was not detached completely from all this; many Corporation members were involved privately in charity for the poor, and the Corporation borrowed money on behalf of the almshouse in Philadelphia. But the authority of the Corporation over this aspect of urban life diminished consistently over the course of the century.[36]

The public streets were the care of the Corporation for a relatively long part of its existence. Here too the political situation worked to the Corporation's disadvantage. Laying out and maintaining roads was the job of county commissioners all through Pennsylvania, except in Philadelphia. The city streets were to be built and maintained by the Corporation, which in practice meant that the householders of the town would contribute their labor, under the direction of a committee of the Common Council. This arrangement might have worked initially, when street construction was vital for commerce. But as men grew busier with their private affairs—and wealthier—they understandably lost their willingness to labor on the streets. The procedure was altered to permit the contribution of money rather than labor; some money went to purchase materials, but the rest, as in the case of the night watch, was spent to hire substitute labor. This was never an adequate solution. Cooperation with the tax assessors was never smooth, and the county commissioners were seldom generous when roads ran into the city. Private householders occasionally paved the street in front of their own houses, but that was voluntary and piecemeal, with no uniform standard. In the late 1730s complaints reached a peak, and some inhabitants petitioned the Assembly to create a statutory body of streets commissioners for the city. This was opposed by the Corporation, which was seeking a solution that did not reduce its own authority. After several other attempts, a solution was reached in 1762 with the establishment by the Assembly of a Board of Streets Commissioners. The commissioners cooperated with the Common Council in deciding what work was to be done and with the tax assessors in deciding how much it would cost.[37]

All these statutory authorities had strong points and weak. The single thing that made each of them able to work successfully was that they had limited responsibilities, which in nearly every case were specified in detail in the law. So in contrast to the Corporation, each statutory body had a manageable job plus access to tax money. The other striking feature of these agencies, however, is the extent to which their actions were circumscribed by the need to consult, agree with, or get the approval of some other body, frequently the Corporation. Thus, the possibilities were immense for delay, inaction, and political one-upmanship. For instance, the streets commissioners had the power to contract with someone to clean the streets, but they could do so only when directed to by the mayor, recorder, and aldermen (who presumably could withhold that direction until they thought the streets were suitably dirty). Money for the town watch was collected through a stultifying process of checks and balance. Wardens and assessors agreed together on the money amounts and the tax rates, and then the money was gathered in by collectors who were appointed by the assessors alone—but the householder who wished to appeal his assessment had to appeal to the wardens. If the collector was forced to distrain property and sell it for the amount of the taxes, he needed an authorizing warrant, which he could get only from the wardens. Over all these bodies there was no coordinating agency; each was independent of supervision. Failure to perform could go unchecked until public discontent reached a high level.[38]

In the areas where no statutory authority was ever established, voluntary associations played a major role. As in any community where the activity of the authorities was modest, the tradition of self-help was strong in Philadelphia. The town was small enough that an alert person soon knew who the influential citizens were.[39] There were able channels of communication for the man with something on his mind who was looking for sympathetic supporters. Newspapers and printed handbills were the most formal methods, but they were useful for mass appeals. The coffee houses were places for the informal exchange of information, which might include a proposed civic reform as well as the price of flour or the fate of a ship. An energetic reformer would also have access to the network of Quaker meetings or religious gatherings of other denominations. Private clubs might also be the nucleus for measures of public benefit. The citizen who reflected on some clear public need, as Benjamin Franklin worrying about the undefended state of Philadelphia during King George's War in the early 1740s, had reasonable means of devising and publicizing a solution and reasonable hope that prosperous and prominent men would lend their support in both money and prestige.[40]

Thus, there was in colonial Philadelphia, as in many settlements both earlier and later, "a widespread sense of personal competence to make a difference" in public matters.[41] Eighteenth-century Philadelphians did not confront the problem of the twentieth-century urban man, who grapples with the frustration of trying to make some impact on a large and seemingly inert system; his problem was merely to define what he wanted to do and devote some modest energy to getting others to help him do it. So long as his project did not run drastically afoul of the local political structure, his was a very manageable task. Franklin, facing down the Quakers on the issue of military defense, was able to generate popular support for a lottery to raise money to fortify the port with cannon and blockade the passage upriver and for a voluntary military association for self-defense.

As the eighteenth century passed, Philadelphians began to enjoy many services that were provided by essentially voluntary efforts, either long- or short-term. These services were not always public in our modern sense of the term, that is, available to all residents. But they were public in the contemporary sense of the word—anyone might join if he had the membership or initiation fee. The Library Company was an association of friends who pooled their private libraries and promised regular contributions for the purchase of new books; membership was open to all who paid the contribution. Beyond that, any other group of friends might do the same thing, so that colonial Philadelphia had a number of small libraries of this kind, specialized perhaps by subject matter or drawing members from certain classes or trades. Each library remained small enough to be managed by its members as a spare-time activity and to afford them an agreeable sense of companionship as well as supplying a useful service.[42]

Perhaps the most famous of the voluntary associations to supply a solution to a public problem were the fire companies. Fire was a grave threat in an eighteenth-century community, especially where houses were constructed so close together as in Philadelphia. The Corporation was aware of the problem and made efforts to deal with it. Chimneys were to be inspected regularly for safety, the owners of unsafe chimneys were to be fined, the fines were to be used to buy fire-fighting equipment (small-scale, such as buckets and ladders), the Corporation was to store the equipment and keep it in good repair, Corporation members were to turn out to fires and coordinate the efforts of volunteers, and so on. The Corporation did purchase a fire engine in 1718, and in the 1730s it dickered with the assessors to raise money to buy several new engines. Had this system worked well, it would probably have been inadequate; but it worked badly. Inspection was largely ignored, fines were rarely paid, collection of fines through lawsuits was self-defeating—it cost more than the amount of the fine to take the case to court. The shortage of money meant, of course, a shortage of equipment, so reliance had to be placed on ordinary citizens having their own equipment and being willing to come with it to fight a fire. The supervision of fire-fighting by the Corporation members was confusing, particularly if they arrived late at the fire. As the Corporation became more detached from the city's interests, there was no reason for the volunteer firemen to defer to a Corporation member while the fire raged.[43]

But the problem remained. The city needed an efficient and affordable system of fire protection. The solution came not from a statutory board but from an assortment of volunteer fire companies, beginning with the Union Fire Company, established in 1736. These groups were reasonably efficient fire fighters because they had equipment, a fairly clear chain of command, and the advantage of having practiced and performed together. They raised money for their equipment by membership fees and also by selling their services in advance to the householders, like a kind of insurance. But the work was also attractive to as many as seven hundred Philadelphians, eventually enrolled in seventeen fire companies. The attraction was partly in the excitement of the work, but it also stemmed from the companionship of fellow members. Many fire companies were made up of a common nationality, such as the Hibernia Fire Company (Irish) or the Neptune Fire Company (German, organized through

Zion Lutheran church). They adopted splended uniforms, paraded together, picnicked and frolicked together, and in general enjoyed a sense of group identity that was an important satisfaction. Personal needs were met at the same time that a public service was provided.[44]

It is worth stressing the point that this "public" service was not for all, only for those who had bought it. As in many social and political arrangements, it was most satisfactory for the well-to-do and moderately prosperous; it did little or nothing for the poor, unless a fire company was inclined to be charitable and put out the fire in a poor man's house gratis. Still, this service reached more people and was unquestionably more effective than the efforts of the Corporation.

There were other areas in which voluntary activities either supplemented the work of the Corporation and the statutory authorities or carried nearly the whole burden. Public health, education, and various aspects of public welfare were almost entirely handled by voluntary efforts. A temporary crisis, such as the threat of bombardment by the French in the 1740s or the passage of Acadian refugees or the brief quartering of British troops before they marched west, was frequently dealt with by voluntary, semiorganized action, gotten together by a few active citizens using their own resources and those of their friends, perhaps appealing to the townsfolk by newspaper or handbill. The distressed and destitute of any particular nationality or religion might reasonably expect assistance from an association of fellow nationals or coreligionists. Concerned citizens pooled energy and funds to organize an insurance company and established several societies that provided annuities to the widowed, the orphaned, and the elderly. Public-minded citizens, many of them Quaker, founded a hospital that provided a variety of medical services, many of which were free to the poor. The object was sometimes to provide a needed service for themselves and others of like mind and pocketbook, sometimes to provide a service to the poor as a contribution to the general welfare of the town. Free smallpox inoculation for the poor, for example, was both a charity and a prudent protection for the whole population.[45]

These governmental arrangements were interrupted in Philadelphia by political independence. It is interesting to see how the government of Philadelphia, with its medieval origins, responded to and survived the American Revolution. When momentous changes were in progress throughout the colonies little meaningful change occurred in Philadelphia.

First of all, one should separate the response of individual Corporation members to the revolutionary crisis from the response of the Corporation itself. Individuals followed their interests and their conscience: some were great patriots, like George Clymer; others, like Andrew Allen, were finally loyalists. But the great majority fell under the heading of moderate in Pennsylvania: far more absorbed in the question of who should rule at home than in the grand imperial question of home rule, they tended to favor colonial union and oppose public resistance, to favor the status quo and oppose any departure from law and order. As a body the Corporation was moderate in tone and conservative in attitude. It was also politically inactive on the great questions of independence, resistance, and organization of the colonies. When the selectmen of Boston wrote in 1761 to the Corporation, suggesting the need to encourage self-sufficiency in manufactures and reduce the dependence on British goods, the Corporation responded in platitudes about the general interests of the English colonies and the need for a "Spirit of Industry and Frugality." Public measures might be suitable for Boston, a well-known locus of rash action, but they were hardly suitable for staid and conservative Philadelphia. The insulation of the Corporation from the pre-Revolutionary activities in Pennsylvania was nearly complete, despite the involvement of individual members.[46]

It should not be surprising, therefore, that as men debated the nature of government, the problem of how to make a government respond to the citizenry, and the right to change a government that did not meet the needs of the governed, their glance should at last fall closer to home than royal George. The Corporation was a kind of tyranny, at least on paper: it too was unresponsive; it did not derive its power from the consent of the governed. The Corporation had no reservoir of good will left to draw on in 1776. When public antagonism focused on it, it was defenseless.[47] As the Assembly went about the business of converting Pennsylvania from a proprietary province to an independent state, it voided Penn's seventy-five-year-old charter of municipal liberties and the Philadelphia Corporation ceased to be. It makes a dramatic picture in the mind's eye—the new government, thrilling to the idea of popular sovereignty, casting out this medieval relic that had long since ceased to have the interest of the town at its center, and replacing it with—with what?

The vision is deceptive, for there was no great popular attack on the Corporation. It was not important enough to claim much energy in a year like 1776. A few individuals, animated perhaps by philosophical concerns or by past grievance against the Corporation, got the matter through the Assembly, but no great to-do was made of it. And it was replaced with—nothing. From 1776 to 1789 the city of Philadelphia had no actual legal government. The statutory bodies remained and functioned as best they might under wartime conditions. The state legislature, sitting much of the time in Philadelphia, had a committee to watch over the city's interests. Committees of public safety functioned for the city and surrounding districts and then were somewhat supplanted by a military government during the British occupation. The Philadelphia merchant elite, which had controlled the Corporation and much of the rest of Philadelphia life, survived the war handsomely, with only a few individual losses. The county commissioners remained; so did the voluntary associations, except for a few of the least viable. Life went on much as before, except where the war forced changes. The evidence certainly tells us how little importance the Corporation had, that its disappearance after seventy-five years was almost entirely without impact.[48]

This coin has another side, however, which became apparent in 1789, when a new city government was established by the legislature. It too was a municipal corporation, "The Mayor, Aldermen, and Citizens of Philadelphia." The corporate form had made the transition from a closed medieval structure to one that was more modern and inclusive. It was composed not just of self-selected members but of all inhabitants. Yet the striking thing about the new government of Philadelphia is not how different it was from the past but how similar. Councilmen were to be elected by the freemen, but there was no clear definition of a freeman. The best guess is that a freeman was a city resident who was eligible to vote for state representative. Many of the inhabitants were thus not qualified to vote for city officials. Aldermen were elected by the freeholders (defined by a property qualification) and for a term of seven years. Aldermen still filled the bench of judges in the city court. The mayor was still chosen from among the aldermen and still had no executive power (although after 1799 he had a good deal of power in appointing officials); the mayoralty of Philadelphia did not become a popularly elective office until 1839. This new corporation did take over the responsibilities of the watch wardens and the streets commissioners in a sense. These independent bodies became dependent on the new Common Council, which appointed the wardens and commissioners and received their reports. It is questionable whether this system was more effective for the average citizen, and it gave him less rather than more control over such practical matters as the quality of the water he drank and of the streets he walked on.[49]

Even more striking is the continuity of government in Philadelphia by the well-to-do merchant families and other members of the upper class. The structure of the government, little changed though it was, seems to have altered more than the individuals that made the structure work. Many men of the early Corporation, or their relatives, are to be found in the post-Revolutionary government, duly voted for by a much larger segment of the citizenry than was earlier the case. Samuel Powel III, the last mayor of pre-Revolutionary Philadelphia, became the first mayor under the new government, having been elected as an alderman. The thirteen-year interregnum was not a period of chaos in which new classes rose to political power, or even new families; it was rather a period of business as usual so far as war and occupation permitted. When the business of the city government was resumed, the same men came forward to take part in it because they had been there all along, active in the life of the city —its business, its financial life, its social life, its political life. And these men were readily accepted by a citizenry that now had a chance to vote for someone else. Popular discontent did not remain sharply focused on the city government, and both form and personnel remained strikingly unchanged. Whatever the American Revolution meant elsewhere in the way of political change or changes in leadership, it meant virtually nothing in Philadelphia.[50]

One can only speculate why. The general citizenry of Philadelphia, having little experience of self-government before independence, remained true to its habits after 1789. Changes that seem remarkably modest to us may have seemed more impressive to them and satisfied a demonstrated political temper of moderation. In ordinary times men feel no pressure to change, and in extraordinary times they feel fearful of change; thus, political and social crises do not necessarily force innovations. Political development of class interests was not very far along in eighteenth-century Philadelphia but had to await a later time.[51] Philadelphians may have been satisfied by the sense that many of the voluntary associations were responsive to them; hence, they were deflected from any popular assault on the elitist character of the city government. All these factors and others, particularly the continuing bitterness of state politics, may have influenced individuals and groups within the population.[52] Local government and local politics, to the Philadelphians of the eighteenth century, were always subsidiary to the economic growth of the town and to the pursuit of personal prosperity.[53] In this sense the medieval character of the municipal corporation cast its shadow from centuries earlier.

NOTES

1. Early Philadelphians had an alternative model of "self-government" at hand in the Quaker meeting. Such a model was informal and dependent far more on personal interaction and group pressure than it was on law and formal rules. The Quaker meeting could not offer specific and reliable outcomes to the practical and personal expectations of citizens if it were transformed into a secular government. In New England the model of church organization was more nearly the prototype for town government than was ever the case in Philadelphia.

2. The term "privileges" has an aristocratic connotation to our twentieth-century sensibilities, but it was in fact the eighteenth-century equivalent of our concept of "rights."

3. John Patterson Davis, *Corporations: A Study of their Origin and Development*, 2 vols. (New York, 1905, reprinted New York, 1961); J. H. Thomas, *Town Government during the Sixteenth Century* (London, 1933); Sidney and Beatrice Webb, *English Local Government* (London, 1906–1929, reprinted Hamden, Conn., 1963), vol. 2 and 3, *The Manor and the Borough*.

4. Charles W. Colby, "The Growth of Oligarchy in English Towns," *English Historical Review*, V (1890), 633–53; Thomas, *Town Government;* Webb and Webb, *Local Government;* for specific examples, see George Chandler, *Liverpool* (London, 1957); Bryan Little, *The City and County of Bristol* (London, 1954), Wallace T. MacGaffrey, *Exeter, 1540–1640: The Growth of an English Country Town* (Cambridge, Mass., 1958).

5. Charles Wilson, *England's Apprenticeship, 1603–1763* (London, 1965), pp. x–xi; David Ogg, *English in the Reign of Charles II* (Oxford, 1934), 49–50; David Ogg, *England in the Reign of James II and William III* (Oxford, 1955), chapter entitled "Freehold and Status"; Webb and Webb, *Local Government*, II, 285.

6. Catherine Peare, *William Penn* (Ann Arbor, 1966); Joseph E. Illick, *William Penn the Politician*, (Ithaca, N.Y., 1965); Gary B. Nash, *Quakers and Politics: Pennsylvania, 1681–1726*, (Princeton, 1968); William E. Lingelbach, "William Penn and City Planning," *Pennsylvania Magazine of History and Biography*, 68 (1944), 298–418; A. N. B. Garvan, "Proprietary Philadelphia as Artifact," in *The Historian and the City*, ed. Oscar Handlin and John Burchard (Cambridge, Mass., 1963); Judith M. Diamondstone, "The Philadelphia Corporation, 1701–1776," Ph.D. diss. (University of Pennsylvania, 1969), 37–41.

7. Diamondstone, "Philadelphia Corporation," 42–44; 54–61; Hannah B. Roach, "The Planting of Philadelphia: A Seventeenth-century Real Estate Development," *Pennsylvania*

Magazine of History and Biography, 92 (1968), 3-47, 143-94; Gary B. Nash, "City Planning and Political Tension in the Seventeenth Century: The Case of Philadelphia," *American Philosophical Society, Proceedings,* CXII (1968) 54-73.

8. Diamondstone, "Philadelphia Corporation," 45-50; Roy Lokken, *David Lloyd* (Seattle, 1959), 42, passim; Edward P. Allinson and Boies Penrose, "The Early Government of Philadelphia and the Blue Anchor Tavern Landing," *Pennsylvania Magazine of History and Biography,* X (1886), 61-77.

9. *Colonial Records of Pennsylvania, Minutes of the Provincial Council of Pennsylvania* (Harrisburg and Philadelphia, 1852), II, 35-36 (hereafter, *Col. Recs.*)

10. Diamondstone, "Philadelphia Corporation", 50-65; *Col. Recs.,* II, 39ff; Pennsylvania Archives, 8th ser., *Votes and Proceedings of the House of Representatives of the Province of Pennsylvania,* I, 282ff (hereafter, *Votes*).

11. The charter of the Philadelphia Corporation is reprinted in *Votes,* I, 393-401; and also in *Ordinances of the Corporation of, and Acts of the Assembly Relating to, the City of Philadelphia,* (Philadelphia, 1851); see also Garvan, "Proprietory Philadelphia," and Edward P. Allinson and Boies Penrose, *Philadelphia, 1681-1887,* Johns Hopkins Studies in Historical and Political Science, 1887, extra vol. II. See also Diamonstone, "Philadelphia Corporation," 65-74.

12. Many of these early small towns, for example, Moyamensing and Kensington, and others more distant, such as Germantown and Manayunk, became part of Philadelphia with the consolidation of 1854, which made the city coextensive with the county. They are preserved only as distinct neighborhoods.

13. The freemanship, or "freedom," of the city had been an important privilege in a small medieval town. Without it a man could not set himself up in business or practice his trade. In a sense, purchasing the freedom of the town meant buying full membership in its activities. A brief effort was made in Philadelphia to require merchants and artisans to become freemen, but it was more a fund-raising than a regulatory device and fell into disuse by 1720. It could be enforced only against men chosen to be on the Common Council; according to the charter, they had to be freemen before they could take their seat. Thus, it became a kind of ceremonial initiation fee for councilmen, negligible as a source of money.

14. For the names of the original members, see the charter in *Votes,* I, 393-401; see also Diamondstone, "Philadelphia Corporation", 293-301. See also the official records of the corporation meetings, *Minutes of the Common Council of the City of Philadelphia, 1704-1776* (Philadelphia, 1847, hereafter, *MCC*). The minutes for the years 1701-04 are missing and their fate unknown. For the city council's handling of the matter of freemanship, see Diamondstone, "Philadelphia Corporation," 85-90, 130-31, 209-10.

15. Thomas, *Town Government,* 19; Webb and Webb, *Local Government,* II, 406-14, 443-74, 481-91; Colby, "The Growth of Oligarchy"; R. E. Brown, *Middle-class Democracy and the Revolution in Massachusetts, 1691-1780* (Ithaca, N.Y., 1955); S. C. Powell, *Puritan Village* (Middletown, Conn., 1963); Diamondstone, "Philadelphia Corporation," 29-35.

16. E. Digby Baltzell, *Philadelphia Gentlemen: The Making of a National Upper Class* (Glencoe, Ill., 1958); Frederick B. Tolles, *Meeting House and Counting House* (Chapel Hill, N.C., 1948). See also R. R. Palmer, *The Age of the Democratic Revolution: A Political History of Europe and America, 1760-1800,* 2 vols. (Princeton, N.J., 1959), I, 27-29, 40-47; and Leonard W. Labaree: *Conservatism in Early American History* (New York, 1948).

17. Diamondstone, "Philadelphia Corporation," 75-136, 200ff.

18. *MCC,* passim; Diamondstone, "Philadelphia Corporation," 77-100, passim.

19. *MCC,* passim; Diamondstone, "Philadelphia Corporation", 101-11, passim.

20. *MCC,* passim; Diamondstone, "Philadelphia Corporation," 112-32 and chapter 4, "The Corporation Magistracy."

21. Carl Bridenbaugh, *Cities in the Wilderness* (New York, 1938), 143–44; E. B. Greene and D. Harrington, *American Population before the Federal Census of 1790,* rev. ed. (Gloucester, Mass., 1966), 117–18; Curtis Nettels, "The Economic Relations of Boston, Philadelphia, and New York," *Journal of Economic and Business History,* III (1930-31), 185-215.

22. For examples, see *MCC,* 28, 37, 145, 178, 206, 365.

23. For a description of the Corporation's income and the manner in which it was collected, see Diamondstone, "Philadelphia Corporation," 94–98, 127–29, 227–30.

24. *Votes,* I, 393–401.

25. Webb and Webb, *English Local Government,* vol. 4, *Statutory Authorities;* E. S. Griffith, *History of American City Government: The Colonial Period* (New York, 1938), I, 69–70; Nash, *Quakers and Politics;* William S. Hanna, *Benjamin Franklin and Pennsylvania Politics* (Palo Alto, Calif., 1964), each documents for a specific time period the factionalism of provincial politics.

26. Diamondstone, "Philadelphia Corporation," 132–36, passim.

27. Diamondstone, "Philadelphia Corporation," 210–18, 285–88.

28. This is hypothetical, and hindsight history as well. There is no evidence that the changes I suggest ever occurred to a Corporation member, and certainly no evidence that such changes of similar ones were desired until very late in the Corporation's history. My point is that innovations were not structurally impossible but rather politically and conceptually difficult.

29. Diamondstone, "Philadelphia Corporation," 122–23, 233, 243, 255; see also chapter 6, "The Corporation Members."

30. For particulars on the individuals mentioned, see ibid., appendix "Biographical Data on Corporation Members."

31. For evidence of these developments, see Tolles, *Meeting House and Counting House;* Nash, *Quakers and Politics;* Hanna, *Benjamin Franklin and Pennsylvania Politics;* and Bridenbaugh, *Cities in the Wilderness.*

32. The detailed history of the Corporation's later years is in Diamondstone, "Philadelphia Corporation," chapter 5, "The Later Years, 1727–1776."

33. How large was Philadelphia? In 1685, only a few years after its founding, the city's population was probably about two thousand. By the 1720s, it was about ten thousand. By the 1770s it was probably thirty thousand. (Greene and Harrington, *American Population,* 117–18; Bridenbaugh, *Cities in the Wilderness,* 303, 305–7, 334–35.)

34. Diamondstone, "Philadelphia Corporation," 165–66.

35. Diamondstone, "Philadelphia Corporation," 204–5; *MCC,* pp. 418–22; Allinson and Penrose, *Philadelphia, 1681–1887,* 29–33.

36. See the summary of eighteenth-century care for the poor in Allinson and Penrose, *Philadelphia, 1681–1887,* 37–40.

37. Diamondstone, "Philadelphia Corporation," 106–8, 152–53; *Statutes at Large of Pennsylvania,* VI, 196–214. See also *Minutes of the Streets Commissioners, (MSS,* Library Company of Philadelphia); and Allinson and Penrose, *Philadelphia, 1681–1887,* 29–33.

38. Diamondstone, "Philadelphia Corporation," 133–35; Allinson and Penrose, *Philadelphia, 1681–1887,* 29–33.

39. See, for instance, Franklin's description of how he made his way with influential Philadelphians in *Autobiography of Benjamin Franklin* (New York, n.d.), 35–36, 71–72.

40. See Franklin's description in his autobiography, 126–28, 136–46. See also Hanna, *Benjamin Franklin and Pennsylvania Politics,* 25–31; *MCC,* 492–93; *Pennsylvania Gazette,* December 22, 1747; January 19, 1748; February 2, 1748.

41. The phrase is quoted from the working definition of democracy in S. Elkins and E. McKitrick, "A Meaning for Turner's Frontier," *Political Science Quarterly,* LXIX (1954), 325.

42. Carl Bridenbaugh, *Rebels and Gentlemen* (New York, 1942), 86–95.

43. Diamondstone, "Philadelphia Corporation," 104–6, 206–7; *MCC,* passim.

44. Daniel Gilbert, "Patterns of Organization and Membership in Colonial Philadelphia Club life, 1725–1755," Ph.D. diss. (University of Pennsylvania, 1952), 45–87, 186–89; H. E. Gillingham, "Philadelphia's First Fire Defences," *Pennsylvania Magazine of History and Biography,* LVI (1932), 355–77.

45. Bridenbaugh, *Rebels and Gentlemen,* 225–62, 296–97; Gilbert, "Patterns of Organization," 154–85.

46. *MCC,* 723–26.

47. Diamonstone, "Philadelphia Corporation," 213–18, 248.

48. Allinson and Penrose, *Philadelphia, 1681–1887,* 52–59.

49. Allinson and Penrose, *Philadelphia, 1681–1887,* 60–139; Sam Bass Warner, Jr., *The Private City: Philadelphia in Three Periods of Its Growth* (Philadelphia, 1968), 99–123.

50. There were short-term changes, of course, but they were important more in terms of state and national developments than in city affairs. See David Hawke, *In the Midst of a Revolution* (Philadelphia, 1961; and R. L. Brunhouse, *The Counter-Revolution in Pennsylvania, 1776–1790* (Harrisburg, 1942).

51. Warner, *The Private City,* 3–21; see also Baltzell, *Philadelphia Gentlemen,* 49–69, 81–92.

52. Brunhouse, *The Counter-Revolution,* passim.

53. Warner, *The Private City,* ix–xii, passim; Baltzell, *Philadelphia Gentlemen,* 364–65, passim.

Contributors

Wayne L. Bockelman is Research Associate, Division of Legislative Information and Research, Legislative Services Agency of New Jersey.

Lois Green Carr is Historian, St. Mary's City Commission in St. Mary's Maryland.

Bruce C. Daniels is Associate Professor of History at the University of Winnipeg in Winnipeg, Canada.

Judith Diamondstone is Coordinator, Project Learn: An Alternative High School in Philadelphia, Pennsylvania.

David Thomas Konig is Assistant Professor of History at Washington University in St. Louis, Missouri.

William Seiler is Professor of History at Emporia State University in Emporia, Kansas.

Nicholas Varga is Professor of History at Loyola College in Baltimore, Maryland.

Richard Waterhouse is Assistant Professor of History at the University of Sydney in Sydney, Australia.

Robert Wheeler is Assistant Professor of History at Cleveland State University in Cleveland, Ohio.

Index

267

Queen Anne's Parish, Md., 94
Queens County, N.Y., 194, 200, 202, 205,
206

Rate. *See* Tax
Ravenel family, 167
Ray, Daniel, 36
Ray, William, 94
Reade, Gwynne, 139
Record keeping, 112, 120-21, 201, 221
Red Hook, N.Y., 188
Reform, 23, 24, 25, 249-56
Refusal to serve, 74, 79, 95, 98, 99, 114,
174, 209, 251
Regulation, 74, 189, 205
Rensselaerswyck, N.Y., 187, 201
Representation, 191
Representative, 97, 193, 194, 196, 197,
200, 201, 208, 240
Restoration, 138, 139, 151, 190
Rhode Island, 46
Richmond County, N.Y., 194, 200, 202,
206
Ridings, 190
Roads. *See* Highways
Roman Catholics, 94
Roosevelt, Franklin Delano, 203
Royal government, 78
Royal informants, 125
Royal power, 16

St. Andrew's Parish, S.C., 167, 168
St. Bartholomew's Parish, S.C., 167, 168,
173
St. David's Parish, S.C., 165, 166, 168,
169, 171
St. George's Parish, S.C., 167, 168
St. Helena's Parish, S.C., 164-65, 167, 168,
169, 170, 171, 173, 177
St. James Goose Creek Parish, S.C., 167,
168, 178
St. James Santee Parish, S.C., 167, 168, 178
St. John's Berkeley Parish, S.C., 165, 166,
168, 169, 170, 171, 177
St. John's Colleton Parish, S.C., 165, 166,
167, 168, 169, 170, 171, 177
St. Luke's Parish, S.C., 168
St. Mark's Parish, S.C., 168
St. Mathew's Parish, S.C., 165, 166, 168,
169, 171

St. Michael's Parish, S.C., 165, 168, 169,
171-72, 175
St. Paul's Parish, S.C., 166, 168
St. Paul's Parish, Va., 147
St. Peter's Parish, S.C., 168
St. Philip's Parish, S.C., 165, 167, 168, 169,
171-72, 173, 174, 175, 180
St. Stephen's Parish, S.C., 165, 168, 169,
170, 171, 177
St. Thomas and St. Dennis Parish, S.C., 167,
168, 178
Salem, Mass., 25, 27, 28, 33, 34, 35, 36, 37
Saltonstall, Sir Richard, 26, 37
Saltonstall, Richard, Jr., 26
Sanctions, 19, 35
Saunders, Isaac, 231
Saybrook, Ct., 56
Schenectady, N.Y., 193, 201, 210
Schepens, 188, 191, 192. *See also* Magis-
trate
School, 47, 57, 95, 164, 189, 240
Schout, 188, 191, 192. *See also* Sheriff
Schuylkill River, 243
Scruggs, Thomas, 36
Secretary, 48, 75, 121, 122
Selectman, 35, 36, 37, 49, 50, 55, 58, 59-
63, 257
Servant, 27, 35, 80, 85, 86, 89, 90, 116,
120, 123, 149, 150, 165, 218
Services, public, 250, 255, 256
Services, social, 240, 254
Settlers. *See* Colonists
Seymour, Governor John, 92
Shawmut, Mass. *See* Boston, Mass.
Sheldon, S.C., 168
Sheppard, William, 19, 23, 24, 30
Sheriff, 17, 47, 48, 50, 64, 74, 75, 80, 85,
87, 91, 99, 122, 128, 129, 140, 145,
188, 190, 192-93, 195, 197, 198-99,
204, 211, 219, 220, 223, 224, 225, 229,
230, 233, 243
Sheriff's tourn, 15, 16
Shippen, Edward, 232-33, 248
Simpson, William, 163
Slaves, 91, 118, 120, 123, 127, 149, 165,
166, 167, 168, 169, 172, 175, 176, 177,
198. *See also* Blacks
Smith, Captain Thomas, 139
Smith, Thomas Jr., 139-40
Smith, Sir Thomas, 18
Smith, William Jr., 199